AF813721

Love Letters

to

High Road Books

Love letters to the dirty south

the dirty south

Thao Ha

ALBUQUERQUE

© 2026 by Thao L. Ha
All rights reserved. Published 2026
Printed in the United States of America

ISBN 978-0-8263-7017-4 (cloth)
ISBN 978-0-8263-7018-1 (ePub)

Library of Congress Control Number: 2026938423

Founded in 1889, the University of New Mexico sits on the traditional homelands of the Pueblo of Sandia. The original peoples of New Mexico—Pueblo, Navajo, and Apache—since time immemorial have deep connections to the land and have made significant contributions to the broader community statewide. We honor the land itself and those who remain stewards of this land throughout the generations and also acknowledge our committed relationship to Indigenous peoples. We gratefully recognize our history.

Cover adapted from Hoàng Vũ Trần's artwork for Thao. The illustrations he created on the letters and envelopes he sent transformed prison correspondence into canvasses for love and connection.
Designed by Isaac Morris
Composed in Mayence, Skolar, and Timberline

For Hoàng Vũ Trần, whose love, courage, and costly hope shaped these pages; for those who have experienced incarceration, including those who never made it home; for the community whose imprisonments remain hidden; and for those who learn through failures and missteps to reclaim the selves they lost beneath expectation and duty.

Contents

Note on the Text — ix

1. The Dirty Yellow South — 1
2. To Love a Gangster — 18
3. Roots — 39
4. When It Goes Black — 60
5. Reunion Interrupted — 75
6. Life in Millimeters — 84
7. Transformation — 93
8. Unbecoming — 109
9. Love Letters to the Dirty South — 125
10. The Walls They Built — 144
11. A Seat Saved for Him — 166
12. The Red Zone — 189
13. Voices on the Margins — 218
14. Home — 241
15. Incarcerated Love in the Time of COVID-19 — 251
16. I Will Try — 267
17. Smile for Me When It's Over — 290

Epilogue — 313

Acknowledgments — 321

Note on the Text

VIETNAMESE IS A TONAL LANGUAGE, and its diacritics carry meaning, memory, and sound. In this book, I have chosen to include diacritics in names when they were spoken that way, when the tones were present, heard, and held in the moment. There are also places where diacritics are not used. This is intentional. In those moments, the names reflect how they were actually spoken in conversation as flattened, softened, or reshaped by life in the United States. Sometimes we adjusted our own names. Sometimes others did it for us. Over time, pronunciation became something negotiated, something lived. What you see on the page mirrors that reality. It is not a strict system but a reflection of voice, context, and the quiet ways language shifts depending on where we are and who we are with.

1

The Dirty Yellow South

MY FIRST LOVE, VU, ONCE TOLD ME, "We don't get to choose the war, only the wounds we carry from it." Vu and I fell in love when we were barely adults, coming of age in a country that expected Vietnamese refugees to be grateful, to keep our heads down, and to survive without making a sound. But we were rowdy, unruly, and reckless. Houston heat bore us down, the air was thick with cigarette smoke, and our mothers' commanding voices trailed behind us as we both ran wild because it was the only kind of freedom we knew. When we bled or made others bleed, it conferred honor because it was some kind of twisted proof we had control over our own lives. Then Vu got locked up and became a ghost in the system. Almost two decades later, we reunited through the mail. His ID was a six-digit number on a prison roster, his perfect penmanship was on college-ruled paper, and his sweet, raspy voice came through a staticky phone. I had dreams of pressing my palm to the plexiglass, seeing his full lips smirking flirtatiously and his milky smooth skin glowing, imagining I could still touch the boy I once loved before the prison system swallowed him whole.

We met on a warm September night in 1992, the kind of night that carried the quiet buzz of summer slipping away. Looking back, I see it for what it was—a lesson in how love can burn fast and fleeting yet carve itself so deep it never really leaves. It happened at Fu Kim, a dim sum joint by day and an after-hours karaoke bar by night. Inside, the air was filled with cigarette smoke and street war stories. The Park Place Boyz, a Houston Vietnamese gang straight from the cracked asphalt of the inner city, greeted me with slow, deliberate nods. Not out of politeness, but respect, a currency I carried by blood. My dad's youngest brother was their leader. Across the room, the Southwest crew spread out like a kingdom of mythical creatures. Another nod, another unspoken gesture of recognition. I dated one of their guys who had once run underground gambling dens for the Flying Dragons, a notorious Chinese gang from New York City.

I was small, barely above five feet tall, but power isn't always in size. It's in the way you hold yourself, in the names stitched to your history, in the way no one asks twice when you walk through the door.

My sister's boyfriend, Doughboy, greeted us at the door and led us through the haze to our crew—the North Chink Posse. We were three tables deep, each table littered with emerald Heineken bottles sweating on to the plastic tabletops, ashtrays spilling over like offerings to the ancestors. Doughboy introduced us to a few new faces, and that's when I saw him. Vu. I felt it the moment his eyes found mine. It was a slow pull, like a song I already knew. His coy smile, so at odds with his bad-boy swagger, held my gaze. Thick, dark hair framed his face. His bangs fell over his eyes just enough to make you want to brush them back. His skin was smooth and pale in the low light, like something untouched. His eyes were bright, full of mischief, and his broad shoulders filled out his white V-neck T-shirt in all the right ways. But it was his lips I couldn't stop looking at. They were full, almost too pretty, made even more dangerous by the lit Marlboro Red dangling lazily from them. The orange ember glowed with a slow burn, and my insides did the same.

I smirked, and he caught it. His boys noticed, too, their laughter curling through the smoke, nudging at the space between us. The one next to him, Rooster, grinned, then stood, flashing a quick hand signal for me to take his seat. I slid in, close enough to catch the scent of cologne clinging to his shirt. We made small talk, learning bits and pieces about each other. His family was from the neighborhood of Granada on the north side of Houston, while I lived in South Belt on the opposite end of the city. He dropped out of high school, and I was a freshman in college. I was into sports; he was into sports betting. On paper, we had little in common, but none of that seemed to matter. By the end of the night, we had traded two serenades and a slow dance, our bodies folding into the music, swaying under the amber haze of the last-call song. The kind of song that lingers in the bones, that makes you forget what came before and what waits after. When the lights came on, reality flickered back in, but it was too late. I was already his, caught in the quiet gravity of something I didn't have a name for yet.

The following week, he collect-called me from the Harris County jail. Burglary, he said. Just some dumb shit. I pressed the phone closer, as if that could close the space between us. We wrote letters to each other, and I visited him regularly. Time seems to move differently when you're waiting for someone to come home. Three months later, the charges were dropped, and he was released. What followed was a love that was reckless, radiant, and impossible to hold without getting burned. They say first love is bittersweet. Sweet because it imprints on everything that comes after; bitter because there will never be another quite like it. It's the first dance, the first hint of something dangerous, a joyride to nowhere, a night stretched long under the Texas moon. It's the sweet escapes to the mile-long jetty, the waves breaking against the rocks, salt misting our skin, his lips tasting of honey and Marlboro smoke. It's moments that were so bright that I didn't see the darkness coming.

In 1997, everything changed. He was sentenced to sixty years in prison for aggravated assault with a deadly weapon for a vehicular shooting after a scuffle inside a nightclub that started with a look held too long and ended with blood on the pavement. That same year, I took a hollow-point bullet in the arm during a pool-hall brawl that should've been just another night. The streets had finally called in their debts. I dropped out of college, and the cycle of violence that defined so much of my life came full circle. His life sentence, and my near-death experience—two endings, two beginnings—marked a turning point. We parted ways, and I walked away from the gang life for good.

I went back to school, earned a PhD and moved to Oceanside in 2007 to start a full-time position at MiraCosta College. Colleagues warned me that I probably shouldn't live in Oceanside as a single woman. They said it was gritty, seedy with lots of violence. It was a town shaped by Marines and gangs with names: Mesa Margarita, Deep Valley Bloods and Crips, Varrio Posole Locos, and the Aryan Brotherhood. Just outside town, in Fallbrook, Tom Metzger, who was a well-known Klan leader, made his home. Before gentrification smoothed it over, there was the Main Attraction, known as the "purple church," a strip club that once lit up at dusk. Its dancers waited in doorways like saints with nowhere to pray. Some of these women were my students. Oceanside felt like home to me. The roughness was familiar, like an old scar you trace without flinching. Its streets hummed with something I've always known. My colleagues didn't understand. They didn't see the life I had left behind, the darkness I outran.

I call my mother often. She asks when I'll come back to Houston. I offer a soft lie: "Maybe someday, Mẹ." I can't tell her that leaving saved me. Houston still holds ghosts I haven't faced.

Houston had its own pockets of Viet gangland, its own rhythm, like the slow, syrupy beats of Dirty South rap. We were steeped in Viet Pride, chanting our catchphrase, "Yeah, we from da Dirty South!" Even now, decades removed, that life lingers in me, a shadow stretching long at my back. The Dirty South still rattles beneath my ribs, and somewhere deeper. That life echoes inside me, and so does Vu. Some nights, I hear his voice, distant and rasped by time. Memories of him come heavy. I try to hide them, but grief slips in anyway.

Work became my shelter. I built walls out of the hours, and over time, it was all I knew. I was ten years in with the college as a professor when a colleague reminded me that I was four years overdue in applying for a sabbatical. While pondering over the application form and its requirements, I wasn't sure what kind of project I would take on. I certainly hadn't planned to write a memoir, but during a summertime dinner with my writer friend, Làc Sư, he enthusiastically said, "Write it. Our stories get erased too easily!" His memoir, *I Love Yous Are for White People*, chronicled his troubled youth as a Vietnamese refugee coming of age in east Los Angeles in the 1990s. While his words were encouraging, I was still hesitant. My youth always reminded me of Vu, and it's the past, one I had buried, so what's the point of pulling old ghosts into the light?

Làc once admitted to me, "I thought writing about my father would kill me. But not writing about him was already doing that." I knew exactly what he meant.

Ghosts don't disappear just because you keep them in the dark. They linger. They whisper. They slip into your reflection when you aren't looking.

So, I wrote. Like Làc, I wanted to write about coming of age as a Vietnamese refugee in the '90s in Houston's Little Saigon. But my story would follow a slightly different arc than his—*from gang life to professor*, bridging the worlds I once struggled to straddle and the one I inhabit now.

In early summer 2018, I sat at my desk, screen glowing blank. The words didn't come, but the memories did. Sharp and vivid, like a song fully memorized. I thought of Vu and our time together and the time we cut out from each other. I wondered if he remembered it, too. Our stolen nights in his navy-blue Mazda on Galveston Beach. Our first movie date in the musty dollar cinema in Clear Lake. Hand in hand at Sharpstown Mall, weaving through holiday crowds. But memory doesn't stay soft for long. It opened like a wound. I remembered the missed meet-ups, the Vietnamese pool hall with buzzing lights, the prison calls cut short. The breakup. The silence. And the aching *what-ifs* that followed.

What if we had stayed together? What if he was with me the night that landed him in prison instead of out with his friends? Could he have avoided it all? What if I had helped him fight the case and rewrite the ending? Could love have saved him? Saved us? The weight of these what-ifs pressed me forward until reaching him felt like the only answer. I told myself it was only curiosity, just a need to know if his memories mirrored mine. But beneath these thoughts was a longing I couldn't quiet. I wanted to reach out even if time dulled it for him and made us unrecognizable, even if time had turned me into a stranger in his story.

I told a homeboy I was going to reach out to Vu so that I could be accurate in my memories of me and Vu. His response was steady. "Sis, your story is yours. You don't need his confirmation. But be careful if you do reach out. Hey, maybe it's not just memory you're chasing."

I let that sit. But at brunch with my girls, a crew of fierce Asian American women who are smart and sharp but soft when it matters, I finally spoke his name. Told them the story. The room went still. And then the tears came.

"You have to write to him," Thúy said, taking my hand. They all agreed.

"You're probably feeling survivor's guilt. You made it out, but he didn't," Theresa said. They all agreed.

"You still love him, huh? Or at the least, you still care deeply about him. How could you not? Your whole work is about helping the formerly incarcerated community." Yến said. They all agreed.

Because of their warm and endearing nudges, new feelings were unearthed in me. Guilt broke open. I didn't just want to remember. I wanted forgiveness. For forgetting him. For leaving. For surviving.

With shaky fingers, I found Jackie, Vu's sister, on Facebook. Typed out a message, deleted it, typed it again. Hit send before I could take it back. Her response came quickly, and when I read it, I had to sit down.

Vu will be really happy to hear from you! You're the one that got away, Sis. Everyone knows that.

But not everyone saw it that way. Jackie's husband weighed in with a different kind of truth, the kind that stings even when you know it's real. "If I was Vu," he told her, "I wouldn't want to hear from the love of my life, the one that got away. It would just make me sad."

My doubt came roaring back. Because maybe he was right. Maybe reaching out wouldn't be a reunion but a reopening. Maybe what I thought was healing would only be a fresh wound.

Jackie and I swapped numbers fast, no hesitation, like all those years apart hadn't really been years, just a long pause between conversations. Minutes later, my phone lit up.

"Siiis! Damn, I can't believe it's been so many freakin' years!" Her voice hit me like a time warp. It was still bubbly, still electric, like we were back in the '90s, kickin' it at her parents' house, observing the uncles playing cards on a foldable table in the garage as they swore *a đụ má* in different tones depending on the hand they were dealt.

I swallowed, trying to keep my voice steady, like this wasn't opening a door I wasn't sure I was ready to walk through. "It's nice hearing your voice. How's the family?"

"We good, busy, you know how it is. I got two kids now. They drive me nuts!" She laughed, and just like that, the tension in my chest loosened. "You ever come back to Houston?"

I nodded instinctively, even though she couldn't see me. "Yeah, every summer. Holidays, too. Actually, I'll be in town in a few weeks."

"Oh, hell yeah! You gotta come see me. My parents would love to see you too. You were always their favorite," she teased, her voice wrapping around me like a winter throw, soft and fluffy.

I smiled, something warm flickering in my ribs. "Awww," I said, feeling silly, feeling sixteen again.

"It's true!" she laughed, and I let myself laugh too.

For a second, the years between then and now blurred, softened at the edges. Maybe the past wasn't something I had to run from. Maybe, for once, I could just let it meet me where I stood.

"Okay," I replied, feeling the distance between the past and present close in one each other. "I'll hit you up when I'm there."

Houston's July humidity hit like a backhand to the face—thick, heavy, and unforgiving. The kind of heat that made you regret every decision that led you outdoors. I stepped out of the car and walked through Vu's old neighborhood. With each step, the bottom of my sneakers felt squishy against the softening asphalt. Billboards loomed above: smiling realtors, finger-pointing injury lawyers, no-credit car dealers, and plastic surgeons selling beauty on layaway. The same gray shopping plazas lined the street, windows still barred in black iron. The Vietnamese pool hall was still there, its sign faded but intact. Family-owned restaurants filled the air with the scent of fish sauce and *cà phê sữa đá*. Weeds burst through cracked sidewalks, puddles shimmered with still water and swarming mosquitoes. The city felt like it hadn't exhaled in years.

I spotted both Jackie and her mom outside the restaurant. Jackie had grown, but her smile hadn't changed. Her full cheeks and squinty eyes that sparkled like Vu's before he'd do something unforgettable. I hugged her first, then her mom, whose arms were full but firm. Her mom's gold necklace and earrings glinted. Clustered with stones, they were Vietnamese armor, proof of status. But her eyes were dulled and swollen with decades of grief for a son who lived behind concrete.

Inside, bowls of *bún bò huế* steamed on the table. We stirred in herbs and lime, spooned in chili. Jackie beamed, "You're a professor now, right? Mom, she's a professor!" I smiled, warmth rising in my chest.

"Yeah," I said. "It's amazing. Getting paid for something that doesn't feel like work."

Jackie grinned. "You livin' the dream. Oceanside near the ocean?"

"Close enough."

"You taking me to play volleyball?"

I laughed. "You know damn well you can't play. But come be my bodyguard."

She threw her head back, laughing. Then leaned in, mischievous. "Vu would be happy to hear from you, Sis. You never know."

Vu's mom's face tensed, then softened. "Don't say that to her," she said. "*Con*, you'll always be family. Vũ would be happy to hear from you, as a friend."

Her words filled me with a quiet warmth. Jackie agreed, adding she'd once tried setting Vu up by faking a letter from a friend. But her tone shifted. "After his last appeal was denied in 2014, he stopped writing. He was depressed."

"I'm sorry," I said softly. "I'll write to him."

They smiled. I smiled, too, but underneath, I was uneasy. After so long, after decades of "moving on," what would "writing" even mean?

Back home, I found the shoebox where I'd hidden Vu's letters from his time in Harris County jail. Nearly three decades old, they'd sat in the back of my closet. I placed them in my carry-on bag. The next day, I flew back to San Diego. Normally, I sleep on that flight. But not this time. Once airborne, I pulled the letters from my bag. The envelopes had faded, edges worn. I opened the first one slowly. Vu's handwriting was slanted and careful. Jackie always complained that she had a hard time reading his handwriting. But for me, it was easy, and although decades had gone by since I'd read his letters, it was still easy. Seeing his handwriting pulled me back in time instantly, like it was like muscle memory.

I read through each letter, the words and drawings dissolving the years between us. The phone calls from jail had always been brief, cut off without warning. But the letters? They lingered. Holding them was like holding a part of him. They were dated, organized in order. The earliest: October 1992. I flipped through drawings—hearts, arrows, roses with thorns. A birthday card with candles on a deck of cards. A puppy hugging itself. My favorite: a white cotton handkerchief, embroidered with two hearts wrapped in a ribbon. My name was misspelled, and I remembered him confessing he'd paid someone to do it, afraid to mess it up himself. It made me chuckle, remembering our shared joy. Others hurt to read. They were raw and full of longing. The last letter, dated October 9, 1997, marked everything that followed.

> Sometimes I wish I can just fall asleep and not wake up. But it doesn't happen that way. I'm just trying to hold on to what I have left. I'm very scared. I hate talking about my case. It gave me a lot of pain and stress. Plus I go through my trial everytime I close my eyes.
>
> I want to thank you for everything you've done for me. I know there's a lot of things that came between us. I hope I didn't cause anything for you to hold any grudges against me. I'm sorry if I did, you know how I am. I wish you well and best of luck in the future. I hope you find happiness wherever you may be. You deserve it. Please take care of yourself. I'm glad our lives crossed each other. Smile for me. I'll love you always.

The letter wrecked me. Each word cut deeper, my chest tightening until breathing felt impossible. Tears streamed down my face in silence until the sobs broke free. A woman beside me handed me a tissue. I nodded thanks, but the crying wouldn't stop. It felt like my heart had cracked open, its pieces slicing through me. Then, suddenly, numbness. As if my body shut down to survive it. I clutched the letters to my stomach, eyes closed, rocking slightly, overwhelmed by a grief too large to hold. The love I carried for Vu, still alive, felt eclipsed by the distance between us—by time, by silence, by all that couldn't be undone. I was helpless. Hopeless.

When the plane touched down that afternoon, I knew what I had to do. That night, I wrote to him.

July 16, 2018

Hi, Vu.

I hope this letter finds you well and in good spirits. Do you remember me? Thao Ha, your old ass girlfriend in 1992. I have been meaning to write you for years, but I never did. It would be so hard to start the letter because so much time had passed that I didn't know how to begin. Other times, I would start the letter then think to myself, what am I doing? Vu probably forgot about me so what is the point? I guess maybe you wouldn't forget about me but I ask myself why would you want to hear from me anyway? Just strange thoughts that stopped me from writing you. Are you surprised?!

A few years ago your sister Jackie found me on the internet and sent me a message. I don't know if she told you I met with her and your mom for lunch. It was nice catching up with them. Jackie said I should write you. I thought it was strange to reconnect with you because so many years had gone by since the last time I saw you, and I figured that the past is the past. I try not to live in the past. But recently I realized that we are who we are because of our past.

In this old age, I realize a lot of things due to life and the wisdom we gain from experiences and time for reflection. I don't want to disregard an opportunity to say hello and write to you as a friend, as a human being who sees you and remembers you as someone who had an impact on my life.

Recently, I have been working on a writing project and had to revisit the past. It got me thinking a lot and you were a major part of my life. I'll be real, I've dated a lot of guys over the period of my life, and even though you're in prison, when we were young and free and were together, I have to say what we had was really meaningful and remains in my memories very much. Do you remember our time together at all? Some things I remember so clearly, and other things I was able to recall when I went home to visit my family this past week. In my old room at my parents' house, I have a box of old stuff like cards, pictures, and letters. I kept all the letters you wrote me when you were doing some time in 1992. We had just met actually, and started "dating" I guess haha, and so we wrote each other and I visited you. I took the letters you wrote and have them with me. Reading them today, they made me laugh, they made me happy, they made me sad, and they made me feel bad that I didn't write you after all these years. When I think of our time together, I get nostalgic, and it was a crucial time in my life—a time of transition from leaving the gangster life to becoming something clean. It's part of the reason I didn't keep in touch with you all these years.

Eventually, I finished my doctorate degree at the University of Texas (UT) at Austin. My degree is in sociology, and I currently work as a professor at a college in California. Teaching college is definitely my calling, and teaching sociology is my passion. You might be wondering what is sociology? It's the study of society by examining systems and organizations that affect people and how people can make changes to society for a better world. Over time,

I've done many leadership things on campus. But my proudest is something that also inspired me to reconnect with you. It's a program that helps people who are out of prison go back to school. My first graduate is now a radiology technician. He still keeps in touch with me and thanks the program. I know how much it can mean to someone who thinks they are not worthy or that they are lost about how to do the right thing. Part of why I feel so connected to these students is because of my past. Like they once did, you're doing time to pay for your crime. But once the debt is paid, we need to give you a chance to do the right thing this next round in life that you have.

So, that's why I finally had the courage to write you and try to reconnect with you after all these years. I want you to know you are special to me and you were a good person to me when we were together. After reading some old letters from you, it reminded me how much of a good boyfriend you were. You made some really bad life choices, and I wish that I had some kind of influence on you to change, but instead I just broke up with you and I feel like I left you behind. I'm sorry for that. But everything happens for a reason and we are the outcome of our choices. I want you to have hope for your future. Jackie said you'll be eligible for parole in about 10 years. You've already done 20+ years so 10 more hopefully will go by quickly. I know it might be hard for you because prison life is mundane—same thing everyday. Do you have your own cell or do you have a cell mate? What is your schedule like? How do you keep busy? How do the other inmates treat you? How about the guards?

I'm sure your family is always telling you to be optimistic about your future. And I want to reinforce that by telling you there is hope. The world is a different place today, but there are many opportunities for people coming out of prison—if they have a good support system like family and friends who can help them. I want you to know I will help you if you need any advice or assistance when you are released. I'm no longer afraid of my past. Helping the formerly incarcerated students in my school has let me see the light of my past as a part of me. You were my past and are still a part of me. I want to give you hope and optimism and a fire in your spirit to not give up.

I have written a lot and I suppose you might even think, "who is this?" haha. If so, that's okay. It was so long ago and not everyone remembers things the same way. Maybe you're very upset with me for forgetting you after all these years. If so, I hope you forgive me. I was trying to shed an old me that I should have never suppressed. Today, I am proud to be who I am even with my past. I am not afraid to tell the world that gangster life was part of me and gangsters are people, too—that a special person in my life was a gangster. I hope you haven't forgotten me and hope to hear back from you. If not, that's ok. I was able to send my thoughts to you and writing this letter has been very cathartic for me. I wish you well and that you are doing ok in there.

Sincerely and warmly,

Thao

A week after I mailed the letter, Jackie and her older sister, Judi, paid Vu a visit. Jackie called me immediately after the visit and gave me a detailed rundown. She told me they had both been eagerly waiting for him to mention my letter, hoping to see a spark of excitement. Throughout the two-hour visit, they nudged him persistently, peppering him with, "Sooo, anything new?!"

Each time, they were met with his cool composure. It wasn't until the last ten minutes that he finally mentioned it, as if it were an afterthought. "Yeah, I got a letter from Thao," he said casually.

"Ooooh. What did she say?!" they pressed.

He shrugged with a burst of annoyance in his voice. "She had the nerve to ask if I remember her!"

Jackie said they burst into laughter, trying to coax more out of him. "Really? How do you feel?" they asked.

"I was offended!" he replied.

When Jackie told me, I braced myself, afraid he wouldn't write back. But a few days later, there it was: a white envelope in the mailbox, his familiar handwriting untouched by time. I couldn't open it right away. I needed space. So my dog and I headed to the beach. We settled on the curved seawall, a favorite spot of ours. Pork Chop lifted his nose to the breeze, tail wagging when children passed. Around us, the world moved, kids in the waves, joggers in rhythm, couples laughing as the sky shifted from orange to deep blue.

I held the envelope like it might dissolve. Slowly, I peeled back the seal. Inside, the paper was lined, the ink black and slanted, his handwriting exactly as I remembered. As I unfolded the letter, the beach fell away. The waves, the voices, the footsteps, all of it faded. At that moment, it was just me and his words. A quiet reunion after years of silence.

July 24, 2018

Hi Thao,

It is funny how your letters seem to always find me in the darkest places in my life. I shouldn't have been surprised but I am. For some reason I have always known or hoped that you would write me eventually one day. Your letter was very emotional to me to say the least. I have read it many, many times in the past few days. At the moment I am overwhelmed by the feelings and memories it has brought back of our time together. I am not going to lie but it made me smile (or blush hahaha) at the things we used to do together. For some strange reason, it made me feel happy and content with my life. I myself got nostalgic (by the way, I had to look that word up when you wrote it). So you were wrong when you thought I forgot about you. You were also wrong when you thought that I wouldn't want to hear from you. Why would you think I would ever be upset with you for moving on and living your life? You seem to forget that I was once your friend first. I have always wanted what was best for you with or without me. I am so proud of you and the things you accomplished, through all the adversity it is amazing to me. By reading your letter now, I truly know the true meaning of the saying, "If you love something, set it free."

You mentioned in your letter that you try not to live in the past. But it is different with me, the past is all I have for now, and I do reminisce about us from time to time. So I do remember our time together. How can I not? It was once a very happy time in my life. We were young, I was wild, not you, and we were very much in love. On rainy days, I always remember the way you look or smile at me. I have never met another person in my life that wholeheartedly accepted me for me. I once asked my mom to send a picture of us to me but she never did. Through the years that passed, I realized that I didn't need one. The one in my memories are far better and I can bring them up at anytime. Jackie said you are prettier now than you were back then.

How do you know about prison life being mundane, same thing everyday? Have you been pen pal with some inmates? I don't want to write about my life in here yet because it will ruin the joy of your letter. I would like to keep reminiscing some more of the past. Hey, you remember the time I got caught sleeping in your room? You woke me up telling me your dad wanted to speak with me. I was so scared at the time I kept wanting to jump out the window but you wouldn't let me. It is funny now haha.

Thao, this last week was like the perfect week for me. I was able to share some very special memories with you. Sorry, it's short but this is the best I can do for now. Words does not come easily for me. My only goal was to make you smile and laugh. I want you to know that you were always special to me. If nothing else, you will always have a friend in me. Take care and be safe.

Love, Vu.

I read one line over and over. *If you love something, set it free.* I'd seen this line before. In memes. In inspirational quotes. In Instagram posts. But in reading it from him, something in me stilled. Not because I had reservations with his words. But because time and separation had given me the gift of understanding. The words "move on" and "forget about me" that he uttered in 1997 had a new meaning. And it hit me. I understood the *why* behind them. He wasn't pushing me away. He was holding the door open, even from a cage. He didn't say those things to end us. He chose for it to be that way so that he could love me in the only way he could. With distance and with dignity. This wasn't about letting go. It was about giving me a kind of freedom he couldn't have.

And me? Sure, I built a life without him. But reading his letter pulled the curtains aside and exposed what was backstage all this time. Twenty years gone, and with just a few lines, he pulled up feelings I'd buried so deep. Grief, joy, guilt, love, hope—all of it rushing back. In the construction noise of building a new life, these feelings sat dormant, waiting on me to be receptive to memory's quiet nudges. Not loud, not demanding, just a song that was playing in the background, but now I heard it clearly because the volume was cranked up. Maybe I didn't have the freedom I thought I had. Seems that somewhere in the crevices of a broken heart, I tucked him away in the space between what we had and what we couldn't keep.

2

To Love a Gangster

When Vu and I met, I knew I wanted to be with him despite the disapproval from my parents, my volleyball coach, the public, even the police. I'll never forget my first visit to him in jail. Judgment clung to me as I walked in, especially when I spotted Deputy Randy Eng—the Korean officer known for patrolling Houston's Asian hotspots. I'd seen him often at Rainbow Karaoke, a hangout for gang-affiliated youth. My hands shook as I handed over my ID. Deputy Eng looked up from the visitor log, his mustache twitching as he shook his head.

"What's a nice-looking girl like you doing here? Who are you visiting?"

"My boyfriend," I said, trying to stay composed.

He scoffed. "You can do better than a loser in jail."

His words stung, sparking quiet defiance in me. I didn't respond, just held my ground. Later, when I told Vu, he was furious, his anger radiating through the glass during our visit. Driving back to campus, Deputy Eng's words echoed in my mind. Days later, Vu addressed it in a letter, frustration bleeding, like the world had drawn a line we weren't meant to cross.

> Remember yesterday what the officer said to you when you came up here to visit me? He said that you were too nice for me and that you should find a new boyfriend. So what do you think about what he said? I been thinking about that all day and night. I think you deserve someone better than me. Somebody with a better future. Somebody that's not in jail. Do you think I'm worth waiting for? Please tell me the truth. I wouldn't get mad at you. I hope that you're not doing this because you feel sorry for me. I'm just saying this because I want you to be happy. You're falling in love with a gangster. Do you regret it? Hope not. Because I promise to change.

I knew what I was getting into with Vu. He was a gangster, and that wasn't a secret. By the early 1990s, Vietnamese gangs had etched themselves into Houston's streets, claiming space in southwest Alief, northside Aldine, central Park Place, and southside Scarsdale—the dim corners of strip malls where pool halls were next to Vietnamese shops and restaurants. All the young people knew who ran where, and Vu moved through the landscape with ease.

You could spot him and his ilk instantly: baggy Girbaud jeans sagging low, a crisp white Hanes T-shirt, Reeboks scuffed from too many nights spent roaming the parking lots and clubs. Hair high with Aqua Net spray, highlighted bangs, and clean-shaved sides. It showed in the way he moved, too, always scanning, always on edge, like the world had taught him to expect the first strike.

He rolled with the boys who carried knives tucked in their socks and guns hidden under the seats of souped-up Hondas. Nights were spent in smoky billiards rooms where the jukebox bled Chinese melody love songs but a single wrong look could split into a fight. These guys gambled away rent money at late-night card games, boosted cars for quick cash, and cut their teeth in fistfights that spilled out of clubs with neon lights and sticky floors. When the money from those runs wasn't enough, there were drug deals, quiet exchanges in apartment complexes where the blinds stayed shut and neighbors knew better than to look too long.

I asked him to change. For a time, I thought he might. He stayed in with me more, skipped out on a few hustles, let himself lean into something softer. But the streets had their own gravity. He'd come back buzzing with stories, half brag, half confession, about a fight where he defended his friends and their honor or about how he'd outplayed someone at the gambling room. Other times, his voice dropped low, telling me how a deal went wrong because stolen property exchanged with the wrong hands, or a home burglary turned into a robbery when people were surprisingly in the home, about who got locked up or who got jumped at the club or which shop wouldn't pay or who felt some guilt for strongarming an elderly shop owner who couldn't pay that month's protection. In the gravest conversations, he whispered about who shot whom and the root of the dispute and how revenge was a never-ending cycle that would escalate into all-out street wars. Vietnamese gangs in Houston were notorious back then, their names and photos splashed across the city's newspaper, but to Vu these weren't just headlines. Some of these guys were the only family who seemed permanent. One lesson was clear: Respect was earned through fear.

But these stories didn't scare me. They intrigued me. I've spent years wondering why I was drawn to bad boys—the ones who lived by fear, fists, fast money, and fast cars. Maybe it was something in me, some shadow I was chasing. Maybe it was growing up in a refugee family, dropped into poverty and neighborhoods where you learned early that rules bent differently. We arrived in America with dreams, but mostly nothing else. Just our bodies and an environment where bullies made us feel fear and the streets taught us harsh lessons: protect yourself, never fold, and if someone comes at you, you come back harder.

Vu and his homeboys, my uncle and his homeboys, my classmates and their homeboys—they embodied these rules. They were proof that boys who started with nothing could build a shield out of fear and violence, turning vulnerability into power.

I remember one night at Rainbow Karaoke in Houston's Asia town, Bellaire. It's the kind of place where the floors were gooey from spilled liquor and the lights strobed blue, then yellow, then red, slicing faces into fragments. Vu stood beside me, easy at first, his arm around my shoulder like he had nothing to prove. He was laughing with his boys, their white T-shirts glowing under the black light. Then it happened. A quick and careless shove, maybe accidental, maybe not. Vu's body stiffened. A voice snapped back. Another shove. Suddenly, the air split, charged with something heavier than music.

The fight broke out fast. A fist caught Vu's buddy's jaw, and then Vu got into it. He swung and moved with a strange mix of grace and violence that made people step back. I saw his knuckles connect. A bottle shattered on the ground next to my feet. The crowd scattered just enough to give the brawling boys enough space, but no one left. People circled, egging it on, because a fight was as much a part of the night as the music. Every night we went out to party, we came to expect that some kind of conflict was gonna pop off.

Vu looked untouchable, his face lit not by fear but by something close to determination. He had that sharp focus, eyes locked, every punch a statement: Don't test me. I should have been afraid, and I was, my heart pounding so hard it drowned out the bass, but I couldn't look away. Watching him, and watching the others watching him with eyes wide open and hands thrown up in the air cheering on the blood sport, it was captivating. Then it broke apart, bouncers muscled through, bodies pulled back, someone bleeding into a napkin that was already turning red. Vu came over to me, breathing heavy, a thin line of blood ran down his thick lips. He licked it away and grinned like nothing had happened, like he'd just stepped out of a game instead of a brawl. He took my hand, and we sprinted out of the place into the night air. My hands were shaking, but his grip was steady, grounding. He looked powerful, alive in a way that I had learned how to be. And that's what drew me in, not in the danger itself, not the bruises or the blood, but the way violence as survival was made to look like strength. Like control. In a world where some are always cautious, always carrying quiet fear, we moved through chaos as if it bowed to us.

Violence as survival became typical, even predictable to me. Bullies weren't something you told teachers about. They were just part of the walk home. Gangsters made people move aside. They had power. They had protection. And in a fragile world, that looked like certainty. Before Vu, there were other bad boys. Too many. Like Sergeant Big Lips, loud and lanky, who swore to me he wanted out of the gang life. He said I made him want more. But the way of the streets had a hold on him. When I broke up with him and started dating a college boy, Sergeant Big Lips made sure I paid. First, he threatened the college boy with verbal warnings: "Stay away from her," he uttered at a beach outing. Then there was a break-in at the college boy's home. There was never proof that Sergeant Big Lips and his crew did it, but the college boy didn't see it as a coincidence. He stopped calling me, and a few weeks after I heard about the break-in from his friends, I confronted him on campus at the student center. He saw me coming toward him and turned the opposite direction from me. I didn't chase him. I understood that he didn't want to see me anymore. I never heard from the college boy again.

Then there was Bob. Vietnamese like me, but from a whole different world. He ran with the Flying Dragons out of New York. He was organized, dangerous, and polished. Dressed like Wall Street and moved like he owned every room he entered. He never paid for meals we ate at restaurants. Just walked into the back and returned like nothing happened. That power seduced me. Then he asked me to open a bank account. Said it was small, just to move gambling money. That was my line. I wasn't gonna launder a damn thing. I left. He didn't chase me. He didn't need to. Bob was too high in the ranking to bother with a girl who walked away. There were always others willing to play along, to be pulled into his orbit. To him, I was just a footnote, a passing thing, while the empire he was building and the men whom he answered to mattered more. In his world, women were replaceable, but power, money, loyalty, and fear were not.

In the late 1980s and early 1990s, things were menacing. Lots of guns, a lot more grief. I grew up in South Belt, a working-class Houston neighborhood where the Vietnamese community had taken root. It wasn't just hurricane season flooding the streets; it was also violence, mostly from rising Vietnamese street gangs. The city knew. The *Houston Chronicle* covered it relentlessly, painting us as a problem, not people.

I remember reading several articles about home invasions. In one, a headline in the *Houston Chronicle* stretched out in bold font: "FAMILY TERRORIZED AS MASKED INTRUDERS INVADE VIETNAMESE HOUSEHOLD." Beneath it, the reporter detailed a home invasion where a Vietnamese couple had been bound with electrical cords, their teenage son forced to lie on the floor as the intruders rifled through drawers, couches, and mattresses, stealing jewelry and money. The robbers pistol-whipped the father and threatened to come back for the family if they spoke to the police. Neighbors described it as another example of "Vietnamese-on-Vietnamese crime." That phrase stuck, and it stung. I remember people talking about how we brought it on to ourselves. We made ourselves targets of the Vietnamese gangs because we kept our gold bars, our jewelry, and our cash under mattresses, under couch cushions, inside kitchen cupboards and pantries, and even in floorboards. Not because we didn't initially trust the neighborhood and our people, but because we didn't trust America's institutions. Not fully. Not after what Vietnam taught our parents. They didn't trust banks, police, and other systems of supposed order. They remembered what it meant to lose everything in an instant.

Yet despite the headlines, my interactions with Vietnamese gangsters felt raw and real. They bled in front of you and for you. Whenever I told myself I was done with that life, it seemed like it kept finding me. Or maybe I didn't want to run from it. The people I knew weren't born with hate. They were born broke and grew up being bullied and bruised. I remember going to Làng Thái Xuân, one of the roughest parts of the city, with my uncle. The place looked like it had given up. The ground cracked like old skin. The buildings sagged, and the windows were busted out or covered in plywood. Spray paint was everywhere with gangs marking the space like it was the only thing they owned. My uncle's crew partied like they had nothing to lose. And maybe they didn't. Most ran from something. Abuse, poverty, ghosts of war. Their parents didn't talk about the trauma; they just passed it down. The violence might have been a choice. But it was also survival. Inherited. Learned. And even if I never said it, it broke my heart to see them trapped in it, trying to live, be loved, feared, or free. I was trying to love them, fear them, and leave them—all at once.

My parents drilled it into me early: Help people when you can. No excuses. We were the lucky ones, they said. We had steady jobs, AC that worked, a full fridge. I had my own room. It was a luxury among my friends. We got bomb pops from the ice cream truck, treats from 7-Eleven and books from the school fair like it was nothing. I knew Vietnamese kids who had less. A lot less. No bedroom, no food, no extras. I didn't have to show a free lunch voucher or shop with food stamps. And because of that, I felt like I owed something. Like I had to give back. So when the gang was hurting for money because drug deals fell through and rent was due, or when the gas tank of a boosted car got close to empty, or when the fridge of the single room apartment where ten boys slept was bare, I started slipping bills from Mama's purse. Fives and tens, folded like gifts. Just until they got on their feet, I told myself. But guilt sat heavy. Stealing from the woman who made my food and washed my clothes didn't sit right.

I moved on to stores. Big Lots first. Small stuff, easy grabs. No cameras, no guards. Then JCPenney. Then Sears. I gave the guys all the goods I shoplifted and let them hock it for cash however and wherever they could. I told myself it was for something bigger that I was helping. But at Target, beneath the fluorescent lights, the lie I'd been living slipped from my hands like a thread pulled too far, unraveling everything I thought I was.

My purse was stuffed with makeup, jewelry, colored stockings ('90s flair my sisters would've loved). Cheap things, expensive tags. I was near the exit when a hand gripped my arm. Firm, calm. A plainclothes woman. No badge. No smile. My stomach dropped. She walked me into a small white-walled room. Two chairs. One table. She dumped my purse and everything spilled out in plastic and bright colors, loud against the flat gray tabletop. I sat frozen, heart racing, panic choking me. *What the hell was I gonna tell my parents?*

Then came the footsteps. A Houston Police Department officer stepped in. Crisp uniform. Quiet voice. He looked at the pile, then at me with disappointment in his eyes.

"Why?"

I couldn't answer. I was too scared to speak, too proud to cry. The woman filled the silence. "She came in planning to steal. It's obvious."

He waited. I stayed still. Finally, he sighed. "All right, young lady, stand up."

He cuffed me—tight, not cruel—and led me through the store like a warning. Shoppers stared. I heard Mama's voice, *We help people when we can*, and wondered how I'd explain that trying to help had wrecked everything.

In the patrol car, I sank into cold plastic that smelled like sweat and shame and someone's worst day. The door slammed shut, sharp as an exclamation mark. The ride to Harris County wasn't long, but time stretched thin. My wrists were bound, but my thoughts kept running, dragging behind me that snapped line I couldn't pull back together.

Inside the station, the booking officer looked at me like I had no business being there. Like I had interrupted something.

"What's an innocent-looking girl like you doing here?" he said, not like he cared, but like he needed to say something. "You shouldn't be here."

I didn't answer. What was I supposed to say? That I grew up in a house where silence was survival? That I learned to protect people before I learned to protect myself? That stealing might not even be the worst thing I'd done?

He asked me for my information. Name, birthdate, address, all of it, and snapped the mugshot like he was taking inventory. He rolled my petite fingers in ink, one by one and then passed me off to a female officer. I was just part of the process now. She patted me down and took everything—my belt, the jewelry Mama bought me, the keys Dad told me never to lose. My maroon-colored Girbaud jeans sagged low on my hips, and she looked me up and down before cinching two of the side belt loops together with a plastic zip tie, like that was supposed to hold me together. She walked me down a long hallway that smelled like bleach and defeat and then led me to a phone. I called my boyfriend at the time, Sergeant Big Lips, told him what happened and where I was. I had hoped he would come get me, and he said he would. He sounded like he meant it. But they weren't gonna process me until morning, so I had to stay.

They threw me in a holding cell with three other women. No one looked surprised to be there. We learned each other's stories fast. One was in for turning tricks, one for cracking her cheating husband's head open with a plank, and the last one for being high and catching sleep in a house that wasn't hers.

"What you in for, China Doll?" the one with the cheating husband asked me. She had a tired smirk.

"Theft," I said, low.

"What'd you steal?"

"Shit for my gang."

She snorted. Shook her head. "They ain't worth it, honey. They never worth it."

She said it like she was trying not only to convince me but to perhaps remind herself.

That night they moved us to our cells. Real ones. Metal bars, metal beds, no promises. I ended up in a cell with the woman who beat her man. She gave me the bottom bunk. She said I was too tiny to get to the top. I curled up tight with arms wrapped around myself like maybe it could undo the day. The metal was cold. My chest was colder. And when the silence stretched too long, laying in the fetal position, I started crying, but not like a baby. Not loud. Just small, just short inhales, and silent long exhales. I tried to hold it in. Tried to stay hard. But the sobs came anyway. Ragged little reminders that I wasn't built for this. And I laid there thinking about Mama. About school. About the record they were gonna print with my name on it. About how it might follow me into every job interview, every dream I ever had. For what? For Big Lips? For the crew? No. This one was on me. Nobody forced me. Nobody held a gun to my head. I did it. I made the call. I stole. I got caught. I ended up in a jail cell with strangers who had their own stories and their own regrets.

But the worst part? I still hadn't learned a damn thing.

The next afternoon, I was released. Sergeant Big Lips drove me to my truck that I left stranded in the Target parking lot. My sisters lied to my parents. Told them I ran away. I came home to my parents' relief rather than an ass whooping from them. A few months later, I stood in front of a judge, trying not to shrink under the stupidity of my choices. The court-appointed lawyer leaned in close and said she negotiated a deferred adjudication with no jail time but six months of community service. I took the deal and sorted books at the Clear Lake library alphabetizing other people's stories while mine stayed crumpled in my chest. But even with the charges adjudicated yet contingent on my good behavior, the streets didn't let me go. I was out of legal trouble, but I wasn't out of trouble. I still ran with the North Chink Posse (NCP) and still partied with the Park Place Boyz whenever the wind blew that way. I didn't care about second chances and the price of potentially ruining that.

Downtown Houston had become a bustling Little Saigon, but behind the storefronts and neon signs, the street gangs multiplied. Vietnamese crews with ties to California like the Natoma Boys and ties to New York like Born to Kill either collaborated with or collided with our sets, and the ones out of the fishing villages along the Gulf, like the Little Rascals from Port Arthur, they were notorious for not giving a fuck. I recall a story that made national news. Reporters described the scene of a violent shooting: Givral's, usually bright and bustling with lunchtime chatter, sliced raw by violence. Patrons ducking behind counters, vinyl seats torn by bullet holes, blood pooling into the grease-stained floor. And then came the name: Minh "Tony Playboy" Duy Tong Nguyen—known enforcer for the Nomads, a Vietnamese gang from the nearby fishing towns. He and his gang had opened fired, the culmination of a turf war. Two people died that day, and three were wounded. What made it even more surreal was what followed: his face popping up on *America's Most Wanted*. The small-stature Texas boy who'd shown up to church potlucks and neighborhood markets became a nationally televised fugitive. And he wasn't just some name on the news. He was my uncle's homeboy. After the shooting, he vanished. The cops tried to find him at

Marian Days, the Vietnamese Catholic annual pilgrimage in Carthage, Missouri. It had become the national congregation for Vietnamese gangsters across America. Deals were made under the cover of holy music and rosary beads. Dope moved, guns changed hands. And when they came back home, the violence followed. They never found Tony Playboy at Marian Days. But after his face got plastered on *America's Most Wanted*, they apprehended him in Canada.

The gangs often moved in under the radar for the most part, hopping cities, doing dirt, then disappearing. Police couldn't keep up. Houston PD built out an Asian Gang Task Force, but they didn't have a single Vietnamese cop on it. No one trusted them, and the victims stayed quiet because everybody knew what could happen to people who talked. The gangsters threatened retaliation with sickening certainty. I remember flipping through the *Houston Chronicle* one muggy morning and stopping dead at the headline: "MAN SENTENCED TO DEATH FOR SHOOTING TWO FRIENDS IN THE BACK TO KEEP THEM SILENT." The killer was Son Tran, and the article noted that two others involved had already pleaded guilty—including Dung Tran. His name came with a clear photo of his face. My heart jerked. Dung was a buddy of mine who studied with me at the University of Houston as an undergrad. Reading that he'd been given a life sentence in the killing spree, which prosecutors described as the "slaughter of victims," made the vicious murders feel uncomfortably close. The article described how the killings unfolded: It began with the murder of one man tied to someone at the Rose Club, followed by a woman who was executed on a remote Galveston beach because she "knew too much." Son and Dung then lured two more victims to a fake robbery planning meeting and shot them in the back, worried that the two victims would talk.

I remember staring at his name: Dung Tran. A feeling of dread took over me. We'd had lunch together many times during breaks between classes; he drove me around in his black Honda Accord with a photo cube of his girlfriend Linda, who he said needed sex at least eight times a day. We'd laughed together and played pool together. Now he was part of a story that haunted our entire community.

The fear from stories like that was real, and it wrapped around our community like barbed wire.

In the early years of Vietnamese gangster formations, they didn't engage in organized forms of crime. They were after homes with valuables and vehicles with chop-shop value. They were after the fast money and the Asian baby girls. When they were rewarded, they wanted more, and so, over the years, burglaries, robberies, auto theft and impulsive drive-by shootings became gateways into extortion, sex trafficking, drug trafficking, money laundering, and planned executions. My uncle was into drug trafficking, but he was a drug user, too, and that was devastating to witness. He was lost to that life. I remember Dad went looking for him. I drove Dad to Làng Thái Xuân as he went in search of a brother he knew was slipping through his custody as a father figure. We found him in an apartment that was falling apart, surrounded by glassy-eyed men and women with nowhere else to be. It was clear. My uncle wasn't coming back. A few years later, he rolled up to our house in his faded gray Datsun 280Z. He parked it in front of our house and left the keys, the pink slip, and a note that said he was leaving town.

A couple of months later, the cops showed up at our house with a warrant. They said my uncle had murdered the madam of the Dong Kyong brothel. Stabbed her while high on coke. They said he was dangerous and that he might come back. They asked Dad if he knew where his brother was.

"I don't know. I haven't heard from him in years," he said.

I heard him lie and witnessed the stoicism in his demeanor. This is the same man who preached honesty, who quoted scripture, who told us never to cover for wrong, but he covered for blood. And I got it. That kind of protection doesn't come from logic. It comes from history. It comes from war. From shame. From the kind of love that doesn't need to make sense.

And then I saw it in myself when the cops came for my sister's boyfriend, Doughboy. That was his street name. We called him Doughboy because his cheeks were round, and he had what you would call a baby face. His disposition was kind, sweet, and bubbly. He was polite and respectful of my parents and other elders. He was good to my sister. He took her out to nice meals, talked on the phone with her for hours making her giggle, and encouraged her to keep up with her studies.

His family lived on the north side of town in a trailer park village filled with Vietnamese Catholics. Their three-bedroom manufactured home sheltered a family of thirteen. Two parents and eleven children. His family owned a tuna fishing boat, and the adult men of the family were gone for months at a time on the deep waters of the Gulf of Mexico. Their family experienced one tragedy after another. Doughboy's younger brother, Hạnh, fell into a pool as a child, and although he was saved, he had been submerged too long without oxygen. He ended up with brain damage that impaired his cognitive development and caused a speech impediment. It also caused a physical disability in the use of his hands and legs, resulting in an awkward limp when he walked. A short number of years after Hạnh's accident, their older brother was thrown off the tuna boat and drowned. His body went missing, and after three days the Coast Guard called off the search. I heard their family talking about how they eventually discovered the body. One of the older sisters and Hạnh were on the way to Galveston to speak with the police and provide information for the death certificate. As they approached the beach town, Hạnh began yelling loudly that their dead brother was talking to him and that the sister needed to drive to the seawall. She did as Hạnh directed, and when they stood on the concrete wall and scanned the vast body of water, their brother's bloated cadaver was floating on the surface.

Doughboy was only fifteen when he started dating my sister. He confided in us, almost shyly, that he liked being at our house, not just because of my sister, but also because of how our family seemed like we were close to one another. We ate dinner as a family, and my parents talked *with* us, not *at* us. Dad would tell a story from work, and Mom would poke at his story if it sounded like a fable. My siblings and I would laugh at Dad's jokes and find amusement in Mom's ability to keep Dad in check.

Doughboy also admitted that hanging out with the NCP homeboys pulled him out of his home. Their world gave him a place to belong when his home felt too heavy and dim. I got the sense that he wore that name like a family crest, a declaration that someone would stand beside him when life pressed too hard. Still, he never spoke ill of his blood family. He only shared that they struggled with money and bad luck. The water they worked on had marked them, with two of his brothers already destroyed by it. It's as if water promised survival but had turned to curses.

And then in early 1992, Doughboy's family faced another tragedy. Doughboy was implicated in the killing of a homeowner during a home invasion. I remember hearing the crew talk about it. There was a group of them involved in the robbery, but questions swirled around who the actual shooter was and whether there was pressure for Doughboy to take the fall because he was the only juvenile. We heard the prosecutors would make it a capital murder case, and rumors spread that the adult guys could face a death sentence. The guys went into hiding, and the cops came looking.

The cops pulled my sister out of school and took her home. In front of my parents, they said she was listed as a known associate of NCP and that she was Doughboy's girl. They asked her what she knew. My parents told her to cooperate and to tell the truth. But she said nothing. I didn't know if she knew the truth. But I knew that if she did, she also knew what the truth would cost. Truth is, she probably didn't know. Gangsters don't tell their women everything. Girlfriends aren't often the soldiers. Knowing nothing was ammo for deniability. But when shit went sideways, they often called the girlfriend.

A few days after the interrogation at our home, Doughboy called from a pay phone to speak with my sister. I listened from the second cordless phone in our house. His voice was low and tense. He told us he couldn't go home because the cops were there. My sister's hand shook as she held the phone, her voice trembling when she asked the question that hung heavily between them: Did you do it?

There was a pause, and then he confessed. He had done it. He needed money to buy my sister a Christmas gift. It had been an accident. The homeowner lunged at him, and in the tussle, the gun went off. Doughboy was the only one armed that night, the only juvenile in the crew. The guys had convinced him that if things went wrong, he'd face a lighter sentence because he was underage. Learning this piece of the story enraged me. I thought to myself, these fucking adult guys let this happen to him.

I watched my sister's face contort with anguish. She cupped her hand over her mouth, her sobs silent but fierce, as though the weight of his confession had physically crushed her. Seeing her like that tore me apart. As the eldest sibling, it had always been my responsibility to protect my younger siblings, and I couldn't just stand by. I spoke up and demanded Doughboy's location. He was at a convenience store near Greenspoint. Without hesitation, I grabbed my keys, got into my Isuzu truck, and drove to find him. I didn't see him in the front or on the side of the building. I drove around the back and found him crouched near the dumpster, his face pale and his body tense with fear. He told me he was scared. It was clear to me I had to help. I fed dimes into the pay phone and called Hải, my best friend from middle school, now a student at Texas A&M with her own apartment. She was never involved in gangs, but she had always had my back, no questions asked.

"I need your help," I said with urgency in my voice.

"What happened?" she asked, her voice laced with concern.

"Can I bring Doughboy to stay with you for a few days? He's in serious trouble and needs to lay low."

"Of course," she replied without hesitation. "When are y'all coming?"

"I'm up north, by Greenspoint. We're heading over now."

"I'll be home. Drive safe."

I assumed she knew what harboring a fugitive meant, but she welcomed us anyway. In the eyes of the law, we were aiding and abetting a person wanted for murder. But to me, Doughboy was family, my brother in spirit if not by blood. I had to do what I had to do. It was about the code, the unspoken law of loyalty to your gang, to your people. Doughboy was family, and I willingly took the risk. When desperation hits, the heart takes over, drowning out any sense of logic or self-preservation. We were ride or die, and loyalty always came first.

As we drove toward College Station, my thoughts turned faster than the tires beneath us. Doughboy's choices, if we can even call them that, played out like a reel I couldn't shut off. The worst-case scenario clung to me: a courtroom, a judge's voice sharp as steel, a sentence that could end with death. He was only a boy, but in the eyes of the law that didn't matter. Turning himself in felt like surrendering him to a grave. My mind leaped instead to impossible escapes. Maybe he could flee to Vietnam, a country he'd never really known, but that would mean abandoning his family forever. Or Louisiana, disappearing on to a shrimp boat, but would he be swallowed by the Gulf like his brother, or would he end up working himself to the bone like the other men in his family? I wanted so much more for him, but he was already marked, already wanted for murder. Every road I imagined collapsed into the same dead end. There was no escape. No easy way out. Just the weight of inevitability pressing down on me, like water over my head, one arm fighting my way to the surface while the other is reaching to save my brother who was drowning below me.

"What does your family think?" I asked.

"They want me to turn myself in," he said, his voice quivered. "They said they'll sell the boat if they have to and get me a good lawyer."

"But you did it," I replied, my words harsh but realistic. "You won't get off completely."

"I know. But maybe I can plead to something lower, serve less time," he muttered, the hope in his voice faint, as if he barely believed it himself.

Silence settled between us, thick with anxiety. After a while, I glanced at him and asked hesitantly, "You want me to turn around?"

He didn't say anything, but when I looked over, I saw a tear roll down his cheek. He shook his head, and we drove the rest of the way in silence.

As we sped down the Texas highway, my eyes were drawn to the stunning bluebonnets lining the roadside. Their deep indigo petals caught the fading sunlight, casting a rich purple hue over the fields. The beauty of the flowers was a stark contrast to the chaos in my mind. I tried to focus on the calm sway of the bluebonnets in the wind, willing myself to maintain a steady pace as we continued down the road.

We stopped at a gas station halfway to College Station. While I pumped gas, Doughboy made his phone calls. I watched him from a distance, an unease nagging at me, the heaviness of what he was facing sunk in deeper. We were both caught in this web now, tangled in a mess with an uncertain future and the dread of what inevitably lay ahead.

We pulled up to Hải's apartment near campus, and I saw her waving from the window, a reassuring sight after the tension of the drive. She met us at the door with a warm smile and ushered us inside quickly, her embrace offering a brief moment of relief. As I left Doughboy in her care, I felt a small sense of comfort knowing he was in good hands, tucked away where the police would never think to look.

On the drive back to Houston, my mind raced with thoughts of what was ahead. Doughboy's future was already slipping away, bleak and narrowing by the mile. I thought of his family, how they must have been unraveling with worry and desperate for answers. I thought of my sister, who loved him with the kind of reckless tenderness that teenagers carry, her heart breaking in ways she couldn't have named yet. My chest ached for all of them. And then the grief shifted outward, crashing over me in sobs I couldn't hold back. I wept for the family of the victim. For the mother who would never see her son walk through the door, for the wife who might replay her last words over and over until they hollowed her out, for his children who would forever live in the shadow of his absence. A single act of violence had split their lives in half—a before and an after, with absolutely no way to stitch it back together. It was a sobering reminder of how one wrong decision could unravel into a thousand sorrows. No one escaped it. Not Doughboy, not his family, not my family, not the victim's family. The agony bound us all together, a chain none of us had chosen, but one we would all be forced to carry.

Two days later, the house phone rang. It was Hải. Doughboy was ready to be picked up. I gathered some of my brother's old clothes for him, packed some cash, just in case, and drove back to her apartment.

When I arrived, he greeted me at the door with a tight hug, and I asked him what he had decided.

"Take me back to Houston, sis. I'm gonna turn myself in."

My heart sank as I thought about the harsh consequences that awaited him. Tears welled in my eyes, and I fought to keep my emotions in check, but my throat tightened, and my body trembled uncontrollably. He put his hands on my shoulders, his voice calm and steady.

"It's okay, sis," he reassured me. "I have to face this. If I run, and whether they find me or not, I'll never see my family or Hieu and you guys again. How's she doing?" I could hear the concern in his voice. I didn't have the heart to tell him the truth, that she was barely eating or sleeping.

"She's doing the best she can," I said gently. "My parents called your folks, and they said they'll help pay for the lawyer."

"Really?" he asked, surprised.

"Of course! They love you, bro. We all do. We're gonna be with you the whole way. We ain't leavin' you."

The gratitude on his face was palpable. "Man, I gotta call and thank them," he said, a flicker of relief in his voice.

The drive back to Houston felt both too fast and painfully slow. Every mile that brought us closer to the city made my heart feel sadder. As we crossed the city limits and the landscape shifted from open fields to towering buildings, the reality of what was about to happen became harder to bear. I glanced at Doughboy, his face calm, but his eyes gave away the storm of emotions underneath. I reached over, placing my hand on his shoulder, squeezing gently, offering what little comfort I could.

His baby face, still so young and innocent despite everything, was about to face adult consequences for a crime committed at the age of sixteen. The state would try him as an adult, no matter his age. The thought twisted my stomach.

"Let's get some food before you turn yourself in," I suggested, my voice trembling. I worried it might be his last real meal as a free man.

He nodded.

"You pick," I told him. "You won't be eating anything good for a while."

Vietnamese was his choice, and we sat quietly over bowls of *phở*, the steam rising in tendrils between us. After we finished, we headed to the bail bonds place downtown. The building was unremarkable, built with red brick, a flashing neon sign on its walls glowed in the early evening gray—BAIL BONDS. My heart raced as I parked the truck, the finality of the moment sinking in.

We stood in front of the truck hood, facing each other. I pulled him into a tight embrace, and this time, I couldn't hold back the tears. I sobbed openly, my body shaking uncontrollably as he held me.

"It's gonna be okay, sis," he whispered into my ear, his voice steady despite the fear I knew he felt.

"I know," I choked out between sobs. "I'm just scared for you."

He pulled back slightly, keeping his hands on my shoulders, his face calm and reassuring. "There's nothing to be scared about. I'll be all right. Tell Hieu I love her. I'll call her as soon as I can."

I nodded and wiped away my tears with the back of my hand. I watched as he walked toward the building. He reached for the door handle, then turned back to look at me one last time, raising his hand in a slow, circular wave. I waved back, my heart breaking. As the door closed behind him, I lost all control, the tears flowing freely, my sobs echoing in the silence of the empty street. I stood there, staring at the door long after it had closed, the image of Doughboy's face as he walked away seared into my memory.

3

Roots

My young life rarely felt peaceful, but I found joy in family where I could. During the eight months Doughboy was out on bond, he worked at Phoenix Electrode and brought Vu with him. Those months were golden. Vu, me, Doughboy, and my sister spent a lot of time together. Two schoolgirls and their gangster boyfriends who I believed were trying to change. They got honest jobs, worked hard, stayed away from the gang, and were dreaming bigger for themselves, seeing themselves as more than just gangbangers.

Then Doughboy's court date came. Guilty. Fifty years. It crushed us. But I understood. A family had been broken in a way that no apology and no time served could ever mend. I knew someone had to pay the debt for what had been done, even if the cost felt unbearable for us. My sorrow stretched in two directions at once. Toward the victim's family who would live forever with an empty seat at the table and whose grief had no parole date. And toward Doughboy, just a boy who stumbled into manhood with a gun in his hand and a hunger to belong, now locked away for the rest of his youth and most of his life. Both truths lived in me at once. Doughboy was guilty, but he was loved. The only anger I carried was toward the ones who persuaded him to hold the weapon in his palm. They fed boys like him the illusion of power and family and left him to hold the burden of a crime he could never undo. In the end, Doughboy bore the punishment, but to me, blame stretched farther than the bars of his cell.

At the time, I believed justice was served, although I could never truly know how the victim's loved ones felt or still feel. Their grief was a private country that I could never enter. All I knew was the silence that followed and the hollow space where a life had been. On our side, the side of the perpetrator, we carried loss, too. Doughboy was gone to prison, and with him went my sister's first love, a mother's hope, and the possibility of who he might have become.

It took decades for me to understand that justice isn't only about punishment or time measured in years. Later in life, I learned about restorative justice, and the idea cracked something open in me. Restorative justice begins not with the hammer of the gavel, but with acknowledgment and the courage to face the wound and name it. To allow grief its shape. It asks us to imagine justice not as revenge or erasure, but as a meeting ground, however fraught, where harm is spoken and responsibility accepted. Looking back, I'm humbled by Doughboy's willingness to face his consequences. At a mere sixteen years old, he willingly and knowingly walked into the shadows of a proverbial death. He reassured us he would be all right. That phone calls, letters, and visits would be the shape of our lives together. And that he would do right while incarcerated.

I began to see that whether you stand with the victim or the perpetrator, loss binds you. Both are left with empty chairs at the table. Restorative justice doesn't promise to mend what can never be made whole again. Instead, it asks us to gather the fragments, to sit in the wreckage together and say, *This happened, and we will not turn away from it.* With adult eyes, I see that justice cannot resurrect the dead, and nor can it erase the crime. But it can offer a path, not to wholeness but to dignity. To recognition. To the possibility that even in the wake of unimaginable harm, we might still find a way to live with one another, if not in forgiveness, then in truth.

That summer after Doughboy got locked up, my parents took us to Vietnam for six weeks. It was my first time back since we fled in 1975. I didn't want to leave Vu, but he reminded me how special it would be to meet the family I never knew, especially my maternal grandmother, my *bà ngoại*, who'd believed we were dead after the fall of Saigon.

We stopped in Hong Kong for two days. While wandering the garment district, a well-dressed man handed me a card, called me beautiful, said I should model. I smiled and took it until the tiny shop lady snatched it from me. "Kidnap girls! Don't talk!" she warned. Her words shook me. It hit me how easily girls disappear.

Kowloon Bay buzzed with life. Skyscrapers, neon lights, American stores, fast cars. It felt more like LA than I ever expected. At the hotel, I rushed to the gift shop, grabbed a postcard, and wrote to Vu. I was full of wonder I wanted to share and was already missing him. Three days later, we landed at Tân Sơn Nhất airport. Stepping into the terminal, it felt surreal. We had once fled this place in April 1975.

On April 30, 1975, Saigon fell to the Việt Cộng, and South Vietnam ceased to exist. I was sixteen months old, and this retelling is from long conversations with my parents recounting their memories, stories carried like scars. Dad was only twenty-four, a pilot in the South Vietnamese Air Force who flew C-130 Hercules planes. In those last days, he had just completed his final mission at Tân Sơn Nhất air base. Mom was twenty-three, a seamstress, clutching me in a crowded terminal thick with other women and children. She said fear was etched into every face, eyes darting at the sound of sirens as the military radios stuttered with broken orders. She hadn't seen Dad in days. Hope was thinning. Then, early in the morning of April 29, she heard his voice cut through the noise. He had found us, but there was no time for words. He grabbed our suitcase while Mom wrapped me tight, and together they ran to the open air and leaped into a jeep already packed with passengers. They sped to the runway where planes waited. Then came the bombs. A thunderous flash lit up the sky, forcing passengers to fling themselves from the jeep. Mom hit the ground hard, landing on her knees and rolling while clutching me tight to her chest. Dad threw himself on top of our bodies as artillery shook the earth, shrapnel tearing into his back and arms. He lifted us to our feet again, and together we weaved through the columns of fire that made the runway glow like a torched hell.

Dad led us toward a row of planes he believed were all fueled. A crowd followed us. One of the planes was hit directly, exploding in flames. Some of the crowd fled toward another craft and never made it. They were killed instantly by a strike. Dad pressed us forward toward the explosion, repeating to himself that bombs rarely fall twice in the same place. Then the barrage eased, and we hid in a hangar. Explosions still thundered in the distance, the ground trembling beneath us. Above, one of the last US Air Force piloted-C-130s lifted away, leaving us behind.

At dawn, the crowds swelled, desperate to escape. My family managed to board a C-130 piloted by one of Dad's buddies. We squeezed in with approximately three hundred others. Mom remembered the heat inside, the air dense with blood, sweat, and burns. Her pants were torn and stained with blood from the fall from the jeep. She wept when she saw how pale I was from a recent measles infection. Dad admitted he didn't notice. His focus was on whether the overloaded plane could take off and whether we'd be shot down before reaching safety.

Only six C-130s escaped Tân Sơn Nhất that day. We were on one of them. Official reports say we landed in Thailand, but Dad said our first stop was Côn Sơn island, infamous for its "Tiger Cages." Images from the island where shackled and tortured prisoners were locked in cages had shocked the world in *Life* magazine. Dad said the pilots on our plane still couldn't accept it was over. They planned to drop off the women and children and then return to continue fighting. But the radio calls coming in were now clear. By morning, it was finished. The South had fallen. We had lost the war. Lost our country. Dad said a heavy weight sank into his stomach. Mom said she cried until her body shook, wondering if she might ever see her family again.

Eighteen years later, I found myself back at the same airport, no longer an infant cradled in Mom's arms but a freshman in college on summer break, stepping off the plane with my parents, two sisters, and a brother. It was 1993 and our first trip back to the motherland. The air hit me first, thick and humid, the same air my parents and I once breathed in terror as bombs fell. The runway was a graveyard of memories. For me, it was a place I had only ever known through their stories. I walked on the same pavement where my parents had once run for their lives, and the distance between our past and our present collapsed together. Dad said his eyes scanned the space, not as a tourist but as a man searching for something he described as eerie. Mom had been to Vietnam alone before, many times before, to rebuild her family's home and their livelihoods. Dad stayed back to watch over us, and he had sponsored most of his family to America anyway. We were all together in Vietnam for a family trip, standing on the fault line of our own history.

The airport buzzed with dense crowds, mopeds, voices, and the thick, humid air of Saigon. The scent of Vietnamese food and the sound of my mother tongue wrapped around me like a homecoming. Outside the airport, my eighty-one-year-old *bà ngoại* stood waiting with the rest of Mom's relatives. Her eyes searched the crowd until they found us. She rushed forward, hugged my parents, then took my face in her wrinkled hands, pressed her nose to my cheek, and smiled wide. She had one tooth left, but her joy was unmistakable. I noticed other older women with black-stained teeth and asked my parents. They explained it was from betel chewing, a cultural tradition tied to weddings and ceremonies.

Later, I learned Bà Ngoại had endured deep losses: her twin died young, and she buried children who might've survived with modern medicine. She'd also been a "first wife." Ông Ngoại, my maternal grandfather, had a second, whom she accepted and even cared for. I couldn't wrap my head around it. Was it really her choice, or something expected of her?

The trek to Cần Giuộc, where Mom grew up, was chaos. Our van tore through Saigon like a runaway train, swerving past cars and nearly hitting pedestrians. I gripped the armrests, terrified. Even with my own history of speeding tickets and near-arrests, this was next level. Once outside the city, we transferred to *xe lams*—three-wheeled Lambro 550s with open-air wooden benches. The ride was dusty and rough. At the Cần Giuộc River, we switched again, climbing into wooden canoes with cousins. It reminded me of a Riverwalk gondola ride with Vu but without the charm. Tall grass and open fields buzzed with life. Mosquitoes, chiggers, geckos, frogs, everything singing in a wild, itchy chorus. The river lapped softly, rhythmic and soothing, but the bugs made it hard to enjoy. As we neared a rickety bridge of uneven planks and shaky pillars, I stepped carefully, trying not to look down. The wood groaned beneath me while my cousins crossed with ease, flip-flops whispering, gracefully carrying luggage and boxes of American goods like seasoned dancers. Mom must have noticed our terror because on her next visit, she had the bridge torn down and rebuilt.

As we neared the house, the countryside opened up. Lush fields, rice paddies, banyan trees swaying in the breeze. As a city girl, I felt calm here. The coastal air was cooler than Saigon's heat, and life felt simple. Meals came from the land, and we spent days playing with local kids. My brother, fourteen and towering over the village boys, became a karate teacher. His kicks, chops, and spins inspired by Saturday afternoon Kung Fu Theater and pirated tapes like *Legend of the Condor Hero*. The boys admired him. The girls blushed. My sisters taught dance moves. I taught English and introduced them to Jif peanut butter on baguettes, sending boys to fetch more from the village market. We became village stars.

At night, the skies were inky black, stars glowing so brightly they felt within reach. Inside, the warm glow of a wood fire under a rice kettle filled the bamboo-walled home. The smoky scent reminded me of campfires at Huntsville State Park with Dad. I traced the rattan walls, imagining Vu beside me in the quiet.

We stayed a week. I didn't want to leave. But we had more family to visit in Sóc Trăng, Dad's village, and other places like Đà Lạt, where, years ago, my dad sent my mom a love letter with a pressed flamboyant flower (*phuong vi*) inside. One of the rare stories she ever recalled with a sense of warmth. On our way out of the village, we stopped to visit a distant relative, a cousin by marriage to my sixth aunt. Their home was thatched together with little more than what the land could provide. Inside, the air was thick and dim, and the light from outside barely pierced the small, dark room. My cousin's daughter lay on a mat on the ground, her fragile body motionless except for the slow, shallow rise of her chest. I couldn't tell what her age might have been given her tiny and shockingly frail frame—her limbs thin with just skin stretched taut over bones. But my cousin being a decade older than me, I assume her daughter would be in elementary or middle school had she not had this affliction. Her grotesquely enlarged head startled me, a striking contrast to the rest of her. It was swollen to the size of a watermelon. Her eyes occasionally rolled back, leaving only the whites visible. She laid hauntingly still, but when my siblings and I whispered in English to each other, her emaciated body and tiny lips moved, as if the foreign sounds awakened her. This child, barely clinging to life, stirred something deep in me. My heart ached. I heard there were thousands more like her, children left in the wake of a war fought long before their time. Children who, through no fault of their own, bore the invisible scars of a chemical meant to destroy forests and crops but instead shattered lives. I had learned about Agent Orange in college, its use as a herbicide by the American military during the war. It was supposed to strip the land bare, to expose the Việt Cộng hiding in the jungles. But I had never seen its aftermath on a human body. Now, staring at this child, I saw the cruelest of ironies, that a government that chastises others for using chemical weapons had once unleashed its own devastation in Southeast Asia. More than twenty million gallons of toxic chemicals were sprayed over Vietnam, Cambodia, and Laos, poisoning the land and its people. The legacy left generations of Vietnamese with skin rashes, neurological disorders, cancers, and birth defects, all connected to chemical warfare.

Looking at her, I could only guess her disease—hydrocephalus perhaps, maybe a congenital defect, or some other cruel mutation tied to Agent Orange. In that moment, the diagnosis seemed less important than the truth about what was in front of me: she was living evidence of a war's toxic shadow, a reminder that the past doesn't always stay buried in the soil. Doctors may have had a name, but a medical term felt useless against what I saw. Recalling that haunting scene, I know that, though gone, she was marked by a war she didn't live through and she existed in the legacy of the enormity of loss. It's a loss that belonged not just to my young relative, but to generations of victims born carrying the war inside their bodies, too.

Mom handed a crisp American $100 bill to the family. Their faces lit up with gratitude and relief as my cousin received the cash, her hands trembling. She tucked the money into her pocket and then embraced my mother, sobbing. "Cảm ơn, chị. Cảm ơn, chị," she repeated over and over, her voice breaking with emotion. Mom held her close, whispering softly, her words too quiet for me to hear, but the warmth of her gesture radiated through me.

Back in the van, I kept seeing their faces. They were my kinfolk, by not just blood but also history. They smiled like they were trying to hold on to something slipping. That kind of smile that doesn't know whether to celebrate or grieve. I couldn't stop thinking about the $100 Mom gave them. A hundred. That's all it took to shift something real in their lives. That money didn't feel like charity. It felt like truth. Like reparation. Like shame. I looked down at my shoes. Fancy-ass Cole Haans that I bought because I thought that's what success was supposed to look like. I used to believe shoes could say things I couldn't. But sitting there in a busted van with red dust still clinging to my cuffs, I felt sick. The same money I dropped on leather and shiny logos could carry a family through a whole year. That's not an exaggeration. That's math.

That little girl we'd just seen came back to me. Thin arms, swollen belly, eyes too tired for her age. Her body was telling the truth about everything we pretend not to see. And I—I had spent years pretending. Pretending I deserved more. Pretending my comfort didn't come at a cost. Pretending I was free. I started crying, not loudly, just steadily. Like my body was leaking all the things I never wanted to say out loud. Both my sisters were crying, too. Being identical twins, their whimpers rose and fell in unison. Their faces, so often mirrors of laughter and mischief, now mirrored sorrow instead, streaked with tears they couldn't hold back. I glanced over to see my fourteen-year-old brother crying, too. A burly teenager with shoulders already broad from adolescence, his tears came quietly. His gentle heart often betrayed him. None of us said a word, but I understood that we were feeling the same thing, that heavy, caramelized, thick as–*nước màu* kind of knowing that doesn't leave you once it settles in your chest. Our parents didn't say a word. Didn't offer comfort. Just let us sit in it. Let us cry. Let us reckon. In that silence, I didn't just grieve for that little girl. I grieved the parts of me that looked away. The parts that bought the shoes. The parts that thought proximity to wealth was the same thing as being real and whole and worthy. I grieved the lie and the living I built around it.

Everywhere we went in South Vietnam, struggle was loud. Not the kind from documentaries. This was raw, in your face and unapologetic. Beggars came in waves. Elders, women with babies, kids chasing cars. Observing the kids hit hardest. No shoes, rotting teeth, cracked skin, torn clothes, hair stuck to their scalps like it was tired of growing. They ran toward us, arms out, eyes wide, asking for what we could never give enough of. I gave what little I had. In every town, sorrow wasn't shocking; it was the baseline. Poverty lived everywhere we looked. It felt like trying to stop a wildfire with a napkin.

On the road to Sóc Trăng, we witnessed an accident between a vehicle and a man on a moped. Our driver didn't slow down. He careened through nonchalantly while I looked out the window and saw the man's body sprawled across the road, his head split open. Brain matter in the street like someone dared us to care. Blood and twitching limbs trying to hold on. As we drove past like it was just another turn in the road, I mourned the dead stranger.

But then a few days passed. And my own privilege? It didn't disappear. It just got quiet. It started whispering instead of shouting. We were riding in a Lambro 550, a three-wheeled golf cart-esque vehicle, headed to visit a family near Dad's neighborhood when the sky darkened and heavy clouds rolled in. A sudden downpour caught us off guard. People scattered, running for cover, but even those with umbrellas couldn't escape the torrential rain. Puddles quickly rose past their ankles, soaking everyone in their path. The Lambro, with its open-air cabin, left us exposed. Rain poured in from all sides like waterfalls.

I sat there, getting soaked, my face slapped by rain, thinking about how my Mama told us to dress nice. I had on my Cole Haans. But this time, stepping off that vehicle into mud so thick it tried to trap me, I felt something different. Not guilt. Not sorrow. Just . . . irritated. My branded-ass shoes sank into the wet earth. And me? I was mad they got dirty.

We stepped inside the house and took off our shoes like we were supposed to. Like we were taught. The tile was cold as punishment, and my feet, already aching, curled up against it like they didn't want to be there either. I was on my period, and I was bleeding. Heavy, angry bleeding. The kind that made my whole body throb. My lower back pulsed like it was holding a grudge. My head felt like it was being beaten from the inside. I didn't have a name for what was happening yet. No doctor ever named *adenomyosis* as the thing. A few years earlier, my parents dragged me to the apartment of Mr. Đồng's, the family acupuncturist. He pressed needles into my skin and whispered things about energy flow and balance. I nodded because I was supposed to, because they believed and I wanted to believe, too. But none of it worked. Not the needles. Not the bitter herbs that tasted like old dirt. Not the prayers whispered under breath while curled into the fetal position. The monthly agony remained, and it was with me in the family's home.

So there I was, in a stranger's house, my insides in revolt, my head a battlefield, my mood swinging somewhere between rage and exhaustion. I didn't feel like being polite. I didn't want to smile. I didn't want to be in Vietnam. I wanted my bed. I wanted a shower with hot running water from a shiny nozzle, not a cold splash of rainwater in an outdoor stall with a gecko judging me from the top ledge like he knew I didn't belong. Like he knew I was soft. And, yeah, it showed. I wasn't hiding it. My face told the truth that my mouth wouldn't. And Mom saw it. She always saw it.

The instant moment we got out of that house, she let me have it. Her voice was sharp and disappointed: "You disrespectful child! How could you look so unhappy and rude in someone else's home? What did they ever do to you?"

She was right. And I hated that she was right. I hated the shame curling in my chest. I hated that I couldn't explain the hurt, the heat in my body, the ache I hadn't learned how to name. I hated that she didn't ask what was wrong. She just scolded me for how I presented myself. How I presented our family. I sulked the whole ride back. Angry at her. Angry at myself. Angry at Vietnam for not being America, and angry at America for making me think comfort was the same thing as peace. That foul mood stuck to me for the rest of the trip. Heavy, sticky, mean.

By the time we were nearing the end of our visit, I was conflicted. As the plane ascended away from Saigon, I felt something twist in me. Like guilt. Like maybe I owed something to the people we met. To the kids on the street. To the families who didn't have a door to shut behind them. I wanted to stay. Or at least do something that mattered. But I also wanted my room and my shower and Vu's silly laugh and my soft mattress and not having to apologize for my moody face. I didn't know how to hold all these things at once that could be categorized into two neat desires—this wanting to help and this need to go home. So I just sat quietly on the plane, seat belt tight across my stomach, bleeding silently into a pad I had to change in an airplane bathroom, wondering if I'd ever come back.

We landed in Houston, tired, sleepy, exhausted. But two of our big suitcases never made it off the belt. My parents looked at each other the way parents do when something confirms all their worst suspicions. They muttered something about Tân Sơn Nhất and how the baggage guys probably saw American tags and helped themselves. One of the bags was mine, and, yeah, I felt that pinch of loss. But I also couldn't stop thinking about what we'd just come from. I tried to make peace with it, even if it was forced.

"It's okay," I said. "Whoever took them probably needed it more than we did."

Dad looked over at me, his face softening like a sermon was forming in his head. "Yes, Thảo. The Bible says God will bless those who give, for they will be given in return many times over."

But Mom? Nah. She wasn't buying any of it. "Tsk," she snapped. "We didn't *give* it to them. They *stole* it. Doesn't your Bible say you're not supposed to steal?"

She wasn't wrong. But she wasn't right either. Not all the way. I had just spent weeks seeing people dig through trash and beg with their eyes before their mouths even opened. Watching kids run barefoot on concrete that burned. So, no, I didn't *like* that our stuff was gone. But I couldn't be mad in the same way anymore. My anger had changed shape. And besides, I had something else on my mind. Someone.

The suitcases disappeared from my thoughts. I was thinking about Vu. Six weeks without a single word. Not even a letter. Just one postcard that I sent from our layover in Hong Kong. I'd folded all my missing him into the corners of that trip, but now we were back. That first night, I called. His mom picked up and said he was out. I didn't ask where or who he was with. I said "Thank you" and hung up before my voice cracked. I didn't sleep. I laid there, arms over my eyes like I could block out the wanting. My mind looped through everything. Kids in the streets, Mom yelling at me, geckos on bathroom walls, cold tile floors, the feel of rain in my socks, the girl on her death mat. And underneath all of it, I just wanted to tell Vu. Not to fix it. Just to know I was still me but just a little different, and he was still him, and that we were still something after all of this.

The next day, my body finally gave in. There were no alarms nor any sunlight strong enough to reach me. Just thick, heavy, necessary sleep. When I finally rose, some time deep into the afternoon, the house smelled like warmth. Mom was in the kitchen, and whatever she'd made had wrapped itself around the whole house like a soft quilt. Garlic, ginger, the hush of steamed rice lifting from the pot. I didn't know I was starving until the smell reminded me I was home. We ate slowly. I let the comfort of the food settle into the hollowness travel leaves behind. When my belly was full, the familiar pull of a food coma beckoned me again. I drifted toward my room, and my bed opened its arms. I didn't fight it. And yet, even in the cradle of desire for sleep, there he was dancing in my mind. Vu. His name didn't come as a thought, exactly. More like a murmur rising through my bones. The kind of remembering that lives behind the eyes. I let myself fall with him in mind. Let the dark pull me.

Then tap. And a few more taps. No louder than a breath against glass. *Tap. Tap.* I let it fold into my dream state. But it came again. Sharper now. Persistent. I cracked my eyes open. The digital clock glared: 11:32 p.m. I sat up, heart already skipping toward the possibility. Part of me didn't want to believe. The rest of me already knew. I crept to the window, pulled the stiff plastic blinds aside, and there he was. Lit by moonlight with a smile a mile wide. My heart lurched, stuttered, then raced like it had somewhere to be. I wanted to slide the glass open, reach through, touch the line of his jaw just to believe it. But I knew the alarm would scream and would wake the whole damn house. So I waved. Dumb and happy. I pointed to the front yard. He nodded.

I tiptoed down the hallway, each step a secret. Fingers fast on the alarm pad, careful not to miss a digit. The front door creaked a little as I eased it open. And there he was. We didn't speak right away. Just wrapped into each other. Arms, shoulders, laughter spilling from our mouths that were too full of feeling to say anything right. We twirled like kids who hadn't yet learned the weight of the world. Like we still believed in happy endings. Like love was something you could sneak out the front door and meet in the moonlight without it costing too much.

"I tried to call you, Sweetie," he whispered in his raspy voice, "but your parents said you were sleeping."

"What? They never told me!" I replied, annoyed.

"Probably because they hate me," he chuckled.

"No, they don't. I tried calling you, too, but your parents said you were out."

"Yeah, sorry, Sweetie. The guys needed me."

I nodded, pretending to be nonchalant. "Nah, it's cool." But the truth was, it wasn't cool. I knew what it meant when he said his "guys" needed him. Before I could voice my frustration, he kissed me, and I let it go.

"Let's go inside the truck," he suggested.

I had a riskier idea. "Let's go to my room."

He hesitated. "Uh, what about your parents? It's kinda risky, don't you think?"

"They're asleep," I reassured him.

"If you think it's okay, then okay," he said, though I could tell he wasn't fully persuaded.

Excitement got ahead of my good sense. I brought Vu inside like I forgot where I lived. Like I forgot who raised me. Like I forgot how fast joy can turn into something you might regret. We were in my room, barely breathing, barely touching, just *there*, when the door flew open. No knock. No warning. It was my dad. His face was hot with rage and eyes colder than I'd ever seen. He didn't yell. He didn't need to. He just told us to get out. Sit on the couch. Right now. I sat there next to Vu like the couch was a burning vessel while shame was the smoke filling my lungs. Dad's words came steady and heavy. Mom was quiet, but her silence and her burning eyes hit just as hard. All I heard in their voices was *How could you? What were you thinking? Do you know what kind of girl you're becoming?*

And when it was over, Dad raised his finger and pointed to the front door. Vu stood up to leave, shoulders hunched like he was trying to fold himself into a smaller mistake. Then Dad turned to me and said something I'll never forget.

"I'll never see him the same." He said it like a prison sentence. Like he was done.

Vu tried to take the blame. Said he should've known better. But I knew the truth. It was me. I didn't lock the door. I didn't listen. He told me it was risky, and I took that risk, and now we were both paying for it.

After that incident, everything got harder. My parents watched me like I was a ticking bomb. They asked questions about my every move. So I started lying. Told them I was studying at the library. Said I was driving girls home from volleyball practice. Anything to buy just an hour to see Vu. But Dad got slick and started tracking the mileage on my truck like he was calculating sin. When he confronted me, I lied again. Told him I gave someone at school a ride after we studied late together for group work. He didn't believe me. And this time, he didn't just talk. He slapped me. Right across the face. Not hard enough to leave a mark, but hard enough to leave a memory.

"Tell me the truth," he said.

But I didn't. I wouldn't. I looked him in the eye, tears hot but stubborn, and said nothing. What could he do? Stop me from going to school? Lock me in the house forever? I knew the cost. I knew what it meant to lie to my parents, betray their trust, to break every rule they built around me like a fence. But I wasn't gonna stop. Not for him. Not for them. Not for fear. If I had to lie, I'd lie. If I had to take the hit, I'd take it. I wanted Vu. And I was willing to pay in silence, in distance, in bruises no one could see.

I had already made my choice. Lied to my parents' faces so many times I stopped feeling the sting. Took every ounce of the love they poured into me and rerouted it toward a boy who made me feel like I could breathe outside their rules. I chose Vu over everything. But what happened next upended everything. A few weeks after my return from Vietnam, I heard rumors that he cheated on me. The rumors slid into my ears like poison, but I didn't want to believe it. I *couldn't* believe it. But the truth doesn't always show up with proof. Sometimes it just stays in your chest and refuses to let you sleep. Night after night, these rumors crawled under my skin and eventually grew teeth. It started chewing at the edges of every memory I had of him. I had to know.

We made plans to hang out. I tried to act cool. But as soon as I got in his truck. I didn't even give him time to settle.

"We need to talk," I said, flat. No smile. No warmth.

He looked at me, already scared. "Oh, shit. What did I do?"

"Take me to Bear Creek. I'm not doing this here."

We didn't say a word the whole ride. The silence felt heavier than any yelling ever could. When we arrived, he stepped out and around, reached to open my door like he always did, but I was already out, stomping toward the trail. He caught up, tried to grab my hand as if his fingers could undo what I came there to ask. I pulled away.

We sat on a bench. Wind moving the trees like they knew what was coming. I looked him dead in the face. "Did you fuck around on me while I was gone?"

He didn't answer. Just dropped his eyes like the dirt had something to say. That silence told me everything. But still, I let him talk. Let him give me the slow, slippery unraveling of his version of the truth.

First, it was, "I went out with the boys a few times, but I didn't talk to no girls."

Then, "I mean . . . some girls talked to me, but I didn't flirt back."

Then, "I was drunk, I don't even remember like that."

Then, “We danced . . . but that’s all. Nothing else happened.”

Every sentence was a shovel digging the grave of what we had. Every half-truth made me want to scream, but I didn’t. I just sat there and let the rage calcify in my chest while the betrayal burned slowly. I had thrown away so much. I lied, fought, got slapped, lost sleep, burned bridges for him. And now? He couldn’t even look me in the eye and give me the whole damn truth. It wasn’t just that he might’ve done something. It was that he didn’t respect me enough to say it straight. Every hesitation, every edit, every stammer made me feel smaller. Like maybe I’d been the only one playing for keeps this whole time.

I had sacrificed so much for him, and in return, this fucker betrayed me in a way that cut deep. He couldn’t comprehend why dancing with a few girls meant anything. To him, it was harmless. But to me, it wasn’t about the dance itself. It was about my pride, about the sharp sting of humiliation. It was the knowledge that the world, our world, had seen it, had seen him, my boyfriend, dancing with someone else as if I didn’t matter. It wasn’t just disrespect; it was a public disgrace, a signal to everyone that I didn’t hold his respect. I had been dissed, exposed, humiliated.

If he admitted that he met some girl and fucked around without anyone knowing, maybe, just maybe, I could have managed the sting. But this? This hit different. This wasn’t a private betrayal. It was a spectacle. I could already hear the whispers spreading through town: “Did you hear? Vu was out dancing with other girls while Thao was away.” And that’s what I couldn’t bear—the eyes, the judgment, the confirmation that I wasn’t enough. I was furious, my heart pounding with rage and embarrassment.

“It was a mistake,” he said with a sorrowful tone. “I wish I could take it back.”

But I couldn’t stomach the thought of being seen as weak, as the girl whose man dissed her publicly with another girl wrapped around his body on the dance floor.

"You fuckin' jerk! Goddamn piece of shit! You dirty fuckin' asshole!" I spat out, unable to contain the fury. "I've gone through so much with my parents for you, and this is what I get? I'm done! Just fuckin' done! I fuckin' hate you! Take me home now!"

He looked at me, apologetic, almost pleading. "Babe, I'm sorry. I didn't know dancing with some friends would make you so upset."

"Shut the fuck up!" I cut him off, my voice screeching like a wounded animal. "I don't care what you fucking think. Just take me home!" When he didn't move, I got up from the bench. "Man, I'll fuckin' walk then!"

Without waiting for a response, I stood up from the park bench and ran toward the street. He followed, calling out my name, grabbing my arm when he caught up. I wrestled against him, kicking back to break free. His grip loosened as I stomped on his foot, and I turned to face him, my breaths deep and hard, but my voice now eerily soft.

"Take me home. Now. Please."

His truck rolled slowly and rumbled to a halt in front of my house. I got out of the car and slammed the door shut behind me like a final chapter closed too abruptly. I didn't look back. I didn't want to see his face and didn't want him to see mine. I just walked inside, straight to my room, and let it all go. I cried like crying might wash something out of me. But it didn't. It just sat there, ugly crying with a sour feeling in my chest. That was supposed to be the end. Full stop. No sequel. No soft return.

He didn't let go easily. The calls came first. Then the card, handwritten and pristine with apology and remorse. Flowers showed up next. Then he got my sisters involved and got his sisters involved and then our friends involved. They said he was sorry. Said it wasn't that deep. Said people mess up. Said I should talk to him. Just once. Just hear him out. They all meant well, but they missed the point. They misunderstood the part where my head told my heart to close up shop. I told them flatly, "He could die for all I care," and I said it with my whole chest. But I said it because I had to. Because if I didn't say something sharp, I might have fallen apart again.

But the truth? The truth was uglier. I was hurt. Real fuckin' ugly-ass hurt. Heart cracked and broken and dragging behind me. I missed him like a phantom limb, and I hated that. I hated him. And I loved him. And I hated that I loved him. I was stuck in that in-between messy middle space where you say one thing and feel the opposite. Where your pride holds you together just tight enough to keep you from bleeding out.

Every time I saw him after that, it was like catching a knife between my ribs. I drank too much, hoping the itch from the hives and the sick in my stomach that would spill out from my guts to the ground would cover the sting. I told myself I was fine, but I wasn't.

And then he moved on, like people do when they get tired of trying. And I let him. Or pretended to. Then one night, I saw him out. There was no girl on his arm. Just him, standing in front of his truck of club Bayou Mama's, his eyes daring me to come hither. Of course, I was drunk. Stupid drunk. The kind that makes your feelings louder than your judgment. I stumbled onto him like my body remembered before my mind did. My arms found him, and my mouth betrayed me. "I still love you," I stated, slurred and raw. "But I hate you, too."

I turned around and left before he could say a word, knowing that if I lingered, I'd end up doing something softer and ruin the little bit of pride I had left.

Looking back, I see that what unraveled between us wasn't just about the dancing, or the girls, or even the betrayal I felt. It was about the way I swallowed the hurt until it turned sour, the way I let anger speak for me instead of giving my pain its true name. At nineteen, I didn't know that love requires more than longing; it requires language. To say: I felt abandoned. To say: I wanted to matter enough for you to choose me in moments when I'm not present. To say: I was scared of losing you, so I pretended I didn't care.

With time, I've learned that the words we're most afraid to speak are often the ones that might stitch a wound closed before it festers. That relationships don't end simply because of what happens, but because of what goes unsaid. If I had known then how to sit with my anger, to name my grief without letting it turn into rage, perhaps we might have repaired the crack instead of letting it splinter into distance and disrepair. At nineteen, pride felt like armor. As an adult, I've learned that pride can also be a cage.

4

When It Goes Black

His new girl was a friend of Judi's. That alone was enough to make my stomach tighten. Jackie told me his parents liked her. Not *loved*, just *liked*. Not like they liked me. Jackie always said they *loved* me. I tried to hold on to that. Like it meant something. I thought I had moved on, too. I dated a college boy who wore polos and had a savings account. The kind of boy you could bring to family dinner without your parents flinching. He paid for meals, asked about my GPA, and didn't beat up people just for giving him an improper look. On paper, he was the win. But paper can't hold hearts.

Vu still had his hands around me. Not literally. Just enough to pull a squeeze when I least expected it. Like that night at Bayou Mama's. The club was loud with sweat and lights and bass all bouncing off the walls. My homegirls were dancing with delight, in one hand drinks, the other up in the air, thrown around in unison with the beats. My sisters, who were a little more reserved than our homegirls, bobbed their heads and swayed their shoulders, mirroring each other, of course. My boyfriend stood next to me like we were in a liquor commercial. One arm around my shoulder, drink in the other, grinning like he was good for me. And maybe he was. But I wasn't in that room with him. I was with Vu. Or more honestly, I was watching him.

There he was. Dead center of the floor and gyrating with his girl like he didn't have a past. They were close, closer than I could stand. She laughed, head tilted back, and his hands slid down her waist like they belonged there. Everything inside me turned sour. The crowd, the music, the beat—all of it blurred behind the burn in my chest. My boyfriend leaned into me and said something into my ear about dancing. I shook my head. He kissed my cheek. I didn't even feel it. Because all I could feel was Vu, and all I could see was what used to be mine dancing like it never missed me. This jealousy thing? It crept up slow, then fast, then hard, then all at once. I grabbed my boyfriend's hand like he meant something to me and dragged him to the dance floor. I pushed myself into him and laid my head on his shoulder like I was trying to bury the ache in his shirt. I tried to dance like we were winning. But my eyes kept drifting and kept looking at them and kept wanting something else.

When Vu finally looked at me, his eyes were unreadable with the faintest tightening at the corners of his mouth—it was a flicker of a glance and just enough to burn. He turned away so quickly it was like I was a name he'd forgotten how to pronounce. That look, or lack of one, cut deeper than anything I'd ever felt. And just like that, I was invisible. Like I never mattered. Like all the lies, all the love, all the hurt never even happened. I turned to my boyfriend. Told him I wasn't feeling well. He nodded, concerned, gentle. He thought I meant the music or the crowd or the sweaty heat. But really, I was sick with remembrance and sick with watching someone I still loved dance like he was free. And knowing I shouldn't even be mad. We left the club, but part of me stayed there on the edge of that dance floor, watching my past hold someone else like it never broke me.

WHEN IT GOES BLACK

Eventually, I broke up with the college boy. He carried my books, left notes with sweet words on my windshield, treated me to my favorite dish (Cajun boiled crawfish), and bought me gifts showing that he knew me, like a Kenwood home stereo system. But sitting across from him at the coffee shop, his hand reaching for mine, I felt hollow. I nodded at the right moments, but my mind was back with Vu, back with the ache.

I let my classes go, too. First it was missing a lecture, then two. I told myself I was trying. I'd haul my textbooks to the library, stack them in front of me like a wall. Microbiology, organic chemistry, page after page of dense diagrams and formulas. I'd sit for hours, tracing the words with my eyes but not absorbing a thing. The exams came, and the grades fell.

I told myself I was a grown-ass woman. But the truth was messier. I was stuck. At home, I snapped at Mom for asking if I'd eaten, rolled my eyes at Dad's sighs of concern, and slammed my bedroom door hard enough to rattle the walls. My sisters caught the edge of it, too. My sarcasm toward them was sharper than it needed to be, my patience worn thin. They'd knock at my door, slip inside together, side by side, and ask if I was okay. I'd shrug, look up at them sideways, and toss out some cutting remark. "Do I look okay?" or "Why, y'all writing a report on me?" They meant kindness, but I met them with barbs because it was easier to push them away than admit that I was unraveling. My brother tried, too, in his own way. He'd hover in my doorway with a mix of awkwardness and concern that only a fourteen-year-old could carry. He'd try to lighten the mood by addressing me with a nickname that was reserved just between me and him. I can't remember how the terms of endearment even came to be. But when we're in our lightest selves with each other, we'd use them. "Hey, Nhibbz, you okay?" Our closeness wouldn't let me snap at him or sling unkind words at him. So I ignored him until he gave up and walked away. He had a tender heart, but I shut him out, too, turning away from the one person who might have made me feel better had I allowed it.

It took me too long to understand that the rage didn't come from the breakups or the failures or even the slipping grades in school. It came from way before that. From all the chaos I thought I'd grown past. From the yelling. From the fear. From the way love and violence showed up in the same room and nobody acted like it was strange. Back then, I didn't know I was walking around with trauma etched into my skin. I didn't have the words. I only felt the weight. And when everything started to crumble, I didn't think I was falling apart. I just stayed angry. Because anger, for a while, was easier than grief. Easier than honesty. Easier than sitting still and asking, *How the hell did I get here?* Now, looking back, I see it. I see the kid who didn't know how to ask for help. Who didn't know that survival ain't the same thing as healing. I see her. And I'm trying, slowly, to forgive her. But it's not fuckin' easy. Honesty and telling the truth is hard. Being vulnerable and soft on purpose? Even harder. That's why writing it down feels safer than saying it out loud. Say it out loud to a sibling? Nope. A friend? Nah. A lover? Please. A therapist? Hell no. Ain't no paper in their office thick enough to hold what I'm still too scared to say out loud. Maybe writing is easier therapy. At least the honesty and vulnerability are communicated in a confession that doesn't feel forced like it does when I attempt to speak it.

My earliest memories of anger are rooted in the foundation of 11411 Sagehurst Lane, Houston, Texas. When I think of my parents' marriage, there's no love in the picture frame. I had wondered if they were forced into it as if somebody picked for them. But that wasn't it. They chose each other. Dad used to joke it was a "shotgun wedding." He said Ông ngoại stood on the porch with a rifle pointed at his chest and told him he *had* to marry Mom. He said it with a chuckle, like it was just some funny American phrase he picked up from the guys he chopped it up with at his work where he was a machinist. He tossed their American humor into our family history like salty seasoning. But Mom wasn't laughing. When I translated what he said into Vietnamese, her face turned sharp and her voice even sharper:

"Liar! Don't you dare talk about my father like that! You chased after me like a dog! Don't lie to the children. They'll believe you!"

And then she cried. Mom cried a lot.

She cried when she couldn't get a message through to her family to tell them she was alive. She cried when Dad said he'd be home after dinner and didn't come back for two days. She cried when she saw pictures of him by a lake, sitting shoulder to shoulder with a woman she'd never met. She cried when the woman whose house she cleaned accused her of stealing a brooch that had been lost for years. She cried when she found out she was pregnant with twins. Said it was supposed to be lucky—Twin Dragons—but still cried, like luck wasn't something she trusted anymore because we were dirt poor and she cried because she didn't want her tiny children to go hungry.

She cried because she had no one to talk to. She cried because she was so alone even in a house full of people because Dad sponsored his siblings and left hers behind. She cried when her nephew drowned in the ocean trying to escape Vietnam. She cried when Dad blamed *her* for his sister's abortion. She cried when her brothers-in-law, grown men living rent-free under our roof, talked to her like she was less than them and expected her to cook, clean, and carry them toward their futures like she didn't have her own to fight for. She cried when she miscarried what would have been her fifth child. A boy. She cried when letters from Dad's family came from Vietnam, asking for money. Well, not really asking, more like demanding.

She cried when Ông ngoại died. She had a ticket booked to Vietnam and she hadn't seen him since we left in 1975, and he died just a few months before she was set to fly back. She was furious when she found out what he asked for before he died. It was a radio. All he wanted was a good radio that could pick up a strong signal. She wanted to send him a nice one, something solid and reliable. But Dad talked her down and said the cheap one would do. Said he'd handle it, but the radio never picked up anything. Mom never forgave Dad for that. Not just because of the radio but also because he made her feel powerless in a decision that mattered to her. Because he told her not to spend too much to connect to the man who raised her, the man who blessed her name, the man who asked for sound and got static. Mom's fury never ended. It still hasn't.

And me? I witnessed it all. Every tear. Every slammed door. Every lie wrapped in a joke. Every silence that turned into screaming when no one else was around. We never talked about love in that house. Just sacrifice. Just survival. Just what you owe and what you swallow. And Mom? Mom cried for all of it.

I learned early how to quiet my mother's crying. As a young child, I'd crawl into her lap and we'd rock, back and forth. I held her while she held me. I was her daughter and her comfort, her child and her consolation. That was our rhythm. By the time I was in middle school, her cries got louder and heavier and angrier. They turned from weeping into wailing and then into something that didn't sound human anymore. And my father, a Vietnamese-born, Southern Baptist-made man, thought submission was her job. And he let her know that. When Mom roared, he responded with fists, with hammers, with destruction. When she came at him with the scorching truth—about the money he pissed away, the secret wire transfers to his family back in Vietnam, the fact that her children were growing up scared—he broke shit. He broke the air with curses. He broke the sound with smashed-up electronics. And he broke her with his fist.

They fought like animals. He the Tiger born in 1950, and she the Cat born in 1951. Mom's tongue could cut deep. She screamed words that clawed at every failure he tried to bury. She talked about his weak spine and his obsession with pleasing everyone except his wife and children. She called out the way he gave everything to his side of the family and left her side begging for scraps. She'd call him a coward, a disgrace, a puppet of a man to his mother who couldn't hold his own in his own home.

And then, he would snap. He broke things when he got mad. I mean *really* broke them. Smashed the mirrored walls in the dining room like he was breaking the truth's reflection. Took a hammer to the ceiling lamp, smashing the glass casing and the bulb. Threw the VCR into the wall like it had cursed him. Tossed the wood framed Zenith television across the room like it had been watching too closely.

And then he tried to break Mom. He'd rush at her and grab her by the neck with both hands. I saw her body snap back against the wall, then crash to the floor. His fist tangled in her hair, yanking her head while her tiny hands clawed at his grip, trying to pry herself free, but they slipped uselessly against his strength. The sound of her body slammed to the ground was sharp, like a loud slap. But even as she lay curled on the floor, she spat fire at him, her words a stream of curses that scorched not just Dad but also his siblings, his mom, and his whole bloodline. Her voice shook, but it never broke. I stood frozen, watching them and knowing I was too small to stop him and I was too scared to move. My fists balled tight at my sides, nails digging into my palms. I held my breath, chest burning, as if the smallest sound from me might set the whole room off again. The air buzzed with the violence of both their bodies, and it felt like the walls themselves were trembling with me. I remember these moments not only as visions, but also as sounds—the thud of his rage and the spit of her defiance.

By the time I entered high school, my body had changed—hours in the weight room, on the volleyball court, and on the track made me feel stronger. It made me think I could step in between my parents. The first time I tried, I wedged myself between them. Dad's arm reached past me grabbing Mom's shoulders. Mom was shouting over my shoulder. I pushed my forearms against Dad's chest and shouted, "Stop!" They both froze, maybe even startled, or just thrown off at the sound of my voice breaking through their violence. Sometimes that pause was enough. And sometimes they stopped because they ran out of steam. Sometimes they stopped because they saw me and my siblings standing there, shaking, trying not to cry. And after? I cleaned up. Swept up shards of glass. Pulled wires from the carpet, picked up knobs and busted-up remotes with the batteries on the other side of the room. Then I made sure Mom was okay. Brought her ice. Sat with her and held her.

The worst was always when they fought in the middle of the night. It's the kind of fight that doesn't creep in. It crashes and wakes you up and makes sleep a distant memory. I'd jolt up, heart thumping, ears wide open, body already knowing before my mind caught up. I'd slip out of bed and stand outside their bedroom door, frozen, listening. Mom's voice was sharp and high. Dad's voice was low but heavy. I'd scream through their door, not knowing what else to do and thinking that maybe if I yelled "Stop!" loud enough and enough times, it might make a difference.

They'd yell back at me. *Go to bed, Thảo. You got school tomorrow.* Like sleep was something I could return to after hearing what I'd heard. As if fuckin' literature and algebra were more urgent than fear and dread. But they were right about one thing: I was tired. Tired in my bones. Tired in my brain. Tired in the way only a child forced to carry adult things can be. Sometimes, if their yelling faded into silence long enough, my body gave in. I'd fall asleep again, like surrendering.

But the fights never stayed gone. That's the thing. They always came back. Same wounds, just dressed up differently. What they never resolved got recycled.

The worst night, the one that still revisits me like a perpetual haunting, was when Mom screamed my name like it was the last word she'd ever say.

"Thảo! Thảo! Your father is going to kill me!"

I ran to the door, beating on it with both fists, kicking at it until the frame shook, and screaming at it as if the sound of my desperate voice could bust open the lock. My throat burned from begging, tears streaking down my face. I heard the lock turn, and the door creaked open slowly. I stood there, barely breathing.

The room was dark, but the hallway light spilled in just enough to carve the scene. Mom was curled on the far edge of the bed, knees pulled up like a shield, her hair like a curtain, hanging over her face and covering her eyes. Dad stood closest to the door with a rifle in his hands. Not sure why, but my sobs cut off instantly. At the sight of the gun, panic should have rushed in, but instead, a strange, icy calm spread through me. I stepped forward and said, softly as I could, "Daddy, what are you doing? You need to put the gun away. Please."

I didn't look at his face. My eyes were fixated on the shape of the weapon, long and lean, but its menacing presence made it feel larger than anything else in the room. Dad didn't say a word. He just stepped forward, moved past me, slow and deliberate, and walked to the closet. He put the rifle back, and I exhaled the long breath I was holding. Without a word, he left the room, footsteps heavy on the floor. In the silence, I heard his body collapse on the upholstered couch in the living room. I climbed into bed with Mom and pressed my body against hers and felt the tremor still shivering through her body.

Morning came with a pale light leaking through the blinds. I hadn't slept. Mom was sleeping, her breathing finally slowed, soft and steady, almost peaceful. I checked the living room and Dad was still there, sleeping and breathing soundly, too.

When they both woke up, they told me and my siblings we could stay home from school. Their voices were gentle and careful. We all said no. I didn't want to miss school. I think I needed normal like the routine of bells in between classes and noises like lockers slamming instead of the kind of slamming that sounds like war. My siblings also acted as if they didn't hear anything. But they did. We all did. They admitted to me later they had stayed in their beds, crying under the blankets, waiting for the house to go quiet again. That was the signal. Quiet meant we survived the night and the storm had passed. We went to school like nothing happened. Like we hadn't all just witnessed what it meant for our father to pick up a gun.

As the eldest, I became the buffer and the referee. I was the girl with the towels blotting up spilled food, with a broom sweeping and gathering shards of broken dishes. The peacekeeper negotiating a war between two factions of a supposedly unified party and the broken heart trying to not take sides, even when I wanted to. I told myself I was being fair. But what I was really doing was surviving and trying to explain the behaviors of two people and making sense of two people who didn't make sense together. In the language of a child, it was that Dad did something wrong. Mom yelled. Dad got mad about the yelling, so he had to break stuff. Sometimes "stuff" was the electronics. Sometimes "stuff" was Mom. That was the logic I carried into adolescence and into womanhood. That violence made sense and could be explained, even excused, if it was provoked. That women got beaten when they got too loud. That being right didn't keep you safe. That love could look like war. And the hardest part? The part that I still carry? Even after the brokenness, the bruises and the blood, I loved them both. Even in all that. Even after all that. My parents are still together. Time has weakened their bodies but not their voices. What was once war fought with fists and broken glass has been reduced to sparring in words, the quarrels still sharp but fleeting. The battles have softened, though it seems their version of love and stubbornness keep them bound together, weathered by decades, still circling like wind and rain in the same storm, never at rest but never apart.

I'd like to think I went to school like nothing happened. But rage and violence and war must have been the lessons I took with me, just like the essays and geometry proofs I kept in my Trapper Keeper. When I was bullied at school, I fought back. When my friends were bullied at school, I fought back. When my sisters got bullied, I fought back hard. Each time I fought back, I remember my body impulsively acting out with a rage that felt fiery red, but my mind, it went blank, like everything went black. And every time, I got away with it because I was the Vietnamese girl who made straight A's and was an undisciplined but rising star on the volleyball team.

By the time I entered college, I hadn't changed. One night, when my sisters came home from a party, I saw the scratch right there, on my sister's face. She said some girl named Abby came at her over some boy. Some dude whose attention floated in the wrong direction, and that was enough for Abby to put her hands where they didn't belong. That was all I needed to hear. I didn't even think. I just felt. For months, I prowled for her like a bounty hunter, scanning faces in smoky clubs, dim-lit parties, crowded karaoke bars, waiting for hers to appear.

Then one afternoon, there she was.

I was on a lunch break with my sister and college mates between classes, sitting at a *phở* shop in downtown Houston's Little Saigon shopping mall. It was broad daylight. My sister spotted her through the giant window, leaned toward me and spoke softly, "Hey, that's Abby." My body was up before my mind caught up. My fists already forming, clenched tight, knuckles aching to make contact, legs already moving. My college boyfriend reached for me, grabbed my arm and spoke low but urgent, "Chill. Just sit down and relax. Let's eat *phở* and act like normal people."

So I sat. But my knees bounced and my jaw was locked tight. Through the window, I watched Abby lingering with her friends, smiling and laughing as if she didn't owe my family anything. My blood was hotter than the soup boiling in the kitchen.

"I gotta go to the bathroom," I said flatly, already pushing my back chair. The bathroom was in the mall hallway where Abby was frolicking with her friends. But I wasn't 'bout to take no damn potty break. I marched out that door and straight toward her, every step with purpose, like justice had a time limit. Walked right up to her, getting in her face close enough to smell her perfume mixed with cigarette smoke, and introduced myself like I was handing her a business card from hell.

"My sister is the girl you fucked with at Kiss. And you're gonna regret it."

She didn't blink. She didn't even flinch. She came at me first, her hands shooting to my throat, like she thought I'd back down. Like I wouldn't go there. But I went there. And my mind went black. I grabbed her shoulder and slammed her into the *phở* shop window so hard the glass rattled in its frame. Folks inside snapped their head at the thud of her body against the glass. To me, it sounded like satisfaction. The clean sound of payback. She dropped, and I dropped with her. I got on top, one hand pinning her down with fingers pressed into her neck, the other hand curled in a fist slamming into the flesh of her face. I unleashed my ire on her with clenched teeth. When I finally stood up and my breath came heavy and ragged, words uttered out of me between gulps of air.

"Don't. Fuck. With. My. Sister. Ever. Again."

I heard people screaming, and someone calling for security. All that noise, but I didn't hear any of it. All I felt was heat rising off me, rising out of me, burning through me. My sister yanked at my shirt, wide-eyed, and we took off sprinting. We broke through the crowd and jumped into my truck. I peeled out of the parking lot, tires screeching like we were escaping more than just a fight.

And I'll be honest: I felt proud. Proud like I'd done something holy. Like I'd defended something sacred. Like violence was more than a reaction, it was more like a legacy. It was a language I inherited, and one I spoke fluently.

Violence was everywhere. It was in the home, the school, the streets. And it was in me. I learned it watching my parents scream at each other into silence. I learned it in the school hallways where the Vietnamese fought the Mexicans and the Blacks. I learned it in the clubs and in the parking lots under streetlights. I learned that if you struck hard and didn't flinch, people would leave you alone. People would respect you. Fear you. And I liked that feeling. I needed it.

They'd say, "Don't mess with Thảo. She's down to fight."

And they were right. That reputation became my armor. It was power. It was something that covered the cracks in me and made me feel like more than just a girl trying not to fall apart. The streets drilled into me that whatever happened to my crew happened to me and that I should defend it for the honor. My parents drilled into me that whatever happened to my sisters would be my fault. If they got hurt, it was because I failed them. The pressure from the street code and the family code pounded in my bloodstream. And the rhythm of violence was the only one it seemed to know.

Looking back, I see what I couldn't see then. That the fighting, the rage, the way I lashed out—it wasn't just reaction. It was communication. It was survival. That's how I learned to move through the world. Violence was clarity. Power. Control in a life that offered little.

When Vu broke my heart, I didn't cry for long. When I felt tears coming, I cursed him under my breath and reminded myself he wasn't to be trusted. And he wasn't to be forgiven but to be punished. I wanted to make him feel the pain I couldn't name by screaming and cursing at him. By refusing his pleas for forgiveness. By rejecting his wishes to get back together and then ignoring his calls for months. By finally accepting his calls only to tell him I tossed the CD of love songs he made for me and the flowers he sent into the trash bin with petals still bright and alive. Because that's what I knew how to do. Hurt others because I was hurt. Strike because I was struck. That was righteousness, that was justice, to me. Back then.

And there was something seductive about it. The way violence could rearrange a moment and force the world to take notice. A clenched jaw felt safer than an open heart. A blow landed with precision said, *You don't get to leave without feeling this.* And in that, I felt strong. Stronger than the girl who was always waiting for someone else to decide her worth.

Even now, some days, I wonder how far I've really come from that girl at the park or in the mall hallways cursing, threatening and throwing fists through gritted teeth. I catch myself, at times, still feeling the heat in my head when I interact with my family, my friends, my intimate partners, my colleagues, my acquaintances, my students, my mentees, the random person in front of me at the checkout line. People I know well, people I don't know well, people I don't know at all. People who I believe are "doing me wrong," doing wrong to someone I care about, doing wrong to others, doing wrong to society. Back then I wanted to hurt people because I didn't know how else to feel *real*. To feel seen. To feel like I mattered. Somewhere in that fury, I mistook fear for power. And sometimes, I still have remnants of those thoughts, sometimes I feel those impulses of wanting to fight, to battle. But I know I've changed for the better. I've evolved. People tell me I'm bubbly, kind, diplomatic, fair, calm, cool, collected, and even charming. It's taken decades of self-reflection, self-awareness, and self-forgiveness to understand the root of the heat I feel burning inside me that makes me want to act with negativity. It's taken decades of active, cognitive reprogramming of the heart and mind.

Today, I turn the want to fight into the want to problem-solve. Managing my emotions, naming them, thinking through the role I have in the conflict, perceived or real, and finding a solution, a resolve—with respect, with clarity, with intention, with care, with compassion, with understanding, with love. And sometimes, when there's no solution, no resolve, no respect left, I say fuck it, and walk away with no regrets that I didn't try to work things out.

5

Reunion Interrupted

IN 1995 I WAS REALLY close to giving up on school. Not like I *planned* to quit. It's just that I drifted further and further from it until it didn't feel like it could be mine anymore. I moved out of my parents' home before I had to hear their lectures. I was scared of the yelling. Scared of the disappointment. Scared of how much it would hurt to see all that love and hope and expectation curdle into shame.

I got a job as a parts manager at a small family-owned computer shop. Nothing fancy, nothing I dreamed of, but it paid enough to keep me from going back to gangster stuff. Sometimes I had to cover the phones when the receptionist dipped out for lunch or got caught up in the back. I didn't love it, but I could fake it. I knew how to smile through my voice, even when I was tired or trying not to think too hard about what I'd left behind.

It was a Thursday evening, almost closing time. The fluorescent lights of the retail office hummed. The air was stale with decades-old, upholstered desk chairs and dust from cardboard boxes we hadn't opened yet. Then the phone rang. I picked it up and put on my best customer-service mask.

"Good afternoon. Thank you for calling Omni Teq Computers. This is Lauren, how may I help you?" I tried to sound smooth and mature, like I wasn't in my early twenties.

A voice on the other end asked, "Hi, may I speak to Thao?"

That voice. It was familiar and beautiful. I knew it was *his* voice. My pulse hit the brakes and punched the gas at the same time. But I tried to sound casual, "This is she. Who's this?"

"Hi, it's me, Vu. Did you say your name was Lauren?" He chuckled softly, the sound sending a rush of warmth through me.

I laughed along, trying to keep it light. "Yeah, they made me pick a white girl name so customers wouldn't have trouble pronouncing Thao."

"How hard is it to say Thao? Damn, it's weird hearing you call yourself Lauren."

"I know, right? I hate it. But it's what the boss wants. Her name's Mai—easier than mine! But she goes by Jennifer!" I laughed, trying to shake the nerves buzzing inside me. "Anyway, this is a surprise. How'd you know where to find me?"

"I called your house. Your sister gave me your work number."

"Oh, cool." I paused, trying to mask the excitement building up inside. "So, what's going on?"

"I know we haven't spoken in a while. It's really good to hear your voice, by the way."

My chest got heavy in that warm kind of way, the kind you feel right before your voice cracks. I wanted to tell him everything. That I missed him. That hearing him again did something to my whole damn day. But I didn't. I just sat there and stayed quiet, heart pounding loudly in my chest, waiting for him to continue.

"I need a favor," he said, his voice soft but serious. "If you're free this evening."

I tried to keep my tone steady. "What kind of favor?" I asked.

"Nothing bad, don't worry. Look, I moved out of the apartment I was sharing with my girlfriend. I'm moving away. Things have gotten pretty hot because of some stuff the guys did. I packed up and left about an hour ago. But I left something behind, something I hid in the AC vent by the bedroom. It's precious, and I need you to go get it for me. I want you to have it. Would you do that for me today? The management won't check the place until tomorrow."

"Are you in trouble?" I asked with concern. "Is everything okay?"

"Everything's fine," he reassured me, though his tone didn't calm my nerves. "I just need you to get this one thing for me. It's important, and I want you to have it. Please, do this for me. For old time's sake."

I sat gripping the phone, torn between the thrill of hearing from him and the fear of what this might mean.

I pulled up to the address he had given me and parked my car on the street. I was surprised by how close his apartment complex was to my workplace, though it felt like another world entirely. The rundown buildings stood in contrast to the soft, pre-dusk light that bathed everything in a warm, golden hue. It was almost beautiful, the way the fading sun softened the edges of a place so clearly worn by time. I stepped out of my car, a mix of trepidation and excitement swirling in my chest as I approached the front door.

Turning the doorknob, I hesitated for a moment, the quiet enveloping me as I stepped inside. The one-bedroom apartment was eerily silent and empty of furniture. The air had a faint odor like old carpet, like the place hadn't had its move-out cleaning yet, but the beige carpet had no stains, the walls—a lighter shade of beige—had no scuff marks, and the white blades of the ceiling fan were dust free. The outdoor light peeked through the plastic vertical blinds from two windows in the living room. I flipped the light switch by the dining area and scanned for the air conditioning vent. It was next to the kitchen, its standard white appliances and honey-toned oak cabinets clean, the countertop bare. My heartbeat quickened as I approached the vent, trying to keep my thoughts steady. I took a deep breath and called out, "Anybody in here?" Silence answered me.

I knelt down and removed the vent cover, my hands steady but my mind buzzing. As I reached in, my fingers brushed against something soft—smooth paper. I gently pulled it out and unrolled a large white scroll. My breath caught in my throat. It was a drawing, a caricature of us. The one we had made at Six Flags Astroworld three years ago when we were still together. I had forgotten about it. The exaggerated cartoon versions of us stared back at me, his big ears, my wide eyes. I couldn't help but laugh softly, feeling a mix of confusion and giddiness.

The colors were soft pastels, the lines black and bold, and I remembered how we had played paper, rock, scissors to decide who would keep it since we couldn't afford two. He had won and kept it, but now, he wanted me to have it. I rolled the paper back up carefully, my heart unexpectedly lighter. I hadn't realized how much of the hurt about our good times together I had been holding on to until that moment.

But as I stood there, a multitude of questions arose. Did this mean he still loved me? Or was this his way of moving on, wanting to let go of the past by giving it to me? If he was moving on, why not just throw it away? Why have me go through all of this to retrieve it? He had called it "precious," after all.

I put the vent cover back on and took a few steps, glancing around the apartment. I peeked into the bedroom, imagining it furnished, picturing him there with someone else. A pang of sadness hit me, an ache that reminded me of what we had once had. I had walked away, and with that choice, I had closed the door on any chance of us getting back together. Regret seeped in, and for a moment, I allowed myself to feel the burden of everything lost. But then pride kicked in, pulling me out of the spiral. *I ain't got time for this shit*, I told myself, shaking off the sorrow. The sky outside was growing darker, and I knew I needed to leave. No sense in risking trespassing charges or something worse. I closed the door behind me, the scroll still in my hands, feeling like I was leaving with more than I had expected.

Back at my apartment, the quiet wasn't just quiet, it was loud with everything I didn't say. The air felt too still, like it was waiting on something I couldn't have. Regret came, like it sometimes did, but this time it sat different. Heavier. I stared at that rolled-up drawing, just paper and ink, but it held more of us than I ever could in words. And that's when it hit me. Yeah, *I was the one who walked away* from him. But some fucked-up part of me stayed. Still missing him. Still holding on. Still wanting to tell him I never really let go.

Another year passed, and the violence around us only intensified. Every week seemed to bring news of another tragedy. Someone we knew was assaulted, robbed, shot at, or worse. Friends were shot and wounded, shot and killed, or died by their own hands. The air was thick with fear and sorrow, hanging over me like a constant, inescapable shroud. Then the merciless winter of 1996 arrived. It was nearly two years after we had last spoken when Vu reached out to me again.

I was at work, surrounded by computer parts while doing the end of year inventory count of hard drives, CPUs, memory sticks, motherboards, cables, graphic cards, and more. The winter months were slow at the shop, and I was counting the minutes until I could close up and head home. The phone rang, and I cringed, hoping it wasn't another service call.

"Lauren, you have a call on line one," the intercom announced. I picked up the phone, using my fake cheery voice. "Hi, this is Lauren. How may I help you?"

And then I heard his unmistakable laughter. "Hi, Thao. It still gets me when you say your name is Lauren."

I rolled my eyes but was unable to stop a smile. "Yeah, well, if you called me at my place, you wouldn't hear me say Lauren."

He chuckled. "I don't have the number to your place. Those pesky twins wouldn't give it to me." I smiled, thinking about how protective my sisters were. "Anyway, are you free after work?"

I hesitated, memories of the last favor he'd asked flickering in my mind. "Why? Need another favor? Last time you called, you had me running an errand. But thank you for the gift you left me."

His voice softened. "No, thank *you* for going out of your way to get it. I hope you didn't throw it away."

"No, I kept it," I replied, the memory of the caricature still fresh in my mind. "It's on my wall, right next to the voodoo doll I made of you."

He burst out laughing, and despite the irritation I still felt about his girlfriend, I found myself comforted by the sound. "My girlfriend wanted me to throw it away, but I couldn't. I couldn't bring myself to put it in the trash. Thanks again for keeping it. But I'm not with her anymore, so it doesn't matter now. Anyway, I'm not calling because I need a favor. Well, maybe it is."

I sensed the shift in his tone, and my heart began to race. "What's wrong? Talk to me," I demanded.

He paused, the silence stretching into what felt like an eternity. My stomach knotted with dread. "I just need someone to talk to. I really need to talk to you in person. Can you meet me at the Viet *bi da* off Highway 249? You know, the one where you used to pick me up when I was too drunk to drive?"

The mention of that pool hall brought back a flood of memories. I knew the place well. It was where the Viet gangsters hung out, where they smoked, drank, placed bets, and brawled. His request felt different this time. His tone was heavy with something unspoken. "Yeah, of course. I'll clock out now and head over. Do you need anything? Something to eat?"

"No, just get here when you can. Don't rush, and drive safe, okay? I just need to talk to you in person."

I hung up, feeling a sense of urgency pulsing in my chest. I gathered my things quickly and bolted out of my office. As I passed by my boss, Chị Mai, she glanced up.

"You're leaving on time today, Lauren! Got a hot date tonight?" she teased, her eyes twinkling mischievously.

I forced a chuckle, "Not quite a hot date, Chị Mai. Just need to see someone important. Have a good night!"

I rushed to my car, my mind racing as I drove. The heavy traffic around me only added to my anxiety. As I navigated through the congestion, my thoughts swirled, fantasizing possible scenarios. Maybe he wanted to talk about us, maybe this was a chance to reconcile. But bad news always came disguised as casual requests, and my mind veered toward darker possibilities: Was he in trouble? Financial ruin? Got his girlfriend pregnant and was running off to the military like Sergeant Big Lips? But he said they had broken up. Was he in trouble with the law? No, if that were the case, he wouldn't be hanging around a place that cops regularly raided.

The dread led my head to flash through all the people who were gone from my life in one way or another. Doughboy and his fifty-year sentence. Đức's untimely death. My uncle, incarcerated. Marco, shot point-blank for being involved with a drug dealer's wife. Minh, killed at Club Roxy as an innocent bystander. Phương and Mirena, who had dropped out of school with babies to care for. Rosie and Linda Legs, high on coke just to get through a night's work at the "modeling" studio. So many lives gone, destroyed, or broken, and I couldn't save any of them.

I took the exit off the highway, knowing I was close. The feeling of worry was slowly replaced by anticipation, even a glimmer of hope. The thought of meeting up with him at his request, seeing his face, and hearing his voice in person felt like a balm for the wounds that time had never quite healed. Our breakup had left me melancholy, but with time and distance—out of sight, out of mind—I had managed to process some of it. When he asked me to save that old drawing of us, I found myself wanting to forgive him, to forget all the dumb shit from the past, and to start fresh. But he had someone else, and I couldn't say what I wanted to say.

In the moments before reaching him, I started to imagine a new life for us. We could be a working-class couple, nothing fancy. We didn't need to achieve what the world expected of us. As long as we had love, that would be enough. But how would I find the courage to say all this? If he had a new girlfriend, how could I convince him she wasn't the one for him? I rehearsed lines over and over in my head. *I'm sorry. Please forgive me. I know I can be stubborn, but I still love you. I hope you still love me. Can we try again?*

As I approached the strip plaza, the neon sign of the pool hall flickered in the distance. But my attention shifted instantly to the red and blue lights flashing in the parking lot. My heart dropped. As I got closer, the powder-blue patrol cars of the Houston PD came into focus. *Fuck. Fuck. What the fuck.*

A flood of thoughts flashed through my head: Was there a fight? A shooting? Was he involved? Was he hurt? I pulled into a nearby parking spot, scanning for broken windows or ambulances. But there were none. It had to be a brawl gone too far, I reasoned. The cops must've been called to break it up. I looked toward the flashing lights, my heart pounding harder with each step. Then I saw him, sitting on the curb, hands cuffed behind his back. My stomach clenched as I started to tremble.

An officer approached my car, bending down as I rolled the window down, trying to steady my voice. "Can I help you, young lady?" he asked, his tone firm but not unkind.

"Hello, sir," I replied, forcing a calm I didn't feel. "I'm here to pick up my friend. What happened?"

He gave me a tight-lipped smile, shaking his head. "Nothing to worry about—unless that gentleman on the curb is your friend?"

I hesitated, my heart screaming *yes*, but my mind forcing a different answer. "No, sir. That's not my friend."

"Well, we've cleared out the place, so maybe your friend found another ride." His voice was dismissive. "You should get going. This isn't a place for you."

He tapped my door, shooed me away with a backhand wave, and walked back to the scene. My eyes followed him, drifting back to Vu. His shoulders were slumped, his head hanging low, but he turned his face sideways toward me. Our eyes met—his sad, mine desperate. He flashed a half smile, trying to communicate something, but all I felt was an overwhelming wave of helplessness. I raised my hand to wave, but it trembled, frozen in midair before curling into a tight fist. I pressed it to my lips, trying to stop them from quivering.

I watched as the cops lifted him from the curb and led him to the patrol car. His gaze never left mine until they pushed him into the back seat, the door slamming shut. That's when the dam broke. "Oh, God. No. Please. Please, please, please, no!" I wailed, my voice cracking as tears blurred my vision. I hunched over the steering wheel, shaking my head, my hands gripping the leather so tightly my knuckles felt cold. My breath came in gasps as I fought to swallow the tears, wheezing between sobs. I heard the crunch of gravel under tires as the patrol cars pulled out of the lot, leaving in a line. And then they were gone.

I collapsed against the wheel, one hand clutching it, the other pounding the dashboard in frustration and anguish. I don't know how long I stayed like that. I can't even remember what I did after. It's all a blur, everything after that moment seemed to fade to black. I must have gone home, but it's a memory I can't quite recall.

I do know that in the following days I vowed to do better. I wanted to be there for him, support him, comfort him. As it turned out, I couldn't do any of that. I would have my own shit to deal with. Just a few weeks after his arrest, I got shot.

6

Life in Millimeters

POOL HALLS WERE LIKE A second home back then. I knew every table, every warped cue stick, every angle on that green felt. I'd learned to play in the game rooms at the University of Houston, skipping more lectures than I want to admit, letting time stretch out between trick shots and chalk dust. Slick Willie's on Westheimer was busy real estate on weekend nights. On the night of January 10, 1997, I rolled in to Slick Willie's with one of my sisters and my homies Hải, Liz, and Hiệp. Hiệp was the soccer boy who was so into me he offered up his car and time and money like it might buy him something more permanent. I let him orbit.

That night had all the makings of a night out with the homies. We joked. We bet rounds. We shit talked. The balls clicked and scattered like applause. There was laughter, the kind that makes you feel young and untouchable. And for a minute, we were. Just Vietnamese young adults in a pool hall, floating in rhythm, softly lit under buzzed-out fluorescents.

Then it snapped.

The sharp crack of a bottle cutting through the air from the hands of an angry pool shark drowned out the clatter of cue balls. The bottle smashed against someone's head, glass exploding, a wet spray of blood coloring the young man's white T-shirt. Everyone froze, then faces contorted from shock to rage. The room twisted before anyone could even speak. Then a shout ripped through the air, half curse, half challenge, "Motherfucker, let's go!" Chaos didn't ask for permission, it just showed up, like it always did in the Dirty Yellow South. The smack of fists, the scrape of chairs knocked sideways, cue balls hurling, sticks cracking across thin shoulders and backs. It was fury and years of old beef that simmered until it boiled over and burned everyone in that place. Vietnamese gangsters posting up like kings, all pride and posture. Too many egos. Too many hungry young men trying to prove they weren't to be played with.

I'd seen it before. That mix of heat, beer, and bravado? That's a deadly cocktail. And everybody in the room sipped whether they knew it or not. We weren't even four games in, but it didn't matter. The table didn't mean shit once the violence erupted. The chatter and laughter shut down abruptly. And just like that, we were in it. That was Houston. That was Southwest. That was our version of a Friday night. And we called it normal.

We'd seen it too many times. This wasn't new. And it sure as hell wasn't entertainment, for some anyway. If you stuck around too long and didn't run out, you could become a headline, a name from the prison automated collect call operator, or a candlelight vigil where someone screams your name as your casket gets lowered into the dirt. So we made for the door. Fast, furious, and focused. But as we hit the threshold, I looked around and didn't see Liz with us. My stomach dropped. I suddenly remembered she'd gone to the bathroom, probably fixing her lipstick or washing her hands, calm as ever while hell was breaking loose.

I told the others to go. No hesitation. Just go! Then I turned back and scrambled through the madness. I found her just as she was exiting the bathroom and stuck in confusion. "Liz," I said, breath tight. "We gotta get the hell outta here. Now. This shit's bad." She didn't ask questions. We held hands, and we ran.

By the time we were sprinting to Hiệp's gold Mercedes Benz , the fight had spilled outside into the parking lot. Fluorescent lights from the retail plaza lit up the flashes of anger, bodies darting between Hondas and BMWs. Voices screamed out names and curses and threats. We were steps from the Benz when the first shot cracked the air.

Boom! Then another. *Boom! Boom!*

The sound cut the air clean open. Loud screams and high-pitched shrieks followed. Tires screeched as cars peeled out. Somebody yelled "Get down!" but it all came out in one big wave of noise and panic and sweat. People around us hit the ground, others bolted in every direction. We didn't hit the ground; Hiệp's car was so close I figured we could make it. We didn't look back. You don't look back when the world is breaking behind you. You just run. You just get into the car. You just pray your name ain't the one written on the bullet.

"Hurry, get in!" I yelled. Hải was already in the front with Hiệp. My sister was in the back, wide-eyed, shouting for us to get in. Just as Liz and I lunged for the open door, another round of shots cracked through the air. "Boom! Boom! Boom!"

I shoved Liz in and threw myself over her and my sister, shielding them with my body as the shots kept going. For a heartbeat, there was silence, broken only by my own pounding breath. I barked at Hiệp to drive, and as I sat up to survey the scene, I saw the door hadn't closed. I reached over, hands shaking, sweaty palms gripping the handle, and just as I was pulling it shut, *Boom! Boom!* The shots shattered the stillness again.

"Go! Go now!" I screamed. Hiệp hit the gas, reversing with a jolt that slammed us back in our seats. The Benz tore across the lot, jumped the curb and crashed hard onto the street. We sped off into the night, leaving behind the chaos, our hearts still racing in the echo of gunfire.

In the frenzy of screams and gunfire, I yanked the car door shut and felt an impact on my right elbow. I thought I'd slammed it against the door. My elbow locked, felt like it turned into stone but tingling sharply. But as the adrenaline began to ebb, the tingling didn't fade. I tuned into my body and realized something was very wrong. I tugged up the sleeve of my neon orange Nike sweatshirt with my left hand. That's when I saw it. A gaping hole in my right elbow. Thick, dark blood oozed into a puddle, dripping onto the beige leather seat.

"Fuck! I've been shot! I've been shot!" The words tumbled out in a mix of shock and disbelief.

My sister whipped her head and stared me in the eyes, her face contorted with terror. "What?! Oh my God! Shit! Shit! Shit!" she screamed. Her hands fluttered in the air before gripping her head. I felt a fierce heat spreading through my elbow as I tried to bend it, but it was jammed solid, locked in place. Panic flooded the car.

"Oh my God, get us to the hospital, or else she's gonna die!" Liz shouted, her voice edged with hysteria.

My sister, drawing on scenes from movies, asked, "Are you cold, Thao?!"

"No. But it's bad. I can tell."

"Okay, but don't fall asleep! Whatever you do, don't fall asleep!"

I'd seen people get shot before. Some limped away, some never moved again. But this was me, my blood, my bones, and I told myself, *It's only your elbow.* It was a strange clarity, as if the universe flipped a switch inside me. My thoughts sharpened and lined up in order: you won't die, not unless you bleed out; no, you'll be okay. I turned to my sister and said calmly, "Hey, take your sock off and tie it around my arm as a tourniquet."

Liz scrambled to help, hands shaking as she kicked off her sneaker and yanked her high knee sock off her foot. She wrapped it tightly, but in her panic, she tied it below the wound. My sister and I corrected her in unison, "No, above!" My sister added, "Below the bicep!"

From the driver's seat, Hiệp's voice cracked, "Where am I going?!"

"Memorial Southwest!" my sister screamed back, directing him as he sped along the freeway.

I slumped back, whispering to myself, "Shit, this really sucks. Pretty sure I'll never play volleyball again."

In that horrifying moment, we absurdly all managed to chuckle. My sister, clutching my hand tightly, said, "Don't say that. You're gonna be okay. Remember what happened to Dad? He's playing again." An industrial machine had stamped its die onto Dad's right hand, his thumb and pinky pressed flat. Doctors amputated half the thumb and the whole pinky, and after his recovery, he managed to still play volleyball.

The brief moment of respite faded into silence, our breaths punctuating the tense quiet. We arrived at the emergency room, where they whisked me straight to radiology and then into surgery. Under the glare of the bright lights above, my mind drifted to my parents. The pain in my arm radiated outward, sharp and unrelenting, piercing every corner of my body. Yet, the ache of knowing what this would do to them pressed down on me with a weight heavier than any physical agony.

When I awoke, voices filled the room. Blinking, I struggled to focus. Without contacts or glasses, my uncorrected vision left the bodies in the room blurred, hovering around me like soft shadows. I cleared my throat with a faint *ahem*, my voice barely breaking the quiet.

"She's awake," Mom whispered, her voice warm with relief. She and Dad leaned in close, their hands reaching out, grounding me in their touch. Mom's cool fingertips caressed the back of my palm, and Dad's machinist hands brushed the hair from my forehead as if I were still a child. Mom gently slipped glasses onto my nose, the scene sharpening into focus through blurred tears. Mom bent her head low, pressed her face close to mine, her nose brushing my cheek before she kissed me, breathing me in. Dad's hand caressed my head.

"You okay, baby?" he asked tenderly.

The warmth of their voices and touch undid me. Tears rolled down my cheeks freely, my lips moving with broken sounds of gasps and apologies. "Sorry, Ba, Mẹ," I whimpered, barely able to look at them.

"It's okay, *con*," Mom murmured, her words wrapping around me like a lullaby, her Vietnamese words gently activating my obedience, "Đừng khóc, nghe?," and with a profound sense of filial piety, I did. I stopped crying.

The doctor explained what luck meant in measurements. A 9 mm hollow-point bullet had ripped through my arm, tearing it inside out, shattering bone into millimeters of fragments, impossible to reconstruct entirely. He extracted the radial head, doing what he could with titanium screws to piece back what remained. Despite the shrapnel and bone debris scattered throughout my elbow, it was nothing short of miraculous that I hadn't lost the limb or been paralyzed. *You were spared the worst by millimeters.* The main artery and nerve left untouched as if by some unseen mercy. The reality of it all settled in; it was a fragile space between survival and something that could have been far worse, like a quiet blessing amid the wreckage.

The night of the shooting, the police interrogated my sister and friends. Shortly after I awoke from surgery, they hovered at my bedside, notepads open, pens tapping, and questioned me, too.

"Who was there?"

"A lot of people I knew and some I didn't."

"What did you see?"

"A lot of people fighting and a lot of people running."

"Who fired the gun?"

"I don't know."

"You got any enemies?"

"None that I know of."

The following day, a steady stream of visitors trickled in with gifts—crinkled plastic bags filled with fruit, chocolates, and plush animals, bouquets of bright, colorful flowers in glass vases, and bags of my favorite Vietnamese snacks like salted plum candies, haw flakes, and dried squid. Someone tied a get-well balloon to the railing of the bed, its string brushing my arm whenever the AC kicked in. Everyone's smiles brightened the room, but the gravity of what happened hung over us. But the person I wanted to see most never came. Vu was locked up, facing his own reckoning with charges for a shooting from a car after a club fight. Most visitors wanted to talk about the night at Slick Willie's, asking who had pulled the trigger. People knew, but nobody was willing to tell the cops. Some wanted to keep quiet, while others murmured about revenge.

When I was finally released from the hospital, Hiệp stopped by the house with a bouquet of red roses and a box of tea.

"Did you see who the shooter was?" I asked him.

"Yeah," he said, looking away. "A guy named Glenn."

"You're sure you saw him?"

He nodded.

"You gotta tell the cops," I urged.

He looked at me, eyes filled with hesitation. "I can't, *em*."

"Why not?" I pressed, a mix of frustration and disbelief creeping into my voice.

"You know why. I don't want no part of this back and forth. They'll come after me."

Anger burned inside me, and the helplessness simmered. But I understood. A few days later, Liz came by to check in. She sat with me, talking softly until she finally leaned closer.

"Glenn Shelton. That's his name," she said quietly.

"You sure?" I asked, feeling the same frustration rise again.

She nodded. "But no one's saying a word."

"Hiep saw him and won't tell the cops. Chicken shit," I muttered, the bitterness spilling out.

She gave me a small, reassuring smile, eyes steady. "I'll do it," she said.

Glenn was arrested, and that summer his crew came for Liz and me at the beach. We had spread out our towels on the hot sand, the sun baking our skin. Watching the waves crash onto shore was relaxing, but I couldn't shake the anxiousness of seeing the pointed stares coming from a group of young Vietnamese guys walking toward us. Their steps were slow and deliberate. They stopped over us, casting us in shade as dark as their expressions. One of them bent down on one knee, arm over the knee, pointing his finger at us and leaned forward to speak at us.

"Word on the street is y'all talked," he said, his voice low and threatening.

Liz looked at me, fear flickering in her wide opened eyes. My chest tightened. I had promised everyone, including myself, that I didn't want revenge, that I'd face Glenn in court and leave the life of violence behind. But Liz's trembling glance set something off in me, something that burned hotter than fear, a surge of protective fury, stoking a fire I thought I'd extinguished. Slowly, I slid my sunglasses down the bridge of my nose, my eyes locked into theirs with a glare sharp enough to cut.

"What exactly is coming to me, huh?" I said, my voice steady, words dripping with contempt. "Your boy blew up my arm. I had nothin' to do with y'all's beef. Y'all ran up on that other crew. And over what? Some girl. Like y'all always do. Bustin' up dudes over a piece of ass. Tell me, if you got one ounce of decency in you, that you think what happened to me was right!"

Their bodies held their ground, but their hard gazes softened around the edges, their lips twitched with a hint of uncertainty. I pressed on, my voice relentless. "I got people, too. Crews I could call, and they'd take this shit further. But I'm not 'bout to keep going down that road. Do you feel good about intimidating me? Threatening me? Putting me through more hell than I've already been through?"

I heard the sounds of gulls shrieking above but no sounds from the young men standing in front of me, shirtless and speechless. Spineless, I thought to myself.

"What? You think my questions are rhetorical?" I let out a dry laugh, shaking my head. "Y'all don't even fuckin' know what rhetorical means, do ya?" I inhaled deeply, salt air filling my lungs, then leveled with them. "I'm ending this here. I'm doing what's right, which is seeing your boy pay for his crime, just like any of us would. If any of you want to end up like him, go ahead, keep on with whatever plans you've got for me." I straightened up, nodding toward Liz, my voice a protective whisper, "Come on, Liz. We're done here."

We picked up our things, gathered our towels with sand that clung stubbornly, and without a backward glance we walked away.

Glenn was charged with attempted murder. He pled to the lesser charge of deadly conduct and was sentenced to ten years. Rumor was he got away soft because his mother worked in the judicial system and greased the wheels. Months later, Vu wasn't so lucky. He was convicted of aggravated assault with a deadly weapon and sentenced to sixty years.

7

Transformation

After Vu's conviction, we stubbornly clung to the hope of an appeal. While waiting for the legal process to crawl forward, I returned to the University of Houston, the place where my academic journey had once faltered. My GPA was a dismal 2.1, a glaring reminder of past failures. At my first advising appointment, I met a young counselor—a Black man with gentle eyes and an easy smile, and he seemed kind and had an encouraging demeanor. He leaned forward, his hands folded loosely on the desk, and nodded thoughtfully as I explained my goal. I told him my dream of studying law and fighting for my friends ensnared by the justice system.

"You can still do this," he said with unwavering certainty, as if he had already seen the version of me that I was trying to see for myself. "It's okay to start over." His words, simple yet powerful, rooted themselves deep in me and gave me the confidence to begin anew. He suggested sociology as my major, despite my less-than-stellar performance in Introduction to Sociology, where I had earned a D. "It's a fresh start," he reassured me.

Determined to honor that chance, I bought a planner and meticulously structured out my days. On the first page, I drew two faint pen lines, just 2 mm apart—a mini-tribute to the bullet wound in my arm and reminder of the resilience that I would need to drive me forward. Every detail of my life was scheduled: blocks of time for reading dense textbooks, grinding through problem sets, drafting essays, physical therapy appointments, dinner with my family, workouts at the gym, even social time with my siblings and friends. I created lengthy to-do lists and savored the small victories of crossing off each completed task. Those incremental achievements became my lifeline, evidence of steady progress in both mind and body. Physically, my recovery was grueling but necessary. My physical therapist pushed me through painful, meticulous exercises, retraining the muscles around my shattered elbow to compensate for the missing radial head. Sweat beaded down my back as I lifted small weights, the scar tissue burning with every repetition. My wrist and fingers were stuck in paralysis, nearly two months gone by before I could will them to move, a limp wrist extended, curled fingers outstretched, a palm finally fully open.

I had to relearn how to navigate the world with one arm, my awkward, unskilled left arm and hand forced to take the lead. Ordinary tasks turned into an obstacle course. Eating meant fumbling with chopsticks, my grip clumsy, rice grains spilling over the edge of the bowl like scattered sand. Writing turned my once graceful cursive strokes into elementary school-grade print, letters sprawling unevenly across the page, my wrist sore after just a few sentences. I thought driving might be terrifying, but I managed to steer the wheel steadily without jerking it, although my heart still pounded heavily each time I merged into traffic. Even washing my hair became an ordeal, my left hand struggling to lather soap into thick strands, my right elbow throbbing whenever I tried to lift higher than shoulder level. Then there was the Vicodin. I tried to avoid it altogether. But some nights, the aching was just too sharp. On more than one occasion, I'd move one of the pillows under my head to lower the angle before sleeping. My left hand would clumsily toss the pillow on to my right arm, and while the idea of a pillow landing on an arm seems harmless, it triggered an excruciating pain that ran from my elbow throughout my limb and radiated throughout my body. What once took seconds now took minutes, and what felt effortless now required patience I didn't know I had. But I persevered, adapting to this new reality while refusing to surrender the activities that brought me joy.

Volleyball haunted me most of all. Learning to play from Dad, having my sisters as teammates—this was a family affair and deeply personal to me. My doctor shook his head and told me flatly that returning to the court was unlikely. But I could still feel the bounce of the rubber ball off my arms, hear its thump on the ground after a clean spike, and feel the exhilaration of diving for a save. I quietly resolved to prove him wrong. Two years later, after hundreds of hours of physical therapy, and the discovery of a Bauerfeind elbow compression sleeve, I was on the court again.

Law school was another mountain I was determined to climb. My academic record whispered doubts, but I silenced them with each lecture attended, each paper written, and each textbook read. I was no longer a student who stumbled through classes half-committed. With each small triumph, I was rewriting my story, determined to transform failure into a foundation for the future I envisioned and was building.

Some folks say success is about self-discipline. Waking up early. Doing the work. Making the hard choices when nobody's watching. I believe that. I've lived that. There's a kind of quiet power in it, the kind that doesn't need applause.

Other folks say success is about the people who show up. The ones who hold you down, tell you the truth when it's ugly, lend you their hands, their stories, their time. I believe that, too.

One version is about the self. The grind. The silence.

The other is about the village. The witness. The chorus.

I don't think it's either-or. I think it's both. And also something else. Something above or beyond or around us. Some higher power of existence that we can't verify to others but we know within ourselves, a spiritual presence whether one perceives it as a deity, an angel, or an ancestor.

Yeah, I had some grit. Yeah, I made choices that pulled me out of some deep holes. But I didn't do any of this alone. I couldn't have. I had people. A community. A classroom. And a voice that was so warm, encouraging, and intelligent that it inspired something in me. That voice belonged to Professor Jackie Hagan. The class was The Sociology of the Family. But it wasn't just a class. It was a reckoning. A soft explosion. A mirror held up when I didn't even know I needed to look. Up until that point, I had sat in classrooms full of lecture notes that explained the Vietnam War like it was just a foreign policy hiccup. Professors spoke about names of battles, numbers of bodies, presidential decisions. But no one ever said our names. No one ever talked about *us*, or if they did, we were refugees as statistics on a graph. No one covered our families, our survival strategies, our pain as war exiles, or how it shaped the way we loved, the way we stayed quiet, the way we broke open.

Professor Hagan did that. She named the invisible. And something in me, something buried, woke up from its hauntings. Those moments of learning critically about Vietnamese families didn't just guide me toward success. It *redefined* what success meant to me. Because it wasn't just about me anymore. It was about all the people who never made it into the textbook. And all the people who did but never got to tell their story their way. That class didn't save me. But it reminded me I was worth saving and our stories are worth telling.

Early in the semester, Professor Hagan delivered a lecture on family strategies for economic survival, highlighting the experiences of Vietnamese refugees. She spoke of how these families, having lost their homeland and livelihoods, often lived in poverty upon arriving in America. Yet they pooled their resources, collectively navigating economic hardship. As she spoke, she looked directly at me and smiled, and for the first time, I heard something in an academic setting that reflected me—my heritage, my community, my family. In that moment, her lecture illuminated a kind of knowledge that didn't just inform. It resonated, lighting up parts of me I hadn't realized I longed to see represented. It made me feel seen in a way that was as exhilarating as it was grounding.

I rarely visited professors. It felt like being called to the principal's office. Asking for help meant I wasn't smart enough. But something about Professor Hagan's references to Vietnamese families made her lectures feel personal, like she was speaking to my life. For the first time, I was drawn not just to the material but also to the professor herself. She made learning feel both intimate and wide open. That connection taught me success wasn't just about grit. It was also about guidance.

I approached her office to ask about volunteer work for law school. The scent of leather greeted me. She sat in a deep leather chair, reading through brown-framed glasses. Shelves of books lined the room, her diplomas and plaques covering the walls. On her desk: a plant, and a framed photo of her with a striking man, tucked beside a pile of graded papers.

I cleared my throat and said, "Hello, Professor Hagan." She looked up, removed her glasses and smiled. "Hi!" she replied with a cheery voice.

I paused at the door and waited for her to invite me in. "I'm Thao Ha, a student in your Family class."

"I recognize you. Come on in," she said, gesturing to the red upholstered chair in front of her desk. "What can I do for you?"

I mustered up my confidence and spoke up, "I want to go to law school and wondered if you knew of any volunteer opportunities I could do."

She raised an eyebrow, her tone curious. "You want to be a lawyer?"

I nodded.

Her expression turned concerned. "You want to work eighty hours a week? You plan on having a family?"

The question caught me off guard, and I stumbled for a response. "Well, I'm not getting married anytime soon. But I don't mind working hard."

"Do you record my lectures?" she asked abruptly.

"No. Should I?" I replied, feeling uneasy.

"But you take notes," she pointed out.

"Yes."

"I ask because your responses on the essay exams are so thorough that I thought surely you must be recording my lectures. To recall such depth from listening is impressive. You're a natural sociologist," she complimented.

I felt a rush of excitement at her words, reminiscent of the pride I felt as a child when my third-grade teacher displayed my poems in the hallway. "Thank you so much. I love the topics, and the way you lecture is very interesting."

She leaned back in her chair, considering me thoughtfully. "I don't think you should go to law school. You should go to graduate school. Get a PhD. Like me. And be a professor. Like me," she declared.

Her words pierced through me with a resonance I couldn't ignore. The message was sharp and clear, cutting through a fog inside me, striking a place I hadn't touched in years. Until that day, the thought of pursuing a PhD or becoming a professor had never crossed my mind. My memories only stretched back to those childhood afternoons playing teacher with my younger twin siblings. Back then, I would re-create my school lessons, crafting makeshift classrooms and scribbling tests they would ace with ease. They sat cross-legged on the carpeted floor of my bedroom, a small chalkboard our parents bought from Toys "R" Us in front of them, me scribbling math formulas with white chalk, its dust sticking to my tiny hands. Their smiles, and mine, were another link of our childhood bonds. Teaching them brought me joy, and I had forgotten what it felt like to guide, to explain, to see someone's eyes light up with understanding. Yet, here was Professor Hagan, with the steady cadence of her voice and the way she looked at me as if I mattered, reawakening that long-forgotten passion and presenting me with a vision of myself I had never dared to imagine—a professor, a scholar, someone who could teach not just as childhood playtime but as a calling, too.

"What do you think?!" she asked, leaning forward, her eyes alight with anticipation.

I hesitated, my voice faltering under the unknown of the possibility. "I love the idea," I confessed, "but I don't know how."

Her smile was steady, a promise wrapped in warmth. "I will guide you," she said.

And guide me she did. She became not just a professor but also a mentor, opening doors I hadn't even known existed. That summer, she invited me to work on a research project for the university's Center for Immigration Research. As co-lead of the project, she assembled a team of accomplished academics to uncover the history of Houston's Asian immigrant communities. I, a mere undergraduate, was the sole student among them. She entrusted me with researching Houston's Vietnamese community, recognizing that my language skills and cultural insight gave me a unique vantage point. Through her belief in me, she didn't just offer opportunities; she gave me a vision of my future, a future I had never dared to dream for myself.

After the research was complete, I submitted the final report. Months later, her email landed in my inbox with a simple request: to meet in her office. The curiosity churned inside me as I walked through the door, and her greeting was immediate and effusive.

"Thao!" she exclaimed, her voice warm with familiarity. But before I could settle into the chair, she tilted her head and scrutinized my outfit. "You've got to lose those white denim pants that stop at your shins," she said, with the same precision she might critique a research paper. "They make you look short, and you're already short. Long pants past the ankles will elongate your legs. Trust me."

I was caught between laughter and shock, but before I could reply, she shifted gears. "Now, down to business." She leaned forward, her tone turning serious. "I'm going to submit your report to a conference. It was above the rest, and I want you to speak about it."

The thought of standing before a crowd filled me with dread, but her voice cut through my fear with calm determination. "Practice your talk. Don't read the report, okay? Practice in front of a mirror or with someone you trust. Be ready for questions. If this conference doesn't accept it, we'll keep submitting it until one does. But mark my words—you will give this talk."

When I learned the following semester that the report had been accepted, the panic set in. The night before the talk, I roped in my buddy Trí to be my audience. But as soon as I started, I jumbled my sentences and my mind turned into a foggy mess.

"That was . . . pretty bad," Trí said with a teasing laugh, though his kind eyes seemed to still have faith in me. "Come on, Little One. You've got this. I'll stay as long as you need. Let's keep at it."

His patience stretched late into the night as I repeated the speech again and again. By the time he left, I'd run through it a dozen times with him and a few more on my own, pacing the empty office under flickering fluorescent lights. When I finally stepped outside, the cool night air carried memories of other late nights, when I'd told my parents I was studying but had been sneaking off to see Vu. Tonight, I was determined to rewrite that story.

Sunlight crept through my window, painting the walls in rose gold. I heard my parents' footsteps and muffled voices down the hall. Professor Hagan had urged me to invite them and I had, but the fear of failing in front of them churned my stomach. I got up and dressed mindfully in an outfit from Express I'd spent more on than I could afford: coral blouse with sharp collars, cream Editor slacks, matching belt with a tiny, shiny buckle. My boots clicked on the floor as I faced the mirror, hoping to reflect the confidence I didn't quite feel.

The university ballroom buzzed with energy. Lights sparkled above rows of lingering attendees. My heels echoed as I crossed to the stage. Trí was already there, waving from behind a camera. His grin soothed me. My parents arrived just before the session began, taking their seats near the front. Seeing them sharpened my focus. This was my chance to prove something, to them and to myself.

Professor Hagan took the stage, hugged me warmly, and stepped back to look me over. "You look fabulous," she said with a wink.

She opened the panel with grace, describing the project and its significance. Her poise steadied me. When she called me up, my heart pounded. I clutched my notes and began. My voice shook at first, but my parents' steady smiles calmed me. I gained confidence, added personal stories, and let my truth come through—even cracked a joke with some street slang that landed just right and earned real laughter from the crowd. By the end, I didn't feel like an impostor. I felt heard. And seen.

Then came the Q&A. Most questions were manageable, until one person asked about the Cuban community in Miami and how it "juxtaposed" with Houston's Vietnamese population. I froze on the meaning of the word. Guessed it meant comparison, but fumbled.

"That's a great question," I said slowly. "I think . . . "

Professor Hagan jumped in smoothly. "This would make an incredible topic for Thao's graduate studies. Keep in mind, she's the only undergraduate on the research team. She has so much potential. What do you think, Thao?"

I nodded, recovering. "Yes. It would be wonderful to do a comparison and contrast of the two communities."

The room applauded. Offstage, I met Trî and my parents, their faces glowing.

Trî grinned. "Thao, you were incredible. Honestly, after last night, I wasn't sure how you'd pull it off, but you killed it. You're awesome!"

Mom's voice rose with excitement. "I can't believe my daughter did that! A big job! I'm so proud of you, *con*!"

Even Dad smiled with even-keeled praise. "Good information," he said. "And a good speech. You did good."

Professor Hagan joined us, beaming. I introduced her to my parents, who bowed with deep thanks. "She did great," Professor Hagan said. "And she's going to graduate school to get her PhD. You told them, didn't you, Thao?"

I froze. I hadn't.

"PhD?" Mom asked.

"Yes," Professor Hagan said. "A doctorate. She's going to be a professor one day."

Mom lit up. "Doctor professor? Oh, yes! We want her to be doctor!" she said, giggling with joy.

The summer after my first public talk, I got an unexpected email from Dr. Helen Rose Ebaugh, a professor I'd taken a year earlier. She'd heard of my work and invited me to join her research on religion in the Houston Vietnamese community. By summer's end, I'd written a report that became a chapter in her co-edited book, *Religion Across Borders*. When I told my parents, their response was flat. "Oh, good. Nice report in a book," they said, without excitement. I wasn't upset. It was their way. Maybe they didn't understand the significance. Or maybe, like Dad often said, "Stay humble in the eyes of the Lord."

Still, their indifference stayed with me. It told me quietly and firmly that what I did wasn't a big deal. So when I earned my bachelor's, I skipped graduation. It felt like a box checked, not a milestone. Even as I gathered strong recommendation letters for grad school from Professor Hagan, Dr. Ebaugh, and others, I hesitated. I was afraid.

Harvard. Yale. UCLA. Berkeley. Princeton, where Dr. Ebaugh had it tight with the department chair and the admissions committee. Those names looked good on paper. Sounded good in other people's mouths when they said them like proof I'd made it. But my fear wasn't rejection. It was leaving. Leaving Mom's daily cooking. Leaving Dad's quiet nods that meant more than full sentences. Leaving late-night drives through Houston streets that knew me before I knew myself. I wasn't scared I wouldn't get in. I was scared I would. Scared I'd go and something would happen back home and I wouldn't be there. Scared I'd change. Or maybe worse, scared I wouldn't.

When Professor Hagan suggested I retake the GRE to improve my math score, I didn't. I made all kinds of excuses. Princeton? Too cold. Cambridge? Too far. Seattle? Too rainy. Phoenix? Too lonely. I never opened most of my professor's recommendation letters. I sent one application. UT Austin.

If I don't get in, I thought, *fuck it. I'll try again next year.*

I told myself Austin was the only choice. It's a short drive away. Close enough to come back if someone got sick, if something broke, if I broke. I convinced myself it was practical and sensible. But choosing Austin was more than that. I was choosing proximity to the only thing I believed tethered me: my family. I was afraid to be too far from them. It's a unique type of fear when your roots are deep, but the soil never feels solid. It's a paradox of being a refugee. Your roots are undeniable, tangled with history, trauma, and survival, but they cling to an earth that sometimes feels borrowed, like it was promised to you but someone can come along at any moment and remind you that you don't fully belong. When you're told to go back to your country. When a law passes that makes you illegal. When a government entity is authorized to enforce your expulsion even if you once had papers. It leaves you with an uncertainty about where you really stand. To stay close to family wasn't only about care or loyalty; it's about stability. When soil is unsteady, roots bind to the nearest roots, clinging together to keep from being uprooted. Austin was less about a city and more about a philosophy of distance. Upon reflection, I was running toward something yet refusing not to run too far away. Maybe that's what it means to grow up refugee-rooted—you live in the tension between wanting to plant yourself firmly while also fearing what might happen if you do. The ground has already been lost before. Who's to say it won't be lost again?

When the acceptance letter came, I tore open the envelope with shaking hands, eyes racing over the words until they blurred. Then it hit: I'd not only been accepted, but also given a full ride and a teaching assistantship. The sounds that came out of me were part shout, part laughter, and part words whispered emphatically and repeatedly, *Fuck, yeah.*

I packed my essentials into Dad's old white Dodge van he used for deliveries: no passenger seats, an empty cavern filled with the smell of motor oil and cardboard boxes. At IKEA, I wandered the aisles of flat-packed furniture, imagining the construction of a new life in every box. I signed a lease on a one-bedroom apartment and hit the road, the stretched highways ahead like an open invitation.

I wrote to Vu and shared the news. By then, he'd been at Beto Unit for nearly four years, locked in max security. His return letter held pride for me but still heavy with despair. He was still waiting for the long and slow process of an appeal decision. While I moved toward promise, he sank deeper into isolation. The distance between us stretched wider, like two ropes pulling in opposite directions. What kept us connected were only memories and a fragile thread of fading hope.

At orientation, my cohort gathered at a bar near campus. Out on its wide wooden deck, string lights crisscrossed above us, glowing golden against the fading blue of the evening. The smell of grilled burgers drifted from the kitchen, mixed with the sharp tang of spilled beer that soaked the planks beneath our feet. It was happy hour, and there were diverse groups that filled the tables, pitchers and pint glasses passing from hand to hand. My classmates were from a variety of geographic regions. Texas, Tennessee, Wyoming, Korea, Costa Rica, Turkey, and Mexico, to name a few. I sat among them with a sweating glass of iced water and a basket of wings in front of me. I waved off offers of beer, shaking my head as I thought back to the last time I'd let alcohol consume me: a night when I hurled vomit out of a moving car, got home too drunk to reach the bathroom, stumbled into my bedroom, and retched into the first thing I found, a shoebox under the bed. I woke the next morning sticky, my cheeks coated in sour gunk, my head aching and my throat raw. The smell clung to me, to the sheets and pillowcase, the memory. That was enough. I've never touched alcohol again.

Grad school offered its own kind of intoxication. A steady buzz that came from immersion. I devoured reading lists and decorated my textbooks with underlined phrases and notes in the margins. Lectures pulled me in, steps in research methods became a regular sequence of thought, and even theory classes, dense with jargon and abstract concepts, thrilled me. Then there was Professor Gideon Sjoberg, nicknamed "the ghost of Burdine." He only taught late at night and floated into the classroom long after sunset, his white button-up shirt and blue slacks sagging on a body bent with age. He was so old he was buddies with the theorists we were studying. Names like Bourdieu and Goffman were spoken of not as abstractions but as old acquaintances.

My classmates slumped in their chairs, pens idle, eyes staring toward the single window, but I leaned in, eyes scanning back and forth between him and my notebook, pen racing to catch every word. On more than one occasion, he paused, peered at me over his glasses, and said, "You're thinking like a true sociologist."

Not everything came easy, though. Statistics were my nemesis. My first professor, an elderly white man, filled the board with messy formulas. Chalk dust blended into his white hair. His writing was tiny; even sitting in the front row, it looked like scattered grains of rice. I barely passed. But once we started using computer programs, things clicked. The logic became visible, patterns emerged on the screen that made sense, and my grades improved. The next semester, stats came alive with Professor Arthur Sakamoto. He cracked jokes, told stories and even wore a firefighter's helmet one day. "I wanted to be a firefighter," he laughed. "But my Asian parents said math had better job prospects." That hit home. My parents had pushed biology as a major over English for the same reason.

In one lecture, he broke down disparities in education by race and class, family, income, culture, all of it. It felt personal. I started listing all the variables that shaped my own path. He also loved soccer and invited us to form an intramural team. Dad always said it was too dangerous, so I declined in high school when the coach tried to recruit me. But now, away from home, I didn't need permission. I joined and felt the joy of the game again. After matches, the team would go out to eat with Professor Sakamoto. Our casual dinners turned into office hours. They became the best part of my week.

Toward the end of the semester, he emailed me to come by his office. By then, I knew that kind of message usually meant something good.

"Thao," he said, leaning back in his chair, hands clasped behind his head, thin lips holding a grin, "how about publishing some research with me on Asian Americans in the South?"

My heart raced with excitement. “Yes, absolutely!” I replied without hesitation.

We dove into the data—public-use microdata samples from the census, or “PUMS,” as Professor Sakamoto called it. We tracked Asian American population trends, focusing on the South. After weeks of analysis, we co-wrote a chapter for a UCLA Asian American Studies Center book. It was later accepted at a national conference. When Sakamoto couldn’t attend, he urged me to present. I was nervous, but as I spoke, confidence built. The applause felt like proof that all the hard work and doubt had been worth it. Grad school became more than academics. It transformed me. I found mentors, strength, and a belief in my voice. I took on teaching assistantships, built bonds with faculty, and tutored UT’s volleyball team. College football was a religion at UT, and game tickets became both entertainment and income. Every hustle helped me stay self-reliant, easing the guilt of my parents funding my lifestyle.

Twice a month, sometimes more, I drove home to Houston. Family gatherings filled the kitchen with the smell of freshly steamed rice, fish sauce, and garlic. My friends coaxed me out to the clubs, strobe lights pulsing, bass thumping through my chest. But beneath the music and the laughter, I felt hollow. Vu stayed with me in a quiet ache. His birthday and holiday cards came randomly, stirring both warmth and sorrow. I couldn’t return to that life, yet I couldn’t fully let go. Austin was a fresh start. I kept my past buried, never transparent when asked about the scar on my elbow, shrugging it off as an old accident, changing subjects before their curiosity dug deeper. I didn’t want to explain and unravel my entire history. Didn’t want to confess that Vu, while still alive, haunted me. Daydreams turned to nightmares. In one, he was surrounded by a bloodthirsty crowd descending upon him with glinting shanks. I woke drenched in sweat, heart pounding, crying before I knew why. The dreams left me shaken, made me fear he was suffering in ways I'd never understand. He told me to move on, and I tried. Each tear felt like a step toward forgetting. I whispered into the dark, *It's not meant to be. It was never meant to be.*

In 2003, back in Houston, I hit a club with some friends. That's where I saw him. He was six feet tall with a lean athletic build, Vietnamese, and carried himself with a quiet reserve, catching glances with me on the patio but not making moves. His friends wandered inside toward the bar, but he hung back until a mutual friend introduced us. We talked easily. Started dating soon after. Meanwhile, the silence with Vu stretched on. We hadn't spoken in a while, I hadn't written, and neither had he. Maybe too much pain between us, too difficult to maintain what little we had left together, and yet, too many failed attempts at closure. I thought about writing him, but the words felt too heavy, too close to bleeding. The new guy was seven years younger, a student in human development who had dreams of teaching and the Army. The relationship moved quickly, faster than I was ready for. It didn't take long before it felt less like love and more like distraction dressed up as purpose. Less than a year in, he proposed at a military ball. The ballroom glittered and sparkled with hundreds of tea lights, ironed uniforms with shiny rank pins, silky sequined gowns, and a diamond ring in a black velvet box. I said yes. I never told Vu. What was there to say? Six years had passed since we were supposed to let go of each other. We tried to. We meant to. But we hadn't yet. Not fully. So it was time I started to mean it.

8

Unbecoming

WE GOT ENGAGED IN 2003. My fiancé, Hưng, threw away the photos, letters, and cards from Vu. I hid the Astroworld drawing, though, just like Vu had. I rolled it up, placed it in a tube mailer, and wrote the words "UT Project" on it.

My sisters and friends were excited to shop for dresses, but I went alone and bought the second one I tried. It was simple, practical, and under $100. For the reception, I wore a bright-red *áo dài* Mom had custom made in Vietnam. Embellished with faux pearls and sequined flowers, it was meant to symbolize luck. Paired with white silk pants and five-inch platform heels. I stared in the mirror and thought, "Not bad for being made in Vietnam."

We hand made the invitations, bought Party City decor, and filled clear glass vases with red gladiolas. It didn't feel cheap; it felt like how refugees do things. Hưng had just joined the Army, and money was tight. He splurged on a diamond ring that sparkled from five tables away, but I pushed to keep costs low. I'd passed my doctoral exams and didn't see the need for extravagance. Still, expectations ran high. The Ocean Palace reception had eight courses, fancy Martell cognac, and a towering cake for eight hundred guests. It had to meet the community's standard.

Most of the planning was taken from me before I could claim it. For someone who needed structure, that loss of control was unsettling. I wasn't just planning a wedding, I was trying to stitch together two families with different pasts and clashing views. My soon-to-be mother-in-law, quiet and legally blind, somehow still saw everything she didn't like. She butted heads with my parents from the start. All they asked was that their friends—folk singers from Vietnam—perform at the reception. She said no. Flat-out. She'd seen her father executed by the Việt Cộng and didn't trust anyone from Vietnam who wasn't a refugee no matter how sweet their songs. Dad was also a war survivor and anti-communist, but he didn't agree. "They carry microphones, not machetes," he said. But she wasn't listening. And the arguing dragged on, sharp and exhausting. No one really won. No one ever does in those kinds of wars.

Then came the next layer. Religion. His family was Buddhist, unassuming and steady in practice. Mom followed Cao Đài, a syncretic Vietnamese faith with an all-seeing eye and a mix of deities, philosophers, and even writer Victor Hugo. Dad called himself an "identity Christian," stern and rigid in the belief of racial hierarchy and Yahweh named as the savior. To keep the peace, we held two ceremonies: a Christian one at my parents' house led by my scripture-quoting uncle, and a Buddhist one at my in-laws', thick with incense that burned from a fruit-adorned altar. I had quietly left religion during graduate school. Slipped into agnosticism without announcing it to them. I just carried it, like a truth I wasn't ready to say aloud.

Planning the wedding drained me. Conflict piled on with disagreements over the seating arrangement and who should be announced in what order. I lashed out at my fiancé and his family, leaving the dinner table without excusing myself in the middle of one of the disagreements. I wanted to call it off, but everyone ignored my bad moods. They brushed it off, convincing me it was common to have "pre-wedding jitters." I should've listened to myself. I wasn't nervous. I was angry.

In the summer of 2004, two weeks before the wedding, we left a family dinner at the restaurant attached to the wedding venue. The drive home was silent, Mom in the front seat, Hưng in the back, me at the wheel. Then Hưng spoke up, his voice cracking. "If I get shipped out to war and don't make it back," he said, addressing Mom, his words catching on the sob, "I could die happy knowing Thao loves me." I looked in the rearview mirror, his eyes shimmered under the glow of the streetlights, tears sliding down his cheeks. I swallowed hard as the guilt swelled, drowning out the doubt, the hesitation, and the voice in me whispering no. In that moment, guilt won. I stayed the course and kept the wedding plans.

My sisters and friends pulled it together, fussing over flowers and decorations, making sure my hair and makeup were good through the change of outfits. The wedding went smoothly . . . on the surface. Guests clapped, Martell shots clinked, and the camera clicked in steady bursts. The entertainment was good enough, a Vietnamese American troupe. But beneath the carefully crafted choreography, the mood was off. I forced half-smiled through photos. In frame after frame, Mom didn't smile at all, her mouth pressed into a thin line, her gaze heavy with things she didn't say. Across the ballroom, my mother-in-law stayed mostly in her seat, only moving through the event when it required. Maybe if I'd opened up to Mom, she would've warned me. She had lived with in-laws like that, carrying mistreatment in silence and swallowing her resentment.

During our move to Fort Carson, our moving truck was stolen. Among the losses was my Astroworld drawing. Its loss stung sharper than the theft itself. It felt like a reminder of who we were, like anything between me and Vu was meant to end, meant to be taken without our permission.

Three years later, when the marriage ended, the final blows came not in shouts but in demands. My mother-in-law insisted the wedding jewelry she gifted me be returned, even advising Hưng to take the pieces to a jeweler to test the stones, to make sure I hadn't swapped the diamonds for cubic zirconia. My parents were more insulted than I was. I didn't argue. I gave that shit back without hesitation. Not because she was right about wanting it back. But because I was done. Done holding on to something that had been breaking me anyway, piece by piece.

Weeks before I left, I had this dream. He came back from deployment in a flag-draped casket. I woke up gasping, sick with guilt, scared that I'd wished something on him I couldn't take back. But then I read somewhere that death in dreams didn't always mean literal death. Sometimes it meant change. Sometimes it meant truth. My love for us had already died. I just hadn't buried it yet.

We had married in haste, and it was a military marriage. What we knew of commitment was shaped by uniforms, orders, patriarchy, and time zones. He was gone more than he was home. Field training. Deployments. Whole months where I'd wake up and forget what it felt like to have someone next to me in bed. If I mentioned a weekend trip with friends, his emails came back laced with guilt, lines about loyalty and sacrifice written in between questions about friendships with male friends.

When he was back, it didn't feel like home either. Military culture was male, rigid, and loud with rank. It stretched the space between us. I was trying to build something rooted, something real. He was trying to be enough for a system that saw him as a cog in the military-industrial complex. Teaching part time on a semester-by-semester basis at Pikes Peak Community College was good for the situation we were in, but I wanted stability. Tenure. An office with my name on it to hold office hours. Committee assignments. Campus program leadership roles. I wanted to build. I was clawing my way toward a future where I didn't need to shrink. But he felt me growing, and instead of celebrating, he grew resentful. When we met, he had said he'd leave the Army after four years and that we'd start fresh. But then came the re-enlistment. Then his desire for a master's degree to gap our educational distance and fill his feelings of inadequacy. Then the silence that followed anytime I talked about dreams that didn't center him. When I got the tenure-track job at MiraCosta, I thought he'd be proud. Thought he'd see it as our win. I called him from the parking lot of the school and shared the exciting news. His voice was flat, not sharing in the jubilee, simply asking what time my flight home would be landing. Sitting across from each other on the living room couch, his jaw tightened as he spoke an ultimatum: choose the job or choose me. He wanted me to be anchored to his military path, following him from base to base, a shadow to his ambition. I responded with the weight of my degrees and my dreams behind my voice, "I didn't work my ass off to earn a doctorate and get a dream job to abandon it all because you've changed your mind about yourself. When we met, we agreed you'd do four years and that's it. Now you want out of a promise we had built our future on because your misogynistic military world makes you feel small compared with me? Because now you want me to be your standard military wife? Fuck that."

I packed my things and left the next month.

He wanted a wife who would follow orders. I wanted a life where I could be free.

So I left the house, the things, the war. And I chose myself.

The second time around came almost ten years after the first. I thought I'd done the hard part already. Thought I'd survived the storm.

But the truth is, sometimes love shows up quietly just to teach you how loud grief can be.

He was five feet eleven. Athletic. Filipino. A Navy vet who loved to play golf on Saturdays and cheer for the San Diego Chargers with his parents on Sundays. He had a quiet way of being kind without performing it. He played piano by ear. He'd sit on the bench, place his fingers steadily on the keys, and let the music come through him like it had always been there. He wrote songs for me, too. Some beautiful, some corny as hell. But all of them were honest. And honest felt like a kind of miracle.

He worked logistics for a military contractor and spent his days solving other people's problems. He spent his nights trying to be soft with me. He picked the wedding venue, a golf course clubhouse covered in white orchids. He said it felt clean and right. Control had long been my shelter, my way of holding chaos at bay, but it was his first marriage, his first dream of what this day should be, so I stepped back, fingers twitching, heart willing, and let him build it his way. We honored Filipino rituals like the thirteen coins, the veil and cord, the sponsors, and the money dance. A semi-Catholic priest who believed in grace more than guilt stood under that white arch and gave us the kind of blessing I never thought I'd want again. There were fewer than 250 people. Still big in its own way, but nothing like the first time. This time, the crowd felt more like a hug than a performance. This time, I think Mom even smiled. He was a good man. A really good man. And I did my best to meet him there. To be who he needed. To be someone kind. But I couldn't give him the one thing he wanted most. A child.

We tried the natural way. We turned to prayers and apps and candles and hope. Then came the doctor visits. At first, everything looked fine. But then came that word I'd never heard before. *Unicornuate.* One fallopian tube. One half-formed shot at motherhood. A uterus shaped more like an apology than a promise. So, IVF was the only option. And it was brutal.

I shot myself up with hormones until my stomach looked like I'd gone a few rounds in a back-alley brawl. Bruised, bloated, purple, green, and black like rotting fruit. One shot hit wrong, and I couldn't walk right for three days. I had to limp through my own hope. Had to tell my body, *Please stay in this with me*, even when it wanted to shut down. But then, hope made its way again. My ovaries started swelling. The eggs grew inside me like tiny balloons filled with maybe. I watched them on the screen, floating, perhaps forming their way to the edge of possibility.

Egg retrieval wasn't a procedure. It was a reckoning. My uterus was tilted. One of my ovaries was hidden and uncooperative. The doctor had to pierce the uterus with a catheter to get to the right ovary. I screamed. Not out loud, but in the way your body remembers screaming after the pain is gone. For days, I crawled on all fours to the bathroom. Couldn't sit. Couldn't stand. Couldn't tell anyone how much it hurt to hope like that. Then the embryos had to be frozen. My body needed time. More healing. More waiting. Every moment felt like maybe. And then the call came.

I picked up the phone and listened to the nurse's gentle voice. But it was too gentle.

"Mrs. Ha, I'm sorry. The test was negative. You can stop the shots now."

And just like that, it was over. Not the pain. Not the love. But the maybe.

I sat in silence processing the thought of no more shots. No more bruises. No more pretending that trying wasn't changing everything inside me. What do you do with that kind of silence? What do you tell a man who gave you love songs and white orchids when all you have left to offer is your breath, shallow and quiet, on the other side of a phone call letting him know it didn't work?

Tears filled my eyes as I delivered the news to him, my voice breaking into sobs. "I'm so sorry. I'll try again," I whispered, though deep down, I wondered if I could.

There'd never be another *almost* like that one. Not even close.

The next three rounds didn't offer promise the way the first one did. They didn't offer much of anything close to promise. Just more protocol, more injections, more bruises turning purple then yellow then gone, only for new ones to take their place. Another try, another frozen embryo withdrawn from the cryobank like it was a savings account. Same pain. Same prayer. Same ending. Repeat. Then rinse away the failure.

By the time summer came around, I was spent. Not just tired. *Done.* My body wasn't mine anymore. It belonged to the appointments, to the hormones, to the rollercoaster I kept getting on even though the track never led anywhere. The migraines, the nausea, the ache behind my knees and the back of my eyes. And then there was the weight. Yes, there was weight gain, but that was trivial. It was the weight of disappointing everybody that was difficult to manage. Him. His parents. My own damn self. It was like I was failing in surround sound.

Then came the going-away party.

His cousin and their fiancée were headed to Japan. Something about a new life. A new start. The extended family told us they wanted to throw a surprise farewell party. The house was full of family, Filipino food, and music. It was boisterous, the kind of loud that makes you feel like maybe you can be invisible if you just smile long enough. Just twenty-four hours earlier, I had gotten the call. Another canceled cycle. Thin uterine lining was too thin, they said. The one before? Canceled from high estrogen. My body kept building hope and shutting the door before anything could walk through it.

But still, we showed up. Because that's what you do. You show up and smile through the sting like you're not bleeding under your clothes. And then the door opened.

We all shouted "Surprise!" like joy was guaranteed.

But they flipped it on us. They weren't saying goodbye. They were announcing something. "Thank you for coming," they said, "but the surprise is on you. We're staying because . . . we're pregnant!"

Cheers erupted, the room bursting with joy. I glanced across the crowd at my husband. His face remained still, his eyes distant. I wondered if he even noticed me watching. After two years of trying, we had nothing to show for our efforts, and here they were—unmarried, unplanned, and months into a pregnancy.

At the food line, my mother-in-law turned to me. "Thao, what's going on with the medical stuff?"

Apologetically, I replied, "I'm sorry, it didn't work again. I just found out yesterday."

Her look of disappointment cut through me like a blade. Before I knew it, I was consoling *her*, rubbing her shoulders and assuring her, "It'll be okay. We'll try again." But looking back, I wonder, who was there to console me?

Most people knew we were trying but didn't really know the storms we were weathering. My sister cried each time she found out. She cried like it was happening to her. I told her I was fine. Lied to her like I'd been lying to myself. My parents didn't say much. They knew me well enough to wait in the quiet until I was ready. And him? My husband? That man cradled hope like a small flame cupped in his hands, shielding it from the wind. Every failed cycle was, to him, just one step closer. Another turn in the staircase toward some glowing idea of fatherhood he never questioned. His faith in us stayed steady. Mine shook like loose glass in a storm. Every time the phone rang, every time the nurse said, "I'm sorry," I didn't just hear failure, I heard, *You're the problem.*

And I believed it. I started to feel like I wasn't just failing to get pregnant. I was failing him. Failing his parents. Failing the family I said we'd build. Failing the version of myself I promised him at the altar. Failing to deliver. And it wasn't just private. It was everywhere. Grocery store. Family barbecues. Cultural events. Golf charities.

"When are y'all gonna have a baby?"

"Isn't it your turn by now?"

"Just relax. God will make it happen."

I wanted to scream. I wanted to say, *If we were pregnant, don't you think we'd tell you? Stop asking me to smile through this.* But instead, I smiled and bit the inside of my cheek. I allowed the questions to slice me open while I nodded like I was still whole. Family gatherings made it worse. His folks—Filipino, Catholic, loving, relentless. They prayed over me. Passed me teas and oils and whispered Indigenous recipes. One aunt gave me a white scarf and said it had been blessed by some fertility saint back in the Philippines. She told me to wear it under my clothes and sleep with it under my pillow. My husband purchased a tiny wooden statue, placing it on the nightstand on his side of the bed, believing that God would answer. He clutched it every night and said a prayer like it could hear him.

And still, nothing. No baby. No heartbeat. No second line. No medical miracle. Just me, with a body that wouldn't comply. A mind that couldn't rest. A heart that kept turning itself inside out, trying to understand how to keep showing up for a dream that wouldn't show up for me. This wasn't breakup pain. This wasn't *he cheated so I left* kind of pain. This was deeper. Slower. The kind of heartbreak that snakes into your veins and settles there. This was self-doubt that sounded like scripture. This was worthlessness that felt earned. I was tired. Of the hormones. Of the prayers. Of the pity. Of the pretending. And so I gave up. Not with fireworks. Not with a scream. Just a quiet folding in on myself. And that's how it started. It was the beginning of our end.

That summer I went back to Texas like I always did. Same heat, same mosquitoes, same AC humming hard throughout the day and night. But some things were different. My sisters had babies now. Toddlers running wild and infants waking up every two hours to be fed. Bottles, diapers, lullabies. I slipped into it easily, taking the night shifts, nursing my baby nephew with warm milk and rocking him on my chest while the house slept. I went days without a shower. The thought of it was once gross to me, but these little ones were suddenly a priority. I ate what I could, when I could. My body ached, my eyes burned from days-old contact lenses, and my heart started doing something I couldn't quite name. It was beautiful. And it was exhausting.

When I flew back to California, I stepped into my quiet home and felt the relief settle into my spirit like warm bathwater. Meals I could eat sitting down. Silence I didn't have to fight for. Sleep that came deep, hard, and uninterrupted. I rested, and in the stillness, my own voice finally spoke to me. Without the outside noise. Without the voices of others. And without the social constraints of what it means to be a woman.

I don't remember ever dreaming of being a mom.

I hadn't dreamed of it as a child. I hadn't daydreamed about baby names or nurseries. I'd just . . . assumed. Assumed that's what came next. That's what women did. What good wives did. What daughters were supposed to grow into. But sitting there, alone and rested, I realized I'd been chasing a version of joy that didn't belong to me. A version written by someone else. And maybe that version worked for other people—my sisters, my mother, women I love and respect—but it wasn't mine. That joy didn't fit.

I told him, and I tried to be soft with it. "I just don't think I want to be a mom anymore. I don't know if it's right for me."

He blinked slowly. Then he looked at me like I'd disappeared right in front of him. "Why are you giving up on us?" he asked.

But that wasn't it. I wasn't giving up on us. I was trying to be honest. I was trying to stay alive inside my own skin. But to him, that honesty sounded like betrayal. The talks turned to tension. The tension turned to fights. And underneath it all, that same truth kept humming. *He couldn't imagine a future without kids. And I couldn't imagine surviving a future where I had them just to keep someone else feeling whole.*

I watched the women around me. Watched them do mothering with love, with exhaustion, with joy and with sacrifice. I admired them. But I didn't envy them. That mattered to me. Sometimes knowing what you don't want is the clearest kind of knowing. I didn't want children.

But I wanted *the marriage*. I wanted to hold on to something that wasn't already gone. I didn't want to fail again. Not at this. Not at love. So when he stood there with his hand on the new lease, ready to go, I broke. I begged and said all the things I swore I wouldn't say:

"Please don't do this. I'm sorry. I'm sorry for everything. I'll try again. I'll call the doctor right away." And I did. I called. I filled out the forms. Paid the fees and took the prescription home like it was salvation in a bottle.

But then my period came. And I just . . . froze. The thought of starting over, again, made my whole chest tighten like a fist. My breath went shallow. My body screamed in a language I had learned to ignore. It wasn't just the meds, the shots, and the bruises. It was the fear. Not of failure. Not even of pain. It was the fear of succeeding. The fear of becoming something I didn't want to be. I couldn't take the pills.

When I told him, he was calm. Too calm. Like the storm had already passed.

"I knew it," he said. "I knew you wouldn't do it."

After a long silence, I replied with resolve, "Yeah. We're just kicking the can down the road. You have to be true to yourself. And I have to be true to myself. At this point, our visions of the future are no longer the same."

And there it was. Not an explosion. Not a slam of a door. Just a quiet line drawn between two truths that couldn't live in the same house. We were both right. We said the words we hadn't been brave enough to admit to ourselves. In my ownership of this unraveling, I had fooled us both into thinking I could do it just to keep the marriage intact.

A few days later, he wavered. He suggested trips to rekindle the spark, to test whether being childless might not be so bad. We went to San Francisco and visited the spot where he had proposed, the magical Palace of Fine Arts, but the magic was gone. For me, the connection had faded. I could see the divergence in our paths. He needed to fulfill his dream of fatherhood, and I needed to be honest about mine. Mom, ever so wise, offered clarity.

"Perhaps your body didn't allow it because your mind and soul never really wanted it."

Her words struck a chord. I had not considered the deep connection between body, mind, and spirit. As I reflect on this, I realized that the idea of balancing motherhood with my career filled me with stress and fear. Social researchers had indicated what I felt. Under certain conditions, children are tethered to maternal unhappiness, particularly in a country with poor family-work policies. I had asked him to find a job closer to home to help if we had children, but he never did.

His dream of fatherhood was the kind carried by blood, born in a delivery room lined with grandparents' *joya*. It was never possible with me. And what is a dream if not something we eventually have to release, like smoke from the mouth? Letting go became the only direction that didn't tear us both apart. And still, it hurt. Hurt in the quiet way a small crack spreads across glass, unnoticeable until it shatters. I couldn't stop thinking of myself as a disappointment. As a body that couldn't give. As a woman who could not "deliver the goods"—not to him and not to his parents who had already begun to shape their love into grandparenthood even before a child existed.

The thought of him leaving our house in Oceanside, just three miles from the people who raised him, was humbling. That house with its soft light and warm walls. That house where I memorized the sound of his keys in the lock, his footsteps on the tile, his cheering for the Chargers echoing from the other room, his hands brushing across black and white keys and churning out magical melodies that filled the room with a soft energy.

When it was time, I couldn't stay. I left for Houston. I chose absence over watching him fold his life into cardboard. I chose motion over stillness. I chose the buzz of dragonflies outside the window of my childhood room over the silence of a shared drawer being emptied. Weeks later, he picked me up from the airport. Still him. Still gentle. Still reaching for the small kindnesses. He picked up my bag without a word. We barely spoke. The sun spilled through the windshield like it didn't know what had changed. He pulled up to the house. I got out. We hugged. I took my bags and motioned that I could make it to the door alone. I walked inside. The air felt different. The walls leaned a little farther from me. The bed was too neat. The kitchen was too clean. And just like that, I was standing in my suburban house, holding the quiet weight of my second divorce. And silence, again, was the only thing that stayed.

I used to think my divorces meant love had failed and that I'd ruined something sacred. But now, I'm not so sure. Every ending cracked open a beginning: a new city, a better job, a version of me I didn't know I could become. Maybe it wasn't love gone wrong. Maybe it was me leaving a kind of love that was never mine—a version built by culture, country, or church, where women are taught to shrink, to sacrifice, to stay even when it breaks them.

I was stubborn. Still am. I couldn't lose myself chasing someone else's dream of a good life. Their dreams weren't wrong, just not mine. It took two marriages to see I wasn't the wrong woman. I just hadn't met myself yet.

Heartache will show you.

Breakups didn't just break me; they chipped away at who I'd been trained to be. The obedient one. The hopeful one. The empathetic one. The one who acted first and asked questions later. That version got scraped down, breakup by breakup, until I could see the outline of someone I actually recognized.

That pain? That wasn't punishment. That was process. That was me unlearning. Unbecoming. Me shedding. Me letting go of traditions that had never truly fit me and that had only ever made me feel like I was failing at something that was never made for me to win.

I hope he becomes a father. I mean that. On the Father's Day after we split, I saw pictures online. Friends posting their husbands with sleepy-eyed toddlers on their shoulders. Pancakes, cookies, cakes, cards, matching jerseys. I saw him in those photos, even though he wasn't in them. I saw the dad he was meant to be. I know he'll get there. I believe that. And when he does, I'll celebrate that joy. Even if it ain't mine to hold. I was his joy once. And then I wasn't. And that's okay. His next joy will come from someone who can give him what I couldn't. That truth used to gut me. But now, it sits quieter in my chest. Still tender. But not heavy and not raw.

As for me, I didn't know what I wanted. Not really. I just knew what I *was supposed* to want. What I was *told* to want. And when I couldn't hold on to those things, when the marriages ended, I carried that failure like it had my name stitched into the lining. Twice divorced. Twice shamed. I thought it meant I wasn't built for love. That I was beneath the dignity of it. That I couldn't be trusted with it. That maybe I was the kind of person who love passed over.

But what I know now, what I'm learning, is that the hardest part of healing isn't forgiving them. It's forgiving yourself for becoming someone you didn't recognize just to make it work. And now, I'm working on becoming someone I can love, even when nobody's watching.

In the middle of my second divorce, when everything was falling apart again, Jackie messaged me out of nowhere. Years of silence between us, broken by a Facebook ping that felt timed to my unraveling. She said she figured I was divorced. She could tell from the photos I quietly deleted. Then she said his name: Vu.

He'd lost his last appeal. Eleven more years before parole, maybe longer. She said he was slipping, barely speaking, deep in something dark. Maybe a word from me, she said, could pull him back. Just a note. Just something to remind him he hadn't been forgotten. But I couldn't. I was still sorting through the wreckage and trying to breathe through the shame. Reaching out felt like tearing open a wound. So I didn't. I left Jackie on read. Left Vu in his cell without a word. Not because I didn't care, but because I did. Too much. And I couldn't carry both of our pain.

9

Love Letters to the Dirty South

IN 2017, I CASHED OUT what investments I had, sold the house, the furniture, the cars, everything that once signaled stability, and stripped my life down to what could fit inside a moving truck. I bought a condo by the beach. A new space. A quiet one. A bright, light, and airy space where I could start over without explaining who I wanted to be. I wasn't going to talk about it anymore. I was just going to do it. I was just going to be.

The year prior, I had brought home Pork Chop, a tiny shih tzu puppy from Houston who had originally been gifted to my brother after he lost his pet rabbit. My brother, with a softness he rarely shows, told me Pork Chop would have a better life with me in California. And he was right. Pork Chop came into my life for a reason, as if the universe knew I needed a steady soul beside me, a companion who asked for nothing but presence and offered the kind of quiet loyalty that feels like peace.

I filled the condo with some new things. Some old. A few green. A few blue. A few broken things I couldn't leave behind. That space, with Pork Chop's small body curled at my feet, became my promise to myself. It was my way of saying, *I'm still here.*

And as for love . . . people say love's got reasons that reason cannot understand. They say the heart wants what it wants. And I've felt that want. That ache. That ghost-itch for something that used to live inside me. I felt it most in the quiet. In the nights that didn't ask much of me but still wouldn't let me sleep. That wanting crept in like a thief. Sometimes when I was alone. Sometimes when I wasn't. I'd be lying next to somebody, the room filled with our breath, skin still moist from the night before. And still, I'd feel empty. Full of lust, sure. But hollow. Like my body had been spoken to, but my spirit had been left out of the conversation. And the next morning always told the truth. That what I was chasing wasn't love. It was closeness. Or maybe the idea of it.

The older I got, the louder the yearning got. Not for just *someone*, but for *that* someone. For the kind of love that felt warm in its stillness. Love that didn't need to shout to be heard. The kind I used to know. Or thought I knew. The kind that lived in the memory of him. Of us. Back to the days before the divorces, before the bruises, before I started lying to myself just to live up to the world. After that summer of 2018 visit with Jackie and Vu's mom, I wrote Vu that letter. A love letter, sort of. To a person. And to a place. The Dirty South. The place where I first learned how to want. And how to lose. I wrote to him to remember. I wrote to him to ask for forgiveness. I wrote to figure out who I was when I wasn't being what everyone else needed. He wrote me back. And we continued to write, every week, our words circling like past stardust, fragments of what burned bright, still drifting, refusing to settle.

July 31, 2018

Dearest Vu,

I hope this letter greets you in a healthy and happy state of mind. I want to thank you for writing me and for making me smile and laugh. I will honor your request and write about the past to reminisce those days we had together. But before I go down memory lane, I wanted to say I hope your days have been a little brighter than the dark times you mentioned. I'm glad my letter came at the right time. Jackie asked why I wanted to write you after all these years. It was a strong inner feeling that had been lingering in my mind and in my heart. The feeling was that I wanted to reconnect with you because . . . maybe because I missed you and I wanted to know how you were doing. Writing you and receiving a letter from you has brought me great joy. No, I don't write to any other inmates (don't be jealous) except for Doughboy. But on another level, I wonder if I had been sensing your feelings of dark times. Yes, we were young then but surely we were very much in love. I believe our connection never died. Perhaps that is why these feelings are still with me today. I'm glad to have you back in my life. I promise to be a very good pen pal and to write you regularly.

I forgot the names of your friends who lived in Alvin. You were staying with them, and that is where you and I hung out a lot together. I remember finishing class and then driving out there super fast to see you. I put a lot of miles in my truck, and the reason I'm telling you this now is because I never told you how much more trouble I got in with my dad after we got busted in my room—yes, that was terrifying then but yes, very funny now. Anyway, on school days, he asked me why I was out so late. I told him I was at the library studying. After that, he tracked the miles to see how far I was driving. He then confronted me so I had to confess I was going to see you.

I hope you got the picture Jackie sent you of us. She sent me one, too. Both pictures were when we went to San Antonio and hung out at the Riverwalk. That was such a fun time together. We both look so young in those pictures. We also look very happy. I had a picture you gave me of you on a keychain. I lost that picture when my stupid jealous ex threw it away. I really am pissed off about it. Another gift you gave me was a message you wrote on a napkin encased in a glass vial that you made when you were working at that glass factory in Houston off Hillcroft and Hwy 59. You gave me so many gifts from the heart. I kept all the drawings you made me when you were in jail in 1992. I even kept the napkin drawing where you spelled my name wrong haha. I guess Vietnamese isn't your strength LOL.

I'm going to send this to you now and include some more pictures. I will write again soon. Thank you again for writing me. Stay healthy and positive.

With Love, Thao

August 3, 2018

Hey Thao,

I received your letter yesterday but didn't read it until this morning. I wanted to finish my last letter to you first. I was not playing when I mentioned it takes me days to write one letter to you. I'll write something down then change my mind five minutes later (thinking she doesn't want to hear that) so I'll start over and over and over. But it's okay because I enjoy the time and reminiscing. Plus in my mind I'm kickin' it with this one girl that used to go cray of this sexy ass ears of mine. The photo of us in San Antonio that Jackie sent put a smile on my face. I can't believe I finally received it. I guess it's better late than never.

For some reason, I do feel the same way. I have always connected with you also and don't know why. Maybe we were soulmates from a past life. At the time when I'm sad, lonely, and needed someone, your face always pop in my head. Do you remember when I was on the run for this case? I called you from a pool hall because I needed to talk to someone. This was long after we broke up, but I wondered through the years why I called you that night and no one else. I remember seeing you sitting in your car crying when they took me away. I think in my heart, I always knew that you would come if I needed you. When you got there I was arrested, I remember seeing you sitting in your car crying when they drove me away. Thao, in that one moment in time I knew you would always be there for me. Some things are better left unsaid so I'm not going to say more. But I did wanted to share that with you. I also want you to know that I will always care for you no matter what you do in this life. Our time together will always be special to me and last me a lifetime because of the memories. So smile for me when you hear this one country song called "Waiting on a Girl" by Joe Nickel. It reminds me of us. From the time we met, I felt like one of us was always waiting on the other. "If you get there before I do, don't give up on me. I'll get there when my chores are through. Don't know how long I'll be. But I'm not going to let you down. Darling, wait and see. Until now and then, 'til I see you again, I'll be waiting for you, love me." I might have added my own words to it, I'm not sure. People say I wear my heart on my sleeve, and I'm fine with that. I sent you this song in remembrance of our time together. Thao, please know that In No Way Do I Want You To Stop Living Your Life. I am very grateful that you are sharing a part of your life with me. In prison, I can only live and see through your eyes so I like to see that you are happy.

I have a have a very hard time writing about this place because it brings so much sadness to my letter. I will try my best for you. This place will consume me if I let it. Thankfully, you've asked me a lot of questions, and I will answer them in my own time. When I first arrived at Beto 1, I was scared shitless. I think I only survived because I lost the will to live. I heard a lot of rumors about Beto from the county and believe me, nothing was good about it. I was devastated when I stepped off the bus and seeing 60 years of my future. At 24 years old, I did not see the strength, resilience and determination you saw in me. But without the will to live it brought bitterness and hatred in myself. I blamed everyone but myself. For years on, I have fought the world and God himself. At one point I almost went over the edge (never told anyone) but kept recalling this one conversation I had with my niece. She was only 2 years old at the time when she accepted my collect call. For some reason, she knew something was wrong with me because she kept saying "Bác Vũ, it's okay, it's okay" over and over. She does not know it but she gave me the strength to move on and the will to be a better man. So now, I pushed on because of that little girl. I pushed on because of my sisters and my family. I pushed on because I owed it to the people that love and care for me.

Anyway, unfortunately I do not have a cell to myself. My cellmate is Mexican and he's good people but doesn't speak any English. I can't speak Spanish so we can't argue with each other that's for sure. My cell is the size of a closet with a bunk bed, a desk, and a toilet that is also a washing machine haha. I keep my letters, pictures, and books in here. Matter of fact, I still got a Christmas card you sent me a long time ago when you lived in Austin.

My days here are easy. I wake up about 7:00 am and 5:30 am on the weekend (old people do not sleep much haha). I'll have my black coffee and then listen to my 107.3FM R&B radio station while doing 500 sit ups. Afterward I'll read a book. I've been doing this for years. I go from one book to another to the next. It is not a mystery why my face was often buried in a book. They often provide a safe haven or some time to escape from this harsh reality. Nowadays reading your letters and writing to you like I am now. By the way, what music do you listen to? Then I'll go to work from 2pm—11pm. I work 7 days a week as a SSI Porter (basically a janitor). The dorm is three stories high and has 34 cells on each floor so I do a lot of running up and down the stairs all day. Most of the time, everybody else is in their cell or the day room so I'm like an errand boy. Vu, get this for me. Vu, get that for me. I don't mind but it does get tiring. I find time in between errands to work out. At about 8pm I'll go feed my pets :). There's two cats (an orange tomcat and a gray female) that comes by my window everyday for years now. I usually feed them mackerel fish so they're a little spoiled and will not eat any bread. I do feel sorry for them because they are locked in this prison also. At first I hated the job, but now I am beginning to enjoy it. There's a place on top of the stairs where there's a window that I can look past the fences (not much of a view but it's quiet). I can be alone and think if I want. I like sitting up there and reading your letters. By the time I get back to the cell, I am tired and just want to relax. At night I try not to think too much but my mind wanders. What do you think about before you sleep? Sleeping is the best time for me. I like to dream and when I do it is the only time I am totally free.

Your letters always bring me comfort and laughter. Thank you for taking the time out for me. I do appreciate your time and happy thoughts. Good night and be safe, Thao.

Love, Vu

August 13, 2018

Hi, Vu!

Thank you for writing me. And a much deeper thank you for sharing your experience and the tough times you've been through. I can't even imagine what it was like for you, but I'm glad your family has stuck by you this whole time. I get really scared thinking about what it's like for you because there are so many shows on television and so many films about prison that are horrific. I read about cases of prisoner abuse and mistreatment, and it pains me to see how the system can damage people instead of rehabilitate people. I worry about you. I asked you to tell me about life in there because I really just want to know if you're ok. I want to know that you are not being mistreated or abused. I realize it's very hard for inmates to discuss it even if it was happening. Society has taught men to be strong and not show emotion or weakness. This is magnified a thousand times in prison where you have to be tough. Prison gangs, prison abuse, prison violence . . . these things worry me for you.

I just wanted to know you're ok, that's all. Thank you again for opening up to me. I realize it's not easy to do. I appreciate your trust in me.

That sucks that there is a delay in mail services, but it's wonderful that technology allows for mail to come to you through the JPay system. The world is a different place now. When you went in, we were still using pagers and the personal cell phone was a brand-new device. But it is now at the center of human life in society. There are not too many people with "land lines" in their home anymore. Today, personal cell phones are all wireless. The phone can go anywhere with you and you can do pretty much everything with your phone. A lot of people keep their attention on the phone so much that it's starting to cause problems like car accidents and other accidents—for example someone fell over a cliff because they were hiking but paying too much attention to their phone trying to take a picture that they didn't notice the edge of the cliff! I try to stay off my phone as much as possible because I don't want to get addicted to it. Some people say they feel nervous when they don't have their phone. I don't want to be like that!

I'm going to stop here and send this to you. I am happy to hear from you and happy that we reconnected. It's nice to know that our memories of the past can bring us great joy in the present. Until next time, stay healthy, think positive thoughts, and anytime you start to feel down or the darkness creeps in, just remember there are people who love and care for you. Or just think about the way you used to make me smile because I'm smiling today because of you.

August 17, 2018

Hi Thao,

Today is a wonderful day for me. I received a letter from you with some pictures in them. I read your letter and went to sleep afterward feeling content and happy. There's something about you that always makes me feel this way. I could do another 100 years (haha just joking, this 8.5 years I have left is long enough) for another letter like that. Thao, I miss you also. At one point in my life, you were like my best friend and I've missed that also. A part of me is always yours. Even though you devastated us both with your decision back then, you made a very good choice. Seeing how you are now. If I and our past inspired you to be the person you are today, then it is worthwhile. I have always known you had the determination, strong will, and let's not forget the stubbornness to be successful. If not, we'd probably be married and you hating me right now haha. And you would be calling me your stupid jealous ex.

I got back from work early today because it's Friday. I like catching the end of the Sweat Hotel radio program from 10pm—11pm. I want you to listen to these songs since they are my favorite R & B songs. "This One's For You and Me" by Johnny Gil. "Come and Talk to Me" by Jodeci. "Love Like Yours and Mine" by Peabo Bryson. And "I'd Rather" by Luther Vandross. I would like to have the lyrics to them if you can send them to me. I am a hopeless romantic so just imagine me singing them to you haha. Since I can't write poems like you do so I've decided to write a song for you.

"I can't remember why we fell apart. From something that was so meant to be. Forever was the promise in our hearts. Now more and more I wonder where you are. Do I ever cross your mind anytime? Do you ever wake up reaching out for me? I miss you. Still have your pictures in my cell. Still hear your footsteps in my dreams. I swear I hear your voice driving me insane. How I wish that you would write to say I miss you."

If you want to hear more songs from Brian McVu, let me know. I do know one thing for sure. If you are dating someone, you better not let him see this letter. He will surely tear it up.

I see you went and Googled Tennessee Colony. I didn't even know that total population is only 300 people. I know that most of them work here. They complain that the pay sucks but don't have much choices around here. When it's payday, no one shows up for work so they are very much short of staff that day. It's like we are home alone that day. The reason I stayed at Beto and didn't ask to transfer is because I'm an old dog and I don't like changes. Doughboy transferred to Michael unit because it's a newer unit. He always hated being in an old-ass unit like Beto. I'm sorry to hear he was denied parole again. I do also have a feeling he'll get out soon. The prison system is changing with all this budget cut and a lot of prisons are closing down. I heard in California, Governor Jerry Brown signed a slew of bills aimed at criminal justice reform. One is changes to parole process for offenders serving lengthy sentences for crimes committed before the age of 25 (like me). Too bad I'm not in California. Texas is a Republican state and the criminal justice reform here sucks. It's all about money and free labor. But there's a little hope since 2019 is just around the corner and the Texas legislature will be back in session. I am praying for one bill to pass (HB2120) for work time and good time for 3G offenders. On my time sheet I have 21 years flat, 21 years work time, and 21 years good time totaling 63 years but it does not mean a thing.

Anyway, this was a long time ago and I do not feel this way now. But at one point when I thought about Tri, I used to get consumed with hate. I hated that he's married, I hated that he has kids, and I hated that he's successful. All the things I will never get a chance to do or have. I have always thought I was innocent but I am not. That night on my case, I had many choices and as a young man, I made the wrong choice. Someone got hurt that night so a debt is owed to society. I am learning to forgive myself and Tri while I'm paying for this debt. Tri, I guess is paying for it in a different or worse way. I heard his brother died, then his dad, and years later his mom. He and I were once best friends. It broke my heart when I learned. I realize now even in my situation, I am blessed. My family's well-being is more important than anything else in this world to me.

Thao, it's getting late and I want to mail this out to you. I want you to know I am well so don't worry about me. I hope you are well, I hope you are happy. My main goal in this letter was to make you smile and when you do, all is right in my world.

Love, Vu.

Reading Vu's letters and writing to him during those late summer months became a ritual. It's the way some people light candles for a hot bath or pray with hands folded before bed. His handwriting carried a rhythm, each curve was a reminder of the young and wild adolescent I once knew and the man he had become inside those walls. Our letters in September stretched longer and grew more personal—stories of the past, what forgiveness meant, of what was and what might still be waiting for us. Laughter and pain folded together, the way memory often is. By the time autumn came, our words had built something steady together, sturdy enough to hold the weight of hope. Our letters transformed. They became plans. Conversations about forms, visitation lists, and travel routes. The possibility of seeing each other again after nearly two decades felt like hope being realized and dates circled on the calendar.

September 28, 2018

Hi Thao,

I want to first say I hope all is well with you. I am very sorry that Jackie made you emotional and sad because of my conviction. Please do not feel guilty. I would like to believe that if we stayed together then maybe I would be on a different path but who can tell the future? I was young, wild, and the life I was living I can also be dead. So please, don't feel sad because my life took a harsh turn. I myself took these turns, so it's all on me. When you think of me, think of our happy times, think of our fun times, and remember the young boy who you once loved wholeheartedly. It's truly unbelievable to me that the first letter between us started 26 years ago. Looks like we are coming full circle, don't you think? Memories of us are getting clearer, and I definitely remember how much we laughed and joked around with each other. That's one of the reasons we are here now, writing to each other. I cherish those memories and when my days are darkest, they help carry me through the next day. I really started this journey believing I can just be your friend, but who am I fooling? For some reason, I feel we are too strongly connected for that. I do hate myself for feeling this way because reality is with every step you take going forward, you move farther out of my reach. You told me to fight for what I believe in. But as you say, we shall see how this all comes to be.

As I read your letters, I am saddened by your experiences regarding love and relationships. I am very sorry that you were hurt so many times, but who hasn't been hurt at one time or another? I hate to think that I helped cause you to lose faith in love. I don't know what to say to comfort you since my experiences regarding love and relationships are very limited. I only experienced real love one time in my life and was also dumped by that experience. I was really hurt that you never believed me but time does heal all pain, right?

You asked me to put you on my visit list so you could come see me and I thought very hard about this. I already put you on this list months ago but just now telling you this because I needed time to think. The more I think, the more I read your letters and see your pictures, the more I want to see you. So, yes, I would like the opportunity to see you. But do it at your convenience okay? Let me know in advance if you can. I think you need to call the unit classification and notify them that it's a special visit since you are out of state. Do this a couple of days in advance so there won't be any problems. Let me explain why it took so long and hard to decide whether or not to tell you I put you on my visitor list. As I mentioned, I do want the opportunity to see you, but at the same time, it scared me. Not that I think it'll be awkward but because we'll click and what it'll do to me. Someone famous once said that love is devastating and for some reason those words always stuck with me. It describes love perfectly, don't you think? But no matter what the cost is, it'll be worth the chance to see you.

In one of my last letters, I mentioned wanting to learn to write better so I can express myself to you. I would really like to say the things I want without tripping over the words. To be able to express my true feelings, thoughts, hopes, and even my dreams in a way that you can really understand the real me. I realize now that I did have a few women that cared for me but it was my fault that I couldn't express myself or I just never cared. But with you, it is different. You brought me back to life so that I see there's hope. I think my emotions are so strong when I write you because of my old feelings for you, the memories of us together, and the love that never died (for me anyway). I keep remembering how you once fell in love with me through our old letters and in my mind this little voice keeps saying maybe, just maybe. I'm just trying to be honest, Thao. I know what reality is, but I really can't help it. That's me being pessimistic, looking at the glass half empty while I should be optimistic and look at the glass half full. Since you said that you were hurt when you were younger and that now you block your love motion. As me being optimistic and that I have a lot of time on my hands, I'd like to start chipping at this wall you build around your heart. I know you are capable of showing this emotion because I was blessed with them once.

The holiday season is coming and it is the worst for me because that's when I get homesick. I know that sounds funny since this has been my home for the last 21 years. Last night I went to sleep in my boxers and woke up this morning freezing cold. I sometimes hate the Texas weather, one minute it's hot as hell and cold as ice the next. I wonder if it gets cold in the winter where you're at. What do you usually do this time of the year? Do you play volleyball in the winter in Cali? Thao, I'm going to end here. I really hope everything is well with you. Please take good care of yourself for me and know that I am thinking of you. I do miss you, Thao.

Love, Vu.

October 9, 2018

Dear Vu,

Thank you for your most recent letter. I hope this letter finds you well and in good spirits. Jackie told me that she and Judi and the kids came to visit for your birthday. I hope that it was a wonderful time! Speaking of visits, I was happy to read in your letter that you placed me on your visitor list. Wow, you are so sneaky. You kept this secret for a while, huh? To this day, you still manage to be full of surprises. Jackie did a great job keeping your secret, too. She didn't say a word. I completely understand your hesitation and why you had to process it for yourself first. You know, there's a reason for everything happening the way it does. I will be visiting Houston 10-23 to 10-29. My dad has an event in Biloxi, Mississippi on 10-25. He trained as a pilot at Keesler Air Force Base in the 1970s so there is a reunion with the pilot students like him and their instructors. I'm going with my parents to the reunion. We were supposed to go to Florida after the reunion and stay the weekend of 10-27 & 10-28, but my parents decided last week that we will drive back 10-26. If you don't have any visitors coming Saturday, 10-27, then I would love to come visit on that day. Let me know. I read through the procedures and rules so if it's a date, then I will call the warden's office early that week and request a special visit. If it doesn't work that date, no worries, I'll be back for the holidays in December.

I want to also thank you for sharing your very personal thoughts and feelings about us. I completely understand how difficult it is for you to manage and negotiate your feelings when you are in such a very difficult situation. I am always going to be your friend no matter what. Yes, I know we have history together. And love is such a complicated and truly complex emotion for me. The reality is that we live in separate and very different worlds. Our lives are separated by space and time that neither one of us can change. I'm in a relationship, and you are all alone in the confines of a punishment that we both know is your reality for at least another 8 years. You are in a much more vulnerable situation than me. Hell, the truth is that I am the one with all the privileges and advantages. So I don't want to hurt you or to ever make things harder for you. I only want you to have as much happiness and positive things as possible for someone in your situation. I get it—it's great to feel love and to feel cared for, but it is hell to know you cannot "be with" that person for whatever reasons. All I can say is that I offer you whatever I can for the time being. I am committed to writing to you, visiting whenever possible, and being here for you and your family if you all ever need my help. Yes, I have feelings for you; they stem from nostalgia and a past that was a wonderful moment in time but ended for the reasons that it did. Today, we are discovering that feelings can linger and memories can play with our emotions. I've learned from 45 years of life that I can never predict my future no matter how much I plan. So, I try to live in the moment and try my best to just do the right things. I don't want to hurt anyone. I haven't told my boyfriend how I feel about you, and I know I should. I know he will be freakin' pissed off. I don't want to marry him (you already know how I feel about marriage). I don't know if I'll be with him "forever." I just live day to day. Maybe he and I make it to "forever," maybe we won't. For me and you, I cannot say that I will be available when you are free. Hell, I don't even know if I will be around on this Earth! But if I am, and if I'm not with someone else, and you become a free man, then I would be willing to take a chance with you. However, those are a lot of "IFs," and you, my dear, should be open to whatever comes your way. One day, when you are free, someone will love you. I have no doubt about that. When that day comes, whatever place our hearts will be in, we will follow it. Until that day comes, I remain true to you as a friend, as someone who once loved you deeply, and as someone who cares for you very much and still loves you. Can someone love two people at the same time? I believe people have, and do. But I want to make decisions and take actions that don't betray anyone. If the day comes when you are free and you say to me, "Thao, make your decision," then you know I will do so with whatever is truest in my heart.

I hope I haven't hurt you with what I've written. If I did, I'm sorry. It's the truth, and it's not simple, and it's very messy. But to me, the reality is that love is messy and never seems easy. Let me end this by writing that you mean so much to me, that you are always in my thoughts, and I can't wait to see you again soon.

With so much love and care, Thao.

The letters had become a bridge across time, words traveling like small lanterns floating over dark water, each one lighting the distance between what was and what might still be.

After so many years of silence, the ink itself felt like breath returned, like memory learning to speak again. He was a hopeless romantic, writing about love as devastation, as something that survived the wreckage of years, as a wager with his heart that he was willing to risk. I was resistant, stubbornly anchored in what I wanted to believe was our reality, of the walls between us, of the mess that love can make. Somewhere between those truths, I began to remember not just who we were, but who we had been to each other. We were young adults, two souls who had once learned to laugh and love before the world hardened around us. And each letter softened the distance and reshaped the edges around my wounded soul. Soon, I would walk through the gates of a Texas prison carrying two decades of what-ifs and maybes. Soon, his voice would no longer be lines of ink but the sound of my name said aloud. The past and present, him and me—two mirrors facing each other from a long hallway, and from that intimate corridor of memory, he began to call me forward.

10

The Walls They Built

OCTOBER 2018. EXCITEMENT AND DREAD lived in the same space of my chest, pacing in circles around each other. I was going to visit Vu, but my body behaved as if it were meeting an old trauma rather than an old love. Sleep was evasive, and food tasted metallic. Vu wasn't just in prison; he was at the Beto Unit. I had done research with the diligence of someone who knows that information can prepare you and help you feel steady while also scaring the shit out of you. Beto had earned its reputation. They called it the Gladiator Unit, not as just as a nickname but as an indictment. Fights staged by guards were for everyone's entertainment. Blood washed away with the same indifference used to mop up slop off the chow hall floors. Violence was institutionalized so thoroughly it became part of the architecture, by design. Some places shape men. Beto produced headlines. John King entered Beto in '92 for burglary and came out full of hate. He met Lawrence Brewer there, a self-declared white supremacist. King's father told a priest, "Something happened to my boy in prison." Soon after they were released from Beto, they dragged James Byrd Jr. down a Texas road in 1998. It was a killing so brutal it left the nation gasping.

They beat him, chained him to a truck, and dragged him until his head was torn from his body. When King and Brewer were executed in 2019, the state marked it a milestone: the first white men in modern Texas to die for the murder of a Black man. It was a single statistic paraded as progress. And this was the place where Vu had lived for decades. I swallowed the knowledge, and it sat in me like a stone.

The curriculum of violence begins long before a man reaches his cell. At intake, which is the moment one enters the prison walls, the indoctrination begins. I remembered Vu telling me about it, they way someone recalls a childhood lesson that was learned the hard way "You can't smell like fear," he said. Fear wasn't an emotion in there. It was an odor, a signal, something equivalent to blood dropped into a spot in the ocean where the sharks encircle. If you showed the slightest hesitation, the slightest tremor, a hint of weakness, an entourage of inmates were ready to pounce. The guards never intervened. Sometimes, they arranged the spectacle. They had a name for what they did to the newcomers: turning out. Fresh arrivals were presented with two options: fight or break. If you broke, you became property. Raped. Passed around. Reduced to a function rather than a person. Some tried to negotiate a kind of safety by attaching themselves to one man and called it protection. We can call it survival, but it's still bondage. Vu once described it to me as an economy—paid as tax, submission as currency. That's how someone like King became who he was. First punked and humiliated, then remade into the only identity that promised safety. White supremacy became a refuge.

And that was the world Vu inhabited. It's a place where boyhood was stripped away and replaced with whatever could keep you alive the longest and maybe preserve a warped sense of dignity. Knowing all of this, I still went toward him. I still loved him in the stubborn, almost irrational way one loves someone marked by a haunted past. I told myself that love could protect us from what prison does to people, that love might be enough, that it could form a membrane between us and the concrete machine that crushes humans. Maybe I was naïve, but I went anyway. Beto held roughly three thousand men. Most worked in kitchens, the library, the laundry room. Vu first got sent to the fields. Worst job, he said. Worse than scrubbing shit off the walls. I could picture it: rows of men with blades, bent under the Texas sun, no shade, no rest. Just sweat and silence. Above them, guards on horseback, rifles resting casually in their laps, watching like it was still 1852. It didn't matter what year it was. What I was envisioning, through Vu's description, through history's long shadow, was plantation work with a new name.

When I first got here, I was in the field squad for two years. I always hated it because there were so many snakes around here. Everyday, we would clear a large section of land with only an aggie and get it ready for planting. I remember being out there when it rained, something about the rain that is soothing to me. We planted a lot of vegetables that the unit consumes. On a good day, we get to pick blueberries. I ate more than I picked when the man on the horse was not looking. I always got sick afterward. Just like the old days, when you need to use the restroom, they just throw you some toilet paper and make you take a dump in front of everybody.

Men squatting in open fields, taking shits in front of other men while a man on horseback sat still like some kind of overseer resurrected. That wasn't an accident. That was choreography. A whole scene staged to humiliate, to remind, to strip you down until you forgot you were ever anything other than a number. *Dehumanizing. Demoralizing. Despicable.* Because that's the point, right? The point is to make you forget what dignity feels like. Prisoners aren't people in places like that. They're gears. Dispensable cogs cranking out goods and labor for the carceral machine. A well-oiled, profitable, and efficient one.

Vu worked ten, twelve hours a day. Seven days a week. For no pay. No breaks. No choice. Refuse? That's a write-up. Too many, and parole gets further away. Say "Fuck it," and they toss you in solitary to be forgotten in a box. The system didn't need his consent. Just his body. Vu was no longer a son, brother, or first love. Just employee #801576, working for free while companies made money off his labor. They called it rehabilitation. But it was just slavery rebranded. No whip needed. Just a number, a uniform, and a never-ending shift. Convict leasing never ended. It evolved. And men in suits still smiled, because shackled labor was a good return on investment.

The Texas landscape stretched flatly in every direction. It's the kind of openness that makes you feel both free and exposed. I drove my brother Jonny's white Tundra and watched oak leaves swirl and fall like confetti after a Longhorn win. October. My birth month. Vu's, too. Some gift. Some celebration. Heading back into the belly of the system that swallowed him. The last time I visited him behind bars was 1992 at the county jail. The memory pressed against my chest like a dull fist.

I edge past slow-moving cars, chasing time. Prison didn't care when you arrived, but Vu might. Dawn split the gray sky. A thin band of gold light carved through fog-slick fields. Cows alongside the road chewed the cud, tails flicking away flies like factory work. I zipped past small town after small town—Buffalo, Palestine, Tennessee Colony. You remember names like that because they become landmarks for your grief.

Then came the prison unit signs. Michael Unit first. Doughboy was somewhere behind those fences. Then Beto.

The landscape shifted from rural quiet to manufactured menace. First the fences—steel mesh fortified with razor wire that promised pain. Then lights, huge and humming, scanning yards where the inmate's feet rarely touched the grass. Beto kept men locked down. Sunlight was an occasional privilege. Recreation time was a rumor. The walls rose high in concrete, a beige-gray color that faded into the land like it wanted to be forgotten. The rust-red admin buildings bled into the dirt. And then the guard tower stood above it all: armed, watchful, ready. That's how they hold you: through walls, through eyes, through fear. Not just the men inside. But everyone who dares to love them. Beto didn't simply house "violent offenders." It held legacies and the cumulative weight of policy, punishment, and the state's appetite for containment. And I drove toward it. Because to me, even behind wire and silence and shame, he was still someone worth showing up for.

I pulled up to the prison entrance at ten minutes before 7:00 a.m., the designated time for visitation to begin. A long line of cars already snaked along the shoulder—families and loved ones waiting for the security personnel to open the gate with the kind of patience born from routine and necessity. I inched forward as the line progressed. Finally, I reached the first security guard. I rolled down the window and handed over my ID, doing my best to make my voice small and agreeable, to sound polite and subdued, to be something less likely to be scrutinized.

"Mornin', ma'am," drawled the guard.

"Hello, sir," I replied.

I had researched the protocol beforehand: keep the engine running, open the trunk and the hood, step outside, and present your ID.

"California?" the guard asked.

"Yes, sir."

"That's a long way from here. Prolly the furthest I seen in a while."

"Yes, sir. I haven't seen my loved one in over twenty years," I said, my voice quavering.

He smiled. "Well, that's certainly special. Have a good visit."

After searching every cavity of Jonny's truck, the guards gave me the all-clear. The second guard assigned me a number, 22, and told me to remember it for when I left.

The drive from the gate to the lot was maybe a few hundred feet, but it felt like miles. The cars ahead of me pulled into parking spaces with practiced precision. I followed their lead. I stepped out of the truck and followed the people who'd done this so often and for so long it seemed like muscle memory. We walked in a single-file line, as if orderliness could soften what waited ahead.

At the kiosk, I handed over my ID. The clerk typed my information into one of those ancient computers—black screen, green letters, blinking rectangle cursor. "Approval."

Then I looked up and there he was: the guard in the tower. Rifle pointed down. Scanning. Measuring. Methodical. Detached. My hands twitched, my chest tightened, my body reacting before my mind developed thoughts.

A line painted on the pavement led to the entrance of the building. I walked it like a tightrope. Calm. Controlled. Every step, I asked myself if I was sure.

The first metal door had a camera fixed above it. I held my ID up and tiptoed to meet the lens. A harsh buzz sounded, and the door clicked open. It was loud and mechanical. I walked through it, and it slammed shut behind me. Then came a second buzz. Another heavy door, another metallic slam. The building announced its control with every sound. They were the sounds of being shut in, shut down. I hadn't even entered the building yet, and already sweat prickled at my collarbone. My mind went to Vu. This was the soundtrack of his daily life: *buzz, clank,* lock. Twenty years of it.

Two women were behind the glass of the front desk. I slid my ID and keys under the opening. One of them handed back a small slip: date, time, names. And the words "Regular visit." The designation landed with a quiet thud. It meant no contact. No hand to hand. No hug. I wasn't blood, I wasn't a wife. Just someone who still loved him and cared enough to make this drive and walk through these doors. I swallowed the hurt. Folded it inside the joy and anticipation of seeing him. It had been too long, and I had learned to make do with whatever was allowed.

At the conveyor belt, I placed my jacket down, pockets empty. I set down a plastic bag of jingling quarters. I stepped through the metal detector and was relieved it stayed silent. Then I saw "Whoopi," the Black female guard with the warm laugh and the face that made her nickname inevitable. Vu's sisters swore she had it out for Asians, but she was cool with me. She'd been there long enough, and longevity provided a sense of discernment to know who came often and who didn't.

Whoopi's eyes wandered up and down my body with curiosity. "You're new, aren't ya?" she asked with a lilt in her voice.

I nodded nervously. "Yes, ma'am."

"Mhmm, I didn't recognize you. Where you coming from?" she inquired, her tone a mixture of surprise and amusement.

"California," I replied, trying to hide my apprehension.

"California?!" she exclaimed, raising her eyebrows. "That's a long way, young lady!"

I smiled, trying to put on a brave face. "Yes, but I'm happy to be here."

She continued to search me, then suddenly asked, "Who you here to see?"

"Hoang Vu Tran," I responded, my voice faltering slightly.

"Tran?! You know the Tran sisters?" she asked, her eyes lighting up.

"Yes, ma'am!" I said, smiling despite myself.

She rolled her eyes and laughed heartily. "Lawd, them girls always be givin' me a hard time."

Yeah, she's the one who busted Jackie for sneaking food to Vu. First chicken wings. Then egg rolls just to give him a taste of home that prison menus never approximated. Jackie said she kept trying and finally pulled it off. Hid them in her son's diaper bag, tucked inside the diapers. She noticed the guards never checked those. I cracked up when they said Vu asked, "Where's the *nước mắm*?!"

I walked passed a row of humming vending machines and reached another check-in desk. I handed over my paper, and the guards logged my name, marked it as a regular visit, and pointed me to a seat by the glass.

The visitation room stretched long and narrow, a corridor designated as a gathering space. At the far end was the door the inmates came through. I settled into a hard plastic chair, eyes fixed on that door, waiting. One by one, the inmates trickled in.

A young guard named Brian Tran walked by. Pale skin, military haircut. He looked more like a high school senior in an ROTC uniform than a prison officer entrusted with ultimate authority. I smiled, a reflex born of politeness rather than comfort. He smiled back, quick and a bit shy. It was the kind of smile that suggested he hadn't yet learned how to harden his face into the institutional mask worn by some of his colleagues. It struck me, how disorienting it was to feel a flicker of warmth toward someone whose uniform is part of a machinery designed to grind people down. I could see the human being in him, the boyishness, a nervous pride in doing a job he may or may not have fully experienced nor fully understood yet. I have mixed feelings of the memory. I could appreciate the smile in the moment yet still know that kindness in prison had strict boundaries. He was both a person and a cog in a dehumanizing structure, two truths coexisting, like so much else in that place.

"Hi," he said, breaking the silence.

"Hello," I replied, purposely omitting the formal "sir." "You're Vietnamese. I've never met a Vietnamese prison guard before," I remarked.

"Yes, I am," he confirmed. "And you're Vietnamese too?"

"Yes. My name is Thảo, and I'm visiting from California," I introduced myself.

He seemed genuinely interested, "Wow, who are you here for?" he asked.

"Hoang Vu Tran," I replied, hoping to strike up a connection.

"Tran! I know him. He's a good dude," Officer Tran exclaimed.

I was taken aback by his response, "You know him, huh? So I guess you know his sisters and other family members who come in?"

Officer Tran chuckled, "Yeah, they are a rowdy bunch."

I laughed because what he said was genuinely funny, and Officer Tran laughed with me. The shared laughter was an unguarded sound that didn't quite match the setting. His lightheartedness and humor made the room feel less severe and me feel more at ease about being in this place. "Well, he should be coming through any minute now. Hope you have a good visit," he said with a smile. I felt the dissonance arise again. It was a reminder that even inside rigid structures, individual kindness leaks through in unexpected places, though never enough to change the architecture itself.

"Thank you so much," I replied gratefully, feeling a little more relaxed.

He walked off, and I turned back to the room. The visitors looked familiar, not because I recognized their faces, but because I recognized their posture. There's a particular way people sit and twitch when they're waiting for someone in state custody. It's not just their clothes or their tired eyes. Girlfriends with crossed arms and tight jaws, mamas holding purses like life preservers, little cousins swinging their legs, old men with hands that shook either from age or worry or anticipation. All of them in this place that didn't belong to them. It was county jail déjà vu from 1992. Different era, different zip code, same grief.

The men came out of the door one by one. They reached the end of a long-ass, battered wooden table reserved for contact visits, signed in like they were clocking into some job no one signed up for, then disappeared behind another door, into a space I didn't have access to except in imagination. Their people got up, walked through it, too, on the other side from a separate entrance. And when they came back, their body language emanated celebration in a way that made me think they'd just come from a backyard barbecue.

They popped open sodas and poured the snacks onto light green melamine plates. Jackie told me they used to let folks eat straight from the bag. But after people were busted slipping drugs and money into Doritos, they cracked down and the rules changed. Now the contents were poured onto the plates. Now it was control pretending to be cleanliness. I thought of those egg rolls Jackie smuggled in. Thought of Vu holding one in his palm, like a memory you could chew. Breaking it up into fragments, hiding it in a chip bag, chewing and swallowing it slowly, letting the taste remind him of a home that the system could never fully erase.

I blinked it away and turned back to my side of the room. My eyes locked on that door behind the glass. It stayed shut long enough for doubt to gather. Then it opened. And there he was.

His crisp white uniform hit first—like bleach against the dull gray walls. He looked burlier than in the photos, like time had layered itself onto his body. But that walk, that unmistakable rolling strut, had survived the decades intact. Still him. He carried his head high, shoulders back, like he had everywhere to go, as though the prison corridor was just another street from our past. He spotted me and his smile opened wide and easy. He moved toward me like he already knew what his presence could do to me, and of course, he was right.

My chest tightened, air backed up somewhere behind my ribs. Couldn't breathe, couldn't move. My hands hovered uselessly in my lap, unsure whether to rise or stay still. He was real and not real. Memory and presence folded into one—the boy I remembered overlaid on the man he'd become. And then I laughed before I even meant to. Loud, sudden, and stupid, like I was seventeen again, floating on the simple fact of him walking toward me, his name still ringing somewhere in my bloodstream.

He sat down, and for a moment we just stared at each other. No words, just the smirks and incredulous smiles that kept slipping out before we could stop them. A couple of giggles, ridiculous, involuntary, yet they rose between us like steam. It felt like everything we hadn't said in decades was suddenly speaking on its own. For a beat, the room fell away. I was back in 1992, leaning into a rusted vent at the county jail, straining to catch his voice through the metal slits, wishing for the one thing we could never get—touch. Skin on skin, even just a fingertip. And there we were again. Older, weathered, experienced, divided by glass, sound through a metal vent, still waiting for a touch the rules wouldn't allow. Time had carved itself into both of us. I felt it in the way caution had settled into my bones. He looked like a man who had survived a war that had no name, only years. But the ease between us slid back into place. Too easy, like we'd been interrupted mid-sentence decades ago and were only picking up where we'd left off.

I couldn't stop looking. The ringing in my ears buzzed slightly, a thin electrical hum, the way they do when memory runs ahead of breath. I dropped my gaze to the table, to pull my eyes from his, trying to pull air in slowly.

Then he said my name.

"Hi, Thao!" he chirped.

"Hi, Vu!" I replied, giggling in disbelief. The sound of our laughter filled the space, ricocheting off the walls, softening the room for a moment, as if the place didn't belong to the state but to us.

He glanced past me, nodding at someone behind me. I turned to see Officer Brian Tran walking by, hands in his pockets, offering a polite smile. Vu lifted his chin in acknowledgment, a brief gesture that suggested a momentary truce between guard and inmate, a silent acknowledgment passing between them. It was the kind of exchange between two people who knew each other's routines but not their lives.

Then it was just the two of us again. We slipped into conversation effortlessly, words tumbling out as if no time had passed. No warm-up. No awkward preface. Talking felt as natural as breathing, automatic, inevitable, like our voices had been waiting all those years for permission to begin again, the rhythm of our voices finding their own cadence.

Once we settled into our hard plastic chairs, Vu began offering small windows into his life behind bars. Not sweeping stories, just pieces. Fragments. The kind a man parts with cautiously. As he talked, I watched his hands. They were steady, but the way his fingers tapped the table gave him away. Rhythmic, controlled, a habit maybe learned from years of waiting for doors to open at someone else's will. I leaned in, elbows on the counter, catching his voice through the old, grated vent. He told me about the daily count. Men lined up shoulder to shoulder while guards shouted names like they were checking inventory. He mentioned the chow hall and the way trays clattered, echoing off the concrete. He wondered what it would be like to hold chopsticks again or what a metal utensil would taste like. His taste buds had become acclimated to plastic. He told me about the noise that never really stopped. Keys jangling, radios hissing, someone yelling down the tier. He described the cold that settled in his bones on winter mornings and the sweat beads on his neck on heat-infused afternoons. He didn't tell me the worst of things. I could see the edits in the pauses, the places where a sentence began but died on his tongue. He softened the edges for me and shaped the cruelty into something manageable. That he was reprimanded for sneaking off to the top of the stairways to sit and read my letters but not revealing what the punishment was. I didn't ask him to elaborate. I listened without judgment, without interrupting.

The less I questioned, the less I responded, the more comfortable he became with his storytelling. He told me that on occasional nights, he took "bird baths," dipping a towel into the toilet water to wipe off the grime from a day in the field. I felt my skin crawl and asked if the shower water was dirty. He paused, looked around the room to signal he was about to reveal a secret. He whispered, "Sometimes, the showers are out of order," raising his hands and curling his fingers to represent quotes. "That's how you know somethin's 'bout to go down. When the dorm knows a guy's about to get hit, the showers go dark. So they're not broken. Just . . . unavailable." I knew these things happened. The shower violence stories are abundant in prison literature, and the numbers are crunched in academic studies.

I responded, "I've heard this before. Now I'm listening to it from you, like a play by play. It's fascinating, really. Pretend I'm a researcher. Tell me more."

He smirked, "Okay, Dr. Ha. Showers are supposed to be a blind spot. Supposedly no cameras. So if they know someone's marked?" He shook his head. "They shut it down. Keeps the blood from washing into the drain. Makes the investigation cleaner, ya know?" He paused for a moment. I kept my eyes locked on him. He leaned back in his chair, shrugging in a resigned way. "That's just how it works. You learn the signs. You learn the signals. You learn when you need to take bird baths."

"Please tell me you're not speaking from experience. That your blood has never been mopped up in the shower," I demanded.

He snorted and replied with no longer a whisper but rather a commanding tone, "Nah, don't you worry 'bout that, Thao. I keep to myself. I used to be part of a group, a gang. But that was long ago. And I never bled in the shower," he chuckled.

"I'm pretty sure you been in some scuffles, some fights, some brawls. I know you. You're never one to back down. You like to bang!" I retorted with a hint of playfulness.

"Shieet, well, yeah. You do know me, and you know I can't help it if I need to defend somebody. One time I did get my ass whooped for that. A little Hispanic dude was getting' picked on. I told the guy pickin' on him to quit it. So, we banged. I got hit square in the nose, but I got some good licks before that. Well, that night, my nose wouldn't stop bleeding. For twenty-four hours straight, it kept bleeding. Next morning, they let me go to medical, and the doctor was like 'This man needs to go to a free-world hospital!' They sent me to the one in Tyler. And you know what's crazy? The busted nose wasn't the worst part. It was walking down the halls of the hospital in a white outfit full of blood stains and my face full of blood and it's drippin' thick out my nose while I'm chained up hands and feet, shuffling by the nurses who can't stop staring at me. I'm sure I looked like a freak, like some kind of monster. In that moment, I actually felt shame."

I let his words settle, the image of him bloodied, shackled, paraded through a hospital corridor. I let it land on me with its full weight. Then I leaned in, matching his quiet. His eyes flicked back to mine, cautious at first, like a man bracing for judgment. "Vu," I said, voice low and steady, "thank you for sharing. You know you don't have to protect me from knowing about these things. I don't want you carrying this burden of incarceration by yourself. I can hold it with you. The hard parts, the ugly parts, the parts that make you feel shame."

He swallowed, and I watched a small unwinding in his shoulders.

"You're not a monster. You survived something many people can't even fathom. Does sharing it with me and speaking it out loud feel okay? Does it make you feel better in some way?"

His eyes softened, his jaws loosened. "I never told no one. My family don't know, that's for sure. I don't want anyone to worry about me." He paused. Looked up at the fluorescent lights then back to me. "You sure you're okay? I don't even know why I told you. I don't want you worrying about me. But, yeah, for some reason, I feel okay telling you."

I reached closer to the glass, hands clasped, resting flat on the counter, "If telling me these things helps you breathe even a little easier, tell me. I can handle it. I'm not going anywhere. I'm here for you. I know the hard truths of prison life. I got this. Okay?"

He nodded, slow at first then with a quiet conviction. His shoulders settled back against the chair, his spine no longer rigid. One of his hands drifted toward the glass, not touching it, just hovering there like he wanted to meet my hands halfway.

“Okay,” he finally said, voice low. “Yeah . . . okay.”

I took a breath and said, “You know, there was that time I got shot, and for a brief moment, I didn’t think I’d make it. The nightmares that came afterward, the threats by the shooter and his crew, the whole drama before the court date.”

Vu’s shoulders tightened, and his jaw locked as if he were swallowing anger on my behalf. “You never told me it was that bad, but I knew it was,” he said quietly, eyes darkening. “You went through all that alone?”

“Well, I don’t really talk about it. Don’t want my family to worry. Maybe more like I don’t want to show that I’m scared. Like, I got this. I’m fine,” I said, meeting his soft gaze. “But I survived it. Like you’ve survived everything in here.”

He shook his head slowly. “I wish I could’ve been there for you.”

“You were dealing with your own shit. Your case and my incident was the same damn year. We were cursed at the same time. That’s why we get along!” I said infused with chuckles to lighten the mood. I leaned closer to the glass. “Hey, we’re here now. After everything. Look at us. The future meets the past. And we have everything to be thankful for.”

He exhaled, the stiffness easing out of his shoulders. “Yeah, we made it. I’m glad we can talk about these things together.”

In that moment, the past didn’t feel like an open wound. It felt like a map, one that had somehow drawn us back to the same point but also gave us a new direction to a different destination.

He glanced at me softly and calmly said, “Your hair looks nice.”

I laughed under my breath, surprised by the tenderness of the comment. “Thank you,” I said, tucking a piece behind my ear to keep my hands busy. Nervous habit. Without thinking, I ran my fingers through it again, smoothing it back. A single strand floated down and landed on the table. Vu’s eyes caught it the instant it fell.

“Slide it through the vent,” he said.

I leaned forward, searching for a hole slightly bigger than the others, my breath shallow as my fingers skimmed the cold metal. Finally, I found one. Its edge was slightly bent, just wide enough. Carefully, I pushed the strand of hair through. Vu took it between his fingers, holding it up as if it were something precious, something sacred. For a moment, he simply stared at it before tucking it into his shirt pocket.

Emboldened by the quiet defiance of the moment, I pressed my pinky against the vent. "Vu," I whispered, "can you touch my skin through the hole?"

He didn't hesitate. His pinky met mine, flesh against flesh through the tiny opening. A spark jolted through me, a pulse of warmth and rebellion, as if in this minuscule act, we had outwitted the system that sought to keep us apart. It was a message, an unspoken *Fuck you, prison; you can't take this from us.*

Time slipped away, faster than I wanted it to, until Officer Tran's voice interrupted us. His tone was soft, almost apologetic. "Hey guys, sorry, but time's up. You gotta wrap it up." Vu grimaced, and I felt the disappointment settle deep in my chest. The finality of the moment pressed against me, tightening around my ribs. *Endings.* They had always been uneasy for us.

I swallowed against the lump in my throat. "Vu, no matter what happens, I'll always be here for you. I'll always be your friend."

His eyes narrowed playfully, mischief creeping into his voice. "Oh, when I get out, we ain't gonna be friends."

The line caught me off guard. I blinked and heat rushed into my cheeks, quickly and uninvited. I tried to steady myself, and all I managed was a helpless smile. Then, as quickly as the teasing came, his expression softened. A quiet sadness flickered across his face before he let out a small breath and smiled again.

"Thao, thank you for visiting me. Damn, I have missed you. This was the gift of a lifetime." His voice dropped slightly, turning serious, a deeper register he saved for moments of reckoning and truths. "I love you."

"I love you, too, Vu. I promise I'll come see you again soon."

Slowly, I stood, and he mirrored my movements. A familiar smile spread across his face, and I felt my own lips curve in response. "I'm not gonna say goodbye," I told him. "Instead, I'll say see you again soon. Until next time."

His smile widened. "Until next time."

I reached out, pressing my palm against the glass, just like when we were younger, an old gesture resurrected, the same one we'd made as kids on opposite sides of the county jail glass, just like I had seen in my dreams during the years out of touch. He lifted his hand and placed it on the glass in front of mine, our hands aligned on opposite sides of the clear but cold barrier. I held there for a beat longer than I should have before forcing myself to turn away. Each step away from him felt heavier than the last. I walked a few steps and glanced back. He hadn't moved. He lifted his hand in a small wave, his lips forming silent words. *I love you.*

It didn't hit like a ton of bricks. It didn't crash over me. It moved through me slowly, deep and heavy. I felt it in the parts of me I thought had gone numb. His *I love you* landed inside me somewhere like it'd been waiting, quietly and patiently, this whole damn time. Like in my soul with a map to where it had always known the way back.

At the exit, I spotted Whoopi heading my way, her signature grin already in place.

"How was it, Cali girl?" she asked, her voice warm with curiosity.

I couldn't help the way my face lit up. "It was amazing!"

Her eyes widened with delight. "When we gonna see you again?"

"Soon! Very soon! Until next time!" I promised, my excitement bubbling over.

"Until next time!" she echoed, her joy as contagious as ever.

The moment I slid into the car and drove away from what was once a dreary place, now feeling like it was somewhere sublime. I reached for my phone. I had to tell his sisters. The call barely reached a full ring before their voices burst through the speaker.

"Sooo, how was it, Sis?!" they demanded in perfect unison.

I could barely contain myself. "It was awesome," I gushed. "He said we ain't gonna be friends when he gets out!" A roar of laughter exploded from the other end of the line.

"Damn fool," Jackie cackled. "That man hasn't changed a bit."

"How did it end?" Judi asked, still giggling.

I hesitated for a second before letting it out. "He said I love you."

Silence. Then chaos and cackles.

"What?! Why?! Sheesh, he's gonna scare you away!" Jackie shrieked between fits of laughter.

"That damn fool," Judi chimed in, barely able to catch her breath. "He couldn't wait a few more visits before blurting that out? Damn, Vu!"

Their laughter blared through the speaker, mixing with my own. I shook my head, smiling to myself. Some things never change.

Dear Vu,

I miss you so much. I don't know if that visit was good or not now. It's like you said in your letter, it's not the actual visit that was the issue—it's how it would affect you after. And I know what you mean now. I thought it would be wonderful and it was. But I'm missing you more now than before and that sucks. I was so touched to hear you say you missed me multiple times. Your smile, your eyes, your voice, everything about you just fanned the old flames for you that I guess never died. I will try to keep a positive outlook because you taught me that it's possible. In your last letter, you wrote that we can love each other without ever being together again. I guess you are right. I still love you after all these years, and I'll love you from afar even as I'm living my life without you out here. When the day comes that you are free, whether it's here or back in Vietnam, I will be there for you. I will never let you out of my life again, even if we don't end up together. At the least, we are friends. But I keep remembering the words you said, "When I get out, we ain't gonna be friends." You've always had that kind of confidence that I loved. Only time will tell. Until then, I plan to honor my commitment to writing you regularly and visiting you as often as possible.

Dear Thao,

Thank you so much for taking the time out of your life for me. Please know that you really made me feel special because of it. I appreciate everything you went through to see me. Words can't express the feeling I felt when I first saw you standing there. I don't know how it was for you but for me, my heart did a flip just seeing you. After 26 years, you still have the same effect on me but only stronger than before. My body was on fire the whole time. Thao Ha, what the hell am I going to do?

Do you remember when I mentioned what this visit would do to me afterward? It made me feel so alive and happy for once. It brought a very deep feeling of love, a deep longing, and the feeling of despair all at the same time. Is my life always going to be like this, seeing and loving you through a glass window or always watching you walking away from me? Is this your universe's way of punishing me, by giving me something precious and take it away? Yes, loving you is devastating for me in any circumstance. I keep asking myself why our connection is so strong, why someone like yourself would have anything to do with me and what is it that you see in me that no one else does? I am overwhelmed with gratitude and really, really amazed by my good luck. Who would have thought?

Sitting inches away from you was frustrating for me since I can't reach out and touch you. But don't think that you are safe from me because there's a window between us. Your eyes see everything so I'm sure they saw the wanting and longing in mine. There was so much more I wanted to say but I was so lost looking into your eyes. Hearing the sound of your voice and laughter again was mesmerizing to me. I could have sat there for a lifetime listening to you talk. I got mad when people interrupted us because I didn't want to miss a second of your time with me. Remember the guy that was making kissing sounds and flexing his arm? I found out why he was teasing me when I got back to my dorm. Everyone was clapping their hands and whistling at me when I walked in.

Thao, loving you is worth all the pain and suffering I feel right now. Remember, life is short so live it to the fullest and always be happy for me. But please save a small piece of it for me. The heart wants what it wants and you already know what mine wants.

I love you.

I sat with his words like they were a fire I didn't ask for but couldn't stop staring at. What the hell was I supposed to do with this disruption? My life had settled into something manageable. Boring, maybe, but safe. And then *this*. This thrill, this wild rush of something that felt like love but maybe was just memory dressed up in new clothes.

Most things in my life ended clearly. Doors closed. Ties cut so clean it was like we never existed. I made peace with closure, even when it didn't come with answers. But Vu? That never ended. It just . . . paused. Sat there quietly in the corner of my life, waiting for the right silence to step back in.

But had we even started? This old love felt too new, too sharp to be recycled. Was this some kind of redemption? A rerun with a new plot? Or was it just unfinished business showing up late, asking for another chance I wasn't sure I had to give?

My phone pinged, and I thought it was Vu's sisters texting me, maybe to ask more questions, maybe to squeeze more details from me. But it was three missed texts and one voicemail. All from *him*. His name lit up my screen with its usual combination of charm and dread. I could almost picture him. Pacing, overthinking, probably sitting in his sliver blue BMW with the engine running and the radio too loud, waiting for me to resurface from this visit that he never fully understood. He wasn't bad. Just . . . volatile in ways that made me feel like I was constantly catching falling glass. The kind of man who could be tender at noon and unreachable by dinner. A man with champagne tastes on a bottled water budget. A walking contradiction of worn-out jeans and perfectly chiseled abs. He was hot. And also a hot mess.

I exhaled, hard, like the breath alone might solve something. It was the collision of two worlds I pretended didn't overlap. One man behind glass, steady and broken in all the familiar ways. And another in the parking lot of my life, very sexy, very complicated, and very much waiting for answers I didn't have yet. I stared at the phone, feeling the weight of both men pressing in from opposite sides on a life I hadn't quite figured out how to live.

What the hell was I going to do with Mr. Hot Mess? I dropped the phone back into the cup holder and kept driving.

11

A Seat Saved For Him

I DIDN'T REALIZE THE VISIT WOULD rearrange me. Not in the dramatic, cinematic way. It was quieter. The kind of shift you only notice later, when you've arrived home, hugged your dog, unpacked your suitcase, and curled yourself on a couch with your dog at your feet and a mug of hot tea in your hand. Walking out of the prison, I carried something I hadn't walked in with. It was something not quite unfamiliar but not easily recognizable. Like an impenetrable wall between us had been sanded down from both sides so that we'd fit the same way we once did.

When I got home, I knew the old rules wouldn't hold, nor the boundaries I set for myself. Certainly not the boundaries that came with the man I was already with, Mr. Hot Mess, who perhaps thought that the only storms in our lives were the ones he was busy creating. I told myself to breathe, to be reasonable, to put everything back into its neat emotional boxes. But this connection to Vu wouldn't go quietly. A single visit. One room, one look, one conversation. The connection came roaring back to life, and soon, letters would no longer suffice.

In a letter following the visit, Vu wrote that he wished he could just pick up the phone and call. I understood the ache to hear him breathe, laugh, and say my name like he used to.

Jackie said I could be on the call list since I was on the visitation one. She'd signed up so long ago she forgot how it worked, but I was determined. I dug through the Beto Unit site, followed the maze of directions and made an account with Securus. Got approved, and a few days later, the phone rang.

First thing Vu said was he didn't wanna cause trouble. Didn't wanna call too much. Said Mr. Hot Mess might not like it. The way he said it, gentle, almost apologetically, made something twist in me. As if he were the risk and not the man leaving emotional wreckage across my living room. I told him not to worry. We made a plan. Fridays. Early. Before work. Just us. The perfect hour when the house was quiet, when Mr. Hot Mess was still starfished across the bed in his usual dramatic sleep, and I could slip outside on my early morning walks with Pork Chop.

Adding calls to the letters was like lighting a match in a dark room. There was a time when I imagined I'd never hear him again. And certainly not like this. Not every week. His voice was playful and raspy and still him. It used to show up in my mind for no reason. No rhythm. Just there. And with it came joy, then grief, then that ache that said, *This ain't yours anymore.* But now it was. On a prison line, in the crackle of the Securus static.

Mr. Hot Mess was the man I'd let into my life only a few months after the divorce, when distraction masked itself as healing because at least it felt good to the body. He was never meant to be anything serious. A fling with a pulse. A man who was fun in the way roller coasters are. Adrenaline-infused and best experienced in short bursts so you don't hurl your lunch. He had two young kids from two different women. One found me on Facebook and sent messages to me when he was unreachable. His finances were a cautionary tale—the baby mama reported late child support and old past-due slips piled up in a stack on his car seat. He claimed he was in the fitness industry as a coach, trainer, and therapist so his schedule was irregular and so was his paycheck. A normal person would've considered all this a bouquet of red flags. He was just a fuckboy, so I considered the red flags insulation, a sort of proof that this man could never become my problem.

Except he did, just not in the way I expected. Roughly a month after we met, he showed up to my place with his young daughter. Tiny thing. Soft voice. Well-mannered. She always said please and thank you. She wandered into my home like she'd been waiting her whole short life to find a place where someone asked her how her day was. Where someone sliced fruit for her and listened to her stories. She asked me to help her with homework because her parents didn't. And they didn't ask her about her feelings. Said she didn't like it when they screamed at each other. She told me these things matter-of-factly, like someone describing the weather.

Something in me, some old, overdeveloped muscle from years of saving lost causes in male form, kicked awake. Every red flag he waved I ignored because she held on to me like I was the one steady thing in a world that kept shifting under her feet. Her parents rented apartments and moved regularly when the rent increased. The exchange from one parent to the other was often strained. I believe in my heart her parents loved her, but they were struggling, too. She wasn't a planned pregnancy. And while I told myself I wasn't saving men anymore, that my Florence Nightingale era had closed with a hard slam, this was new. This was different. This wasn't about Mr. Hot Mess. This was about his daughter. A little girl who deserved what some adults fail to give their children: attention, structure, tenderness, presence. Love is one thing. Plenty of parents feel love for their children. But love without capacity, without resources, without consistency, without showing up, leaves a child hungry in ways that aren't visible until they start clinging to strangers who make them feel seen.

So I stayed. Longer than I should have. Longer than he deserved. Because she deserved more than she was getting. And I was foolish enough, maybe tender enough, to think I could fill the gap without losing myself in the process. My friends worried about this too. They had been sounding the alarm for months. They were afraid Mr. Hot Mess was using me, pulling from my stability without offering even a fraction back. "He's not good enough for you," they'd say, in that careful tone friends use when they're trying not to sound too judgmental. I'd shrug and reply that I was in a privileged position. Steady job, extra bedrooms, a pension, and retirement funds tucked away like good behavior in a bank. If someone was using me, that was on them. I was only doing good deeds, and that was all I could control. It sounded noble, very Buddhist, very Stoic, very enlightened.

When Vu and I reconnected, I was still under the belief that I could hold everything in neat and organized compartments. But the truth was far less virtuous. It was naïve to believe generosity made me invincible. That I could open all the compartments of my life—pieces of my days, pieces of my heart, pieces of myself—and never feel the weight. Even the most well-constructed person has a breaking point, though we rarely admit it until we've already heard something inside us crack. But that moment hadn't come for me yet. It wasn't until a couple of months later when the holiday season came around.

The holidays rolled in before I even noticed. Folks always say the holidays are hell for the locked up. Loneliness dressed in tinsel. Joy forced down your throat in peanut butter jelly sandwiches inside "Johnny sacks" while the world forgets you. But Vu let me know, this time, he had something more than the mundane prison festivities.

November 19, 2025

Hi Sweetie.

It's three days until Thanksgiving so by the time you receive this letter, you'll be eating leftovers. However you celebrate, I hope it was a happy occasion for you. This year will be different for me since I'll be celebrating with you mentally. I don't know how it's possible that I'm actually happy for once. I am thankful for our reconnecting and it is you that brightens my days. Because of your love, I have no worries. Here's a quote for you, "being deeply loved by someone gives you strength, while loving someone deeply gives you courage." My strength and courage come from you.

Thinking back to the time of our breakup and when you were mad at me, if I knew then what I know now, I would of sat down and wrote you a letter to explain. I realize now that stubborn women never listen but they can read. In the future when you're mad at me, I'm going to run off somewhere and write you a letter. In life, we live and we learn.

Before I send this off, I want to share something with you. When you first wrote me, my intention was just to write you a few letters to let you know how I feel about you and then disappear. Something in me that needed you to know and plus, I needed to know if you ever loved me. Now I know.

The joy of seeing each other again didn't just belong to us. It spilled into his family. That Christmas, Jackie invited me to the Tran family dinner. I would see them again after more than twenty years. After our breakup, I'd occasionally stopped by his parents' house, telling myself it was just to say hello. But really, I was holding on, even after pretending to let go.

My family had celebrated earlier—lunch with warmth, the usual. By night, my siblings were gone to their in-laws. My parents retreated to their rooms to call it a night. I was left with time, memory, and the pull of unfinished history. The drive was firty-five minutes from my home, on the north side of town. Exiting off Veterans Memorial road, I noticed that the neighborhood had changed. The homes were bigger and sleeker. The stores were polished, decorated with holiday art that glistened under bright parking lot lights. It was a picturesque display of a well-to-do suburban shopping plaza. The surroundings changed, but my nerves were the same as when I visited decades ago. Would I be welcome?

I didn't know his nieces or nephews. His siblings, except Jackie, were faces from another life. Though they all knew *of* me, but walking toward the house felt like approaching a room that no longer had my imprint on it. I sat in the car too long, trying to steady my breath the way you do before ripping off a bandage that you yourself put on. Then I got out.

Laughter and voices drifted through the air as I neared the backyard. The sound was warm and familiar. The smell of food pulled me closer—onions, fish sauce, something fried. His mother stood by the stove in the garage, coaxing magic out of a pan the way Vietnamese mothers do. His father, cigarette in hand, glanced my way, then looked again and disappeared into the garage, not recognizing me. But then I saw his brothers Dung and Van. Our eyes met, and their faces cracked open into the kind of smiles people reserve for old friends.

"Long time no see, Thao! So nice to see you!" they exclaimed, their voices filled with genuine joy.

Jackie leaned toward her dad and whispered something in his ear. His face shifted. Surprise first, then recognition, then a softness I hadn't expected. He walked over and hugged me, long and full, like he'd been waiting. Judi came next, then Vu's mother, who touched my face, held it in the palm of her hand, and smoothed my hair like she needed confirmation I wasn't a ghost. Then came Tasia, the niece Vu adored, and Kim, the cousin who wrote him letters and sent him books. One by one, they welcomed me like I belonged. The energy was familiar and electric, like Vu and I seeing each other again. No awkward pauses, no polite hesitation. Just unfiltered joy.

His parents looked older, but the spark was there. His siblings introduced me to their families, saying my name like it mattered, with reverence that made it clear, that after all this time, I still mattered.

"This is Thảo. Bác Vũ's Thảo."

They said it with a kind of pride that startled me, like I was a character who stepped out of the family folklore into their living room. They'd grown up on stories about me, and here I was, breathing, smiling, and hugging them. The hugs were long, their kindness quiet but unmistakable. We sat down to dinner. One seat left empty for Vu. At the head of the table, his father bowed his head, murmured a prayer in Vietnamese, and when he raised his head to speak, his gaze went toward me.

"Thảo," he said, voice steady but soft, "you've always been like a daughter to me. Your return is a gift. If you're still with us when Vũ comes home, I'd love to call you my daughter-in-law."

Before I could even swallow the lump in my throat, Vu's mother chimed in, "Even if that doesn't happen, this is your home. And if you marry someone else, bring him. We'll love him, too."

His sisters cracked up. "Yeah, right. She bring some dude, Vũ gonna beat his ass and end up back in prison!"

Laughter filled the room. Vu's father just smiled with the patience of a man who has witnessed every possible version of his children. "Not a proposal," he clarified, eyes twinkling. "Just a hope. And if it happens, I'll throw the biggest damn party this family's ever seen."

Then the warmth in the room shifted. Vu's father, who'd been jovial just moments before, grew quiet. Regret weighed down his voice.

"Vũ has never had good luck," he murmured, eyes downward, fixated on his plate. He spoke of fate—*số mạng*—and how one moment can reorder an entire life.

Then he told the story. The story I'd heard before but not like this. On the day Vu was arrested, he'd been working with his father. "Trí called. I answered. I gave Vũ the phone," he said. "If I hadn't . . . he wouldn't be in prison."

The table fell silent. The guilt in his voice was unbearable, the kind of sorrow that ages a man in real time. His eyes got watery.

"Bác, please don't," I said softly. "Please don't blame yourself."

His eyes softened and sorrow seemed to have settled. Vu's siblings jumped in, frustration rising in their voices, as if volume and tone alone could shake the trauma out of their memories. They told the story, again, so I'd know, really know, how unfair it all was. That he took the fall for his friend. He had been pulled under by someone else's tide. Their version always circled back to their truth: Vu never stood a chance. I saw it differently. He had a chance, and he chose Trí over himself. But that truth wasn't mine to offer in that moment.

His mother finally raised her hand like she was calling order in the court room. "We are making Thảo sad," she said. Just like that, the conversation stopped.

We returned to our plates. Turkey, egg rolls, green beans—comfort food from two different worlds, but most of us picked at our plates. The table was beautiful, heavy with the symbols of success: red lacquered wood, crystal glasses, apple pie at the center, a crystal chandelier grand enough for a catalog hung above. But nothing filled the empty chair. The ache of Vu's absence sat there instead.

Jackie broke the silence. "This time of year is hard, sis," she said gently. "Vũ usually calls. But it's late."

The sniffles started and napkins dabbed at tears. Then we cleared plates. Washed dishes. Took photos. Like routine would patch the ache.

I told them about our visit, our letters, our calls. The stories seemed to warm the room, everyone wide-eyed in attention and exhaling soft chuckles. It gave the room a heartbeat again.

Then, with cinematic precision, the phone rang.

"Bác Vũ's on the phone! Bác Vũ's on the phone!!!" Tasia shrieked.

The phone was passed around like a precious artifact, each family member taking their turn clutching the phone like they needed proof he was still tethered to them. Their voices overlapped with joy, giggles ricocheting off the walls. The exuberant energy in the room only made the empty chair stand out more to me, like an absence with a pulse, demonstrating how much he'd meant to them.

When Judi got her turn, she held the phone tightly, like it might dissipate out of her hands if she loosened her grip. Her eyes twinkled with mischief. "Anh Vũ, we have a surprise for you!" she said, her voice brimming with excitement. Then she turned and handed the phone to me with the grin of someone giving you the best gift under the tree and knowing it.

"Hi, babe," I said softly. "I'm here visiting your family."

He chuckled, the surprise evident in his voice. "Hi, baby! You really did that for me?"

"Yes, of course. It's been wonderful," I said. "I want you to have time with your family, okay? I'll see you in a few days. Merry Christmas, babe. I love you."

"Babe, this is the best Christmas I've ever had," he said, his voice thick with emotion. "You visiting my family. It's amazing. Thank you so much. Merry Christmas. I can't wait to see you in a few days. I love you."

As the call ended, my eyes landed on his father. He had been studying me, his expression unreadable at first, like the quiet appraisal of a poker player who held his cards close. Then he gave me a small nod and motioned for me to follow him to a quiet corner of the house. His voice was gentle when he spoke.

"Thảo, I hope you know that you will always be welcome in our home." He paused for a moment, glancing around before continuing. "Look around you. This house, it's Vũ's. His mother and I have decided to give it to him when he comes home. We've been saving for him, too. A lot. We want him to have a good life, maybe even start a business. Who knows?"

I listened in silence, absorbing his words, the weight of his hope pressing against my shoulders with reverence, ache, and gratitude.

"But more than anything," he continued, "I hope you will always be there for him." He hesitated, then added, "I'm not trying to bribe you, but . . . just in case you decide to marry Vũ, I want you to know that he will have something to bring into the marriage. And all of this, it will be yours, too." He gestured at the furniture, the television, the future he'd been constructing in his mind for years.

The air between us stilled. Then, in a softer voice, he said, "Your presence here with us. It's a gift from God." He looked at me, his eyes glassy. "You were the only girlfriend of his that I ever loved. He was foolish not to know how to keep a good thing. Every night, I pray that God will bring him home to us someday. But for now . . . He has answered my prayers by bringing you back into our lives."

I didn't know what to say. Not because I didn't have words, but because none of them felt equal to what he offered.

That night, I observed so much and took everything in. The lingering sadness that shadowed Vu's family, the regret that clung to them like an unwelcome guest, the torment of waiting for a Christmas call, the pain of wanting a piece of him for the holidays but knowing it could never be enough while settling for the echo of his voice. The collective fear that this waiting would never end.

But there was joy, too. The kind of joy a family with an incarcerated loved one learns to hold on by creating presence through the construction of memories, photos, and hypotheticals. The way their eyes lit up when I spoke about our letters, our calls, our visit. The way they laughed when telling old stories about him, bringing him to life in the room. The pure elation when his voice finally crackled through the phone, momentarily making the distance disappear. And as I sat there, watching the way they clung to these moments, I wondered what it felt like for Vu. What it felt like from his side of the wall.

Hi Babe.

Today is Christmas and to my surprise when I called home, you were there. I really thought my sister Judi was playing a joke on me until you came on the phone. For the past two days I fought with myself over calling you because of my need to hear your voice. Every time I looked over at the phone, there's always a long-ass line and there's no way I can wait since I'm working at the time. Your universe did a miraculous thing for me by locking the dorm down. I stayed out because I was working. Usually on holidays, they locked up the dorm to pass out Johnny sacks for dinner (two corndogs and a peanut butter sandwich). My co-worker and I broke records passing them out because we both wanted to get on the phone. My reward for my effort was talking to you. I loved every moment of it and just hearing you say you love me made this the best Christmas for me ever. I'd like to know what your answer was when my Dad proposed to you! Now you see where I get my sentimental and hopeless romantic feelings from. Thank you for the Christmas card. It is beautiful and the words touched me deeply. With so much love for you, I can't breathe. Please do not guard your heart with me because if you do, there's no way I will find my way back. For now, love me any way you want but eventually when this comes to a full circle, I would want you wholeheartedly as it was 26 years ago or nothing at all.

Four days later, at 3:30 a.m., my phone alarm chirped. My eyes were heavy, my body laid still, my mind halfway in a dream. I'd barely slept, thinking too much about the visit. The room was dark, and I laid there for a few minutes in the warm cocoon of blankets trying to remember the last time I'd voluntarily seen this hour. The night before, I'd done all the small rituals women perform when they know they'll be seen by someone who matters: showered, laid my clothes out, blow-dried my hair to save myself from a hair crisis, spritzed the roots with Calgon Morning Glory, hoping it'd later drift through the vent, maybe land on him. A few strands of hair had landed on the bathroom counter. I gathered them, rolled them into a bunch, and slipped them into my coat pocket. A Christmas gift, locks of love.

Green tea in hand, I stepped into the cold. Roads empty, sky black. But I wasn't alone. Not really. Christmas had passed, but love still has a way of shepherding people toward prison gates. Nearly three thousand men inside Beto, but there are only forty-five chairs in visitation. Most people get two hours, if they got anything at all. Some waited all day just to be told *Not today*. I was lucky. I knew that I got four hours, an out-of-state special visit. And I got in.

This time, it felt different. Less like dread. More like gratitude. I was third in the line of cars at the gate. The entry guard knew my face. "Welcome back, ma'am," he said, scanning my ID.

They searched Jonny's truck, but my stomach didn't knot. The buzz and clank of the doors didn't rattle me like before. Whoopi smiled wide, called me "Cali girl" again, and patted me down like we'd done this dance before. Officer Brian Tran greeted me, too. "Nice you're visiting him for the holidays," he said, his voice carrying that mix of friendliness, professionalism, and fatigue from a man who worked holiday shifts.

This time, we spoke and got to know each other. He was from Dallas, commuting an hour each way. Working here to pay for school. Wanted to be a physical therapist. This job? Just a stop. I told him my story. That Vu and I went way back. That I was a professor now. That somehow, after all these years, we'd found our way back to each other. Not perfect. But real.

Officer Tran nodded, his smile softening. "Wow, that's pretty amazing," he said. "Hope y'all have a great visit."

His kindness, his genuine interest in our story, reminded me that even in a place like this, surrounded by cold steel and concrete walls, there were still good people. People like Officer Tran, who in their small, quiet ways, were decent. It made a difference. It softened the brutality of the setting. He walked back toward the far end of the room where the contact visitors were checking in. My gaze wandered, scanning the room. The clock on the wall ticked steadily, indifferent to the moment unfolding. The paint on the walls peeled in places, evidence of time's slow erosion. I exhaled, willing myself to stay present, when suddenly, a figure emerged from the door on the contact side. My heart lurched. For a moment, I thought I'd conjured him. A trick of my longing. But no. It was him. He walked with intention, like he belonged there, like he owned the contact visitor corridor. His eyes found mine, he flashed that grin, equal parts trouble and recognition. Then, with a playful flick of his finger, he beckoned me toward him, a silent *Come here* that sent electricity straight through my ribs.

I blinked, trying to make sense of it. My visitation sheet was very clear: regular visit. No contact. I hesitated, stayed glued to my seat, watching as Vu handed his paper to Officer Tran. They exchanged words, something about a *regular visit*, but I couldn't make out the full conversation. Then Vu turned back to me, his eyes steady, reassuring. I heard him say something about Christmas time.

Officer Tran looked at me, then gestured for me to come to him. "Follow me, ma'am," he said. Confused, I rose from my seat, trailing behind him as he led me to the other side of the door. We reached it, he opened the door, looked at me and smirked. "Don't get used to this." I must have looked completely dumbfounded because I just stood there, frozen. He waved his hand for me to walk into the mystery room, his voice amused. "You can go on in. Y'all get one minute."

I stepped into that room, what they called the "contact room," and the temperature of the moment shifted. It was warm and cozy. It made the moment feel humane. My pulse was like drumbeats from a marching band in my ears. And then I saw him. Right there in front of me. Not in a letter. Not behind some thick-ass glass. Not on a call with that annoying automated woman's voice stating, "You have one minute remaining." Nope. He was standing. A few feet away. Looking at me like we hadn't lost all that time. For the first time in decades, he was real. Not a memory. Not a story I kept telling myself to survive the silence. He was there. Alive in the same air I was breathing. Looking at me like the years hadn't carved a canyon between us. And I laughed. For real. From somewhere deep in my gut I forgot I still had. That kind of laugh that doesn't ask permission, doesn't apologize for itself. That kind of laugh that's just disbelief and joy and pain rolled into one and spit out as sound. My head fell back, and I let it loose. I didn't care how it sounded or who heard it.

And Vu? He opened his arms like he knew I needed that before I even took my next breath. And I walked into him. No hesitation. No apology for taking so long to make this moment happen. He folded me in like his arms had been rehearsing for this. Like the distance had just been a long-ass pause and not a state-imposed separation. My face hit his chest, and I stayed. I didn't want to move. His heartbeat thudded through the cotton of his shirt and hit my skin like a message that had been trying to reach me for decades. *Still here. Still here. Still here.* And in that moment, so was I. Not broken. Not trying to be strong. Just held.

"I've missed you so much," he whispered into my ear.

"I miss you, too," I murmured back, my voice catching in my throat.

We held each other, locked in, neither of us moving, as if afraid that letting go would shatter the moment. My body tingled, overwhelmed by the sensation of his arms around me. And then, he pulled back just slightly, his lips hovering near my cheeks.

"So," he murmured, his voice laced with mischief, "can I get a kiss or what?"

The world stopped. My mind blanked like someone unplugged it. And all I could do was nod. His lips met mine, and a jolt of electricity shot through me, igniting something deep inside. It was slow at first, careful and respectful, then deepened, the years of separation between us had dissolved. When we finally pulled apart, I was breathless, my cheeks burned hot, my knees soft, my skin buzzing. He slid his fingers through my hair, and I nestled my head against his chest once more. We swayed gently, back and forth, like we'd found the beat of that old song only we could hear and remember from the night we met at Fu Kim. If I could've frozen time, laminated the air, bronzed the moment in gold leaf, I would've.

But all too soon, Officer Tran's voice cut through the moment. "Time's up, guys. Sorry."

The spell broke. Reluctantly, I let go. As I made my way back to my seat, I could still feel the warmth of his arms, the press of his lips, the whole moment imprinted of on my skin like a brand. I sat down, my entire body humming with glee. Even with the cold glass between us, my excitement was impossible to contain. I leaned closer, my voice spilling through the vent in a breathless rush. "What the hell just happened?!" The question echoed, my heart still racing from the unexpected moment we had just been gifted.

Vu smirked, his eyes dancing with mischief as he leaned in, lowering his voice as if he were letting me in on a secret. "Oh, you know. I got my ways in here."

I raised an eyebrow, still in disbelief. “What did you say to Officer Tran?”

His grin widened. “I told him, Hey man, that’s mah girl. It’s Christmas time. At least let me get a hug for Christmas.”

I laughed, shaking my head. “Wow. Can’t believe he broke the rules for us!”

“No doubt,” he said, still grinning. Then, more softly, “Baby, your hair smells so good.” The warmth in his voice sent a shiver down my spine. I reached up, pulled a few strands from my head, and passed them to him through the vent one by one. Then I remembered the strands in my coat pocket. Took those out and slid them through, too. He took them carefully, held them to his nose, then tied them together before tucking them into his shirt pocket. A silence settled between us, gentle and full. Then, his voice came through, quieter this time.

“Thank you again for visiting my family. It means a lot to me.” He hesitated, then added, “Sorry about them bringing up my case and making you sad.”

I shook my head, offering him a small smile. “It’s okay. It’s all out of love. They care about you.”

I hesitated, the words caught at the edge of my tongue. There was something I had been carrying, a question that had never left me, but I wasn’t sure if now was the time to ask. Still, I had to know. Taking a breath, I finally spoke. “I’m curious . . . we never really talked about it back then. Why did you choose to stay silent on the stand?”

His smirk faded. The playfulness in his eyes dimmed as something heavier settled over him. His gaze drifted, scanning the room as if searching for an escape. I watched as his breathing changed from deep and sharp to shallow and careful. His body tensed, shoulders became rigid, as if bracing for impact. A deep inhale. A long sigh. And then, finally, he spoke. His voice was steady, but there was something underneath it, something unspoken. A hesitation. A history. A wound that had never quite healed.

"Bravado. Honor. I did it for those things that don't mean shit to me anymore. We had a code we lived by, you know. And it was something I stuck with. Yeah, he was about to have a family. My lawyer kept tellin' me that if I just told the truth, that I wouldn't do much time. But that meant that I had to point out the shooter as Trí, and I couldn't bear the idea of him leaving a wife and kid behind. I was single, not really happy with my life anyway, and I figured that my case would land me ten years, maybe a little more, maybe a little less. I had no idea they would slap sixty on me. Then I was sure I would win the appeal when Trí signed the affidavit of confession. But the judge didn't believe it. Said my friend was trying to cover up for me. So I was denied. It's a horrible feeling that my family spent so much money on me for nothin'. But the worst feeling was when I got my sentence and turned around to look at my parents. My mom was cryin' bad. I couldn't do nothin'. I couldn't even cry myself. I must have looked ruthless to everyone in the room. My mom ran to the guards when they was takin' me away and begged'em to let her hug me one last time. They took me anyway. But a little later, after I was in the holding cell, they let her in to say goodbye. She hugged me and cried. I think my body and mind were in shock because I couldn't cry with her. I just kept telling her it was gonna be okay. That I would fight the verdict and win my appeal. I was arrogant to believe I could beat the system and take the fall for Trí with some years inside if it meant he could be with his family. But like I said before, a debt needs to be paid. So I accept my fate."

The gravity of his words just hung there. He sat across from me, and the bravado he used to carry like a shield was gone. What was left was stripped down and repolished. Not weak, but real. The code he used to swear by? That old-school silence and sacrifice? That was some ghost shit now. Yes, it haunted him, but he didn't live by it anymore. He said what he had to say. And I listened. I let that confession stretch out and settle into the hollow parts of my curiosity. It wasn't just what he gave up that gutted me. It was who he gave it up *for*. The man who walked free and built a whole-ass life while Vu's got paused like somebody hit mute on everything but time. And yet, Vu harbored no bitterness. No rage. No "I should've." He'd already made peace with a story that was never gonna be fair.

"You have always loved others and put them before yourself," I said softly. "In one of your letters, you wrote that you were beginning to forgive yourself and Trí. I'm in awe of you because prison could have made you hard and could have turned you into someone else or something else. But you're still thoughtful. You're humble. You're loving. You're selfless. You're a bright light, babe."

He let out this long, tired breath, like his body didn't know how to carry kindness anymore. "I don't know about all that," he said, mouth tugging into something like a smile. "But I'm tryin'." That was the truth of him. He was always trying. Even when hope was rationed like commissary.

We spent the next hour unraveling it all, talking through the shit he used to bury deep—his past choices, the pain of his parents watching helplessly as he was taken away, the rigid pounding of a system that doesn't bend, doesn't give, and doesn't offer much for redemption. Maybe except time for you to reflect. He spoke about the years that followed, the appeals denied, the slow erosion of hope, the long stretches of nothing, and the days he stopped believing he would ever go home. And still, even in all that, he said there was something left for him. A sliver. A flicker. Not loud, not bold. But still, hope. And gratitude.

"I used to think about all the things I lost," he admitted, his fingers idly tracing along the vent. "But now, I try to think about what I still got."

I nodded, my throat tight. "And what do you still have?"

He looked at me then, really looked at me, his eyes steady and unshaken. "You," he said simply.

The word sank into my chest, a quiet truth I hadn't fully allowed myself to believe until now.

We talked about the future—not in grand plans, not in impossible dreams, but in the small, tangible things. The letters. The phone calls. The next visit. What it would feel like to hold each other again without the countdown of minutes hanging over us. The conversation ebbed and flowed, shifting from grief to laughter, from sorrow to warmth. He told me about the men he had met inside, the friendships formed out of survival, the stories he carried that weren't his but had shaped him nonetheless.

I told him about my life outside these walls—the students I taught, the way the Pacific Ocean smelled at sunrise in Oceanside, the songs that made me think of him. He closed his eyes as I spoke, listening like he was trying to etch my voice into his memory.

"I wish I could be there with you," he said after a long silence.

"Same," I whispered. "One day."

The hours slipped away faster than I wanted them to. When the guard signaled that time was almost up, I felt the familiar sense of dread. It was the ache of goodbye. We pressed our hands against the glass, our fingers aligning as best as they could. "No matter what happens," I said, my voice steady, "I'll be here."

His eyes softened. "I know," he said. "You always been there. That means everything to me."

I walked away with backward steps, holding my gaze on him. I wanted to hold on to the moment, to keep it untouched just a little longer. He held his eyes with mine. And in that moment, I knew that despite the years, despite the walls, despite the impossible distance, I wanted this.

I had to figure out what to do about *Mr. Hot Mess*. He had the right to know. The right to hear the truth, not just about what had happened, but about what my heart had already decided. When I got back to

Oceanside, the weight of that truth settled in the room with me. Pork Chop lay curled at my feet, his gentle stillness held me like a warm, anchoring hush, offering a soft, wordless calm that steadied me more than he could ever know.

Mr. Hot Mess asked the question I had been dreading.

"How was it? Did you visit Vu?" he asked with curiosity.

I hesitated for a split second, my hand reaching down instinctively to gently stroke Pork Chop's back. Then I answered honestly. "Yeah, a few days after Christmas. I also visited his family on Christmas Day. How was yours?"

"Not much. I spent the day at my brother's," he said, his voice tinged with sadness. "I'm lucky to have some sort of family . . . even if it's a broken one."

I nodded, understanding the resignation of what he was saying. His family history was complicated, its own kind of labyrinth. There was a white and creole biological father he had never met but existed in rumor and genetics. And then there was his Vietnamese mother who was a refugee, perhaps once a bar girl, maybe something else entirely, who vanished when he and his half brother were young. Disappearance was her legacy. His brother's father, an Iowa-born soldier built from cornfields and military certainty, took the boys in when their mother disappeared. I thought it was a noble deed, stepping up for a child who wasn't yours. But sometimes nobility is partly a costume people wear in public. Behind closed doors, blood really does run thicker, and he raised Mr. Hot Mess with a kind of dutiful distance. Fed him, clothed him, kept him alive, but never gave him the safety or affection a child instinctively reaches for. It was care without closeness. Structure without softness. Enough to survive, but not enough to thrive.

It explained so much, the way abandonment sat in him like a low-grade fever, the way he kept trying to assemble a family of his own even if the pieces didn't match. Unplanned children, baby mamas he couldn't stay with, promises he couldn't keep. He wanted belonging with the desperation of someone who had been given away before. But the hard truth? He could never commit to anything. Not love, not work, not fatherhood, not even himself. The boy who'd been left behind had grown into a man still looking for someone to choose him first.

"I'm glad you have your brother and his family," I said, hoping to offer some comfort. "And that Stella got to see her cousins."

He nodded, but his eyes held something unreadable. "How was the visit?"

I let out a slow breath. "It was really special," I admitted. "You know, it's the holidays. His parents don't visit anymore . . . said it's too hard to say goodbye. So instead, they just don't come at all."

"That sucks," he said. "What about his siblings?"

"They used to go more often, but life gets in the way, ya know," I explained. "Marriage, kids, work. It's a three-hour drive one way. A two-hour visit turns into a full-day commitment."

He nodded. "Yeah, I totally get that." A pause. Then, "And you? How was it for *you*?"

I smiled, thinking back to my conversation with Vu. "I was happy," I said simply. "We talked about a lot of things. About the past, about his case. He shared some really deep and fucked-up shit. It gave me a different perspective of him. A guy in his situation could be angry, bitter, and hateful. But he's the opposite of all those things. It's really admirable."

Silence stretched between us. Then he looked at me for a long moment, his gaze shifting, softening. "So I guess I have your body, and he has your soul," he murmured.

I felt my breath catch. I couldn't deny it. I couldn't tell him he was wrong. Because he wasn't. But I said nothing. Instead, I rose from the couch, placed my hand on his shoulder, squeezed it firmly once, and walked away. That was the last real conversation we had about it. A few months later, he packed up his things and left.

Vu used to call him Ol' Boy. It was his way of acknowledging him without really acknowledging him. I remember when Jackie had told Vu about my marriage back in 2014. She said he had struggled to catch his breath, and that for a long moment, he had just sat there, processing it. And then, his voice tight, he had asked, "Does he look nice?"

Jackie laughed. "What does that even mean? How does someone *look* nice?"

Vu clarified, "Does he seem like someone who would treat her well?"

She sighed, considering. "Yeah . . . He seems like a nice guy. Someone who would respect her."

But when he asked her about Ol' Boy, she hadn't sugarcoated it.

"That motherfucka is fine as hell, Anh Vũ! Sorry, bro, but that's the damn truth. But I can't say he looks *nice*. He looks like a *lot* of trouble. All tatted up and shit. But yeah, he's fine."

I told Jackie about the guilt I carried. How, after our visit, after the long embrace, and the kiss, and the *I love yous*, I felt like I had cheated on Ol' Boy. How it felt like a betrayal.

Jackie tried to comfort me. "Love is complicated, Sis," she said. "It's never just one thing. Never just one way." And then, after a beat, she asked the question I had been avoiding: "What are you going to do about it?"

Ol' Boy was supposed to be the easier choice. He was free, fine, and right in front of me. But I knew. I had to let him go. Even if Vu hadn't come back into my life. Mr. Hot Mess deserved more than just a body. More than just an empty shell of a woman performing routine and normalcy when her heart wasn't in it for him. He deserved a woman who could love him fully. And that woman wasn't me. Letting him go was the easy part. Clean break. But letting go of his daughter, that was the wound that didn't close neatly. She was six, all big eyes and brave smiles, a little girl who walked into my home and told me things no child should have to experience and asked me things no child should have to wonder about. Kids seem to know when an adult is paying attention. It gutted me to step away from her life, to leave her behind with parents who loved her in feeling but not always in practice. I wanted so badly to be the steady thing she could count on. But I couldn't stay for her without lying to myself about him. And that lie would have poisoned my whole existence. Still, I hope, quietly and fiercely, that something might stay with her. Maybe the way I asked about her day. Maybe the nights I corrected her math problems. Maybe the strawberries I sliced into the shape of hearts placed carefully in her lunch box. Maybe the comfort of knowing an adult cared about what she felt. Maybe she absorbed one small example of what parental love could look like. And maybe someday, if she ever needs me, she'll know how to find me.

12

The Red Zone

Friday Night Lights. Hook 'Em Horns. Luv Ya Blue. In Texas, football isn't just a game. It's gospel. It divides, unites, baptizes boys into men who bleed team colors. So, of course, even behind fences and razor wire, football still rules. I never thought about what that meant inside until Vu told me. In a place where every day drags and nothing feels yours, football gives you something to look forward to. Something to feel. For some, it's stats and trash talk. For others, it's fantasy leagues and bets. But mostly, it's survival. It's laughter where there isn't supposed to be any. He told me how for a season, even the hard men eased up. Football brought joy back. Even with its rivalries, it has a way of bringing people together, taming egos, and forging alliances in a place where trust is scarce. It changed the atmosphere inside. The healthy competition, the playful shit-talking, the laughter. These things don't come easily in a place built to strip men of their joy. For a season, the conversations were filled with something other than survival. It helped men endure.

Vu often said, "It is what it is, and you do what you must to endure." After our Christmas visit, he wrote to me about enduring.

January 3, 2019

I know it was shocking to you when I hugged and kissed you, but for me, it was heavenly. I have lived most of my life in total

> darkness with bitterness and hatred. At times I succumbed to it because it was easier but it's a loved one that helped me fight back toward the light. I would like to think there's a reason or purpose that I'm going through all this and have the ability to endure it. Let me share with you a quote that says a lot about my situation. "A person must endure ultimate despair in order to appreciate ultimate bliss. It is necessary for a person to have wished for death in order to know how good it is to live" by Edward Dantz (The Count of Monte Cristo). That moment was my ultimate bliss.

Vu once wrote he was slipping and close to letting the dark win. But then Tasia's voice pulled him back. Her love, her innocence, saved him in a way nothing else could. He once carried envy, especially toward Trí, but he had family and love. And that was enough. Vu had always pushed limits. Wildness was his second skin. Prison didn't kill that. It just gave it rules. His buddy inside, Rene, told me Vu brought life to football season. Contraband cigarettes, cough syrup hooch, Super Bowl spreads. Vu had a way of turning a prison dorm into a makeshift block party. "Your boy cooks better Mexican than me," his dorm mate Rene once told me. Everybody wanted Vu's plate.

Prison gang culture and racial politics forbid men from social interaction unless it was to broker prison politics. But during football season, at Beto, they bent the rules to make pozole with a fusion of ingredients. Vu contributed a ramen packet. To heat the water, he'd purchased a hot pot from the commissary. Once the water boiled, he placed in the noodles and the ramen oil. A former Tango Blast guy brought tortilla chips, and a former Crip brought ketchup lifted from the kitchen which they mixed with spices from the ramen packet to make salsa. Guys who'd never spoken to each other during off season suddenly found reasons to share, not just ingredients and tools, but also time and space and meals.

A cocktail they called hooch was prison ingenuity at its finest. Vu fermented cough syrup with oranges pilfered from the kitchen by a cellmate, added in a packet of sugar and an apple someone hadn't eaten from their Jonny sack. Mixed it in a trash bag, hid it in the back of a locker, and prayed it didn't explode. Let it sit for a few nights until it kicked like a mule. From the way Vu described it, that stuff could baptize a man or authorize him a medical visit, depending on the batch.

Vu obtained unauthorized goods the way some men in there get respect. Quietly, through favors, trades, and the kind of diplomacy that might have made him a successful broker for the United Nations. The commodities were both tangible and intangible, but all were of value in the exchange market. A handful of ramen packets here. A pressed-and-starched custom-tailored uniform there. A few hours of helping someone write a grievance letter. An evening of conversation on the writings of Stoic philosophers. Suddenly, a pack of cigarettes would materialize in a hand-off after chow. All the gathering of goods wasn't just for daily prison life; they were gems for a treasure chest to be opened during football season.

Football was sacred to Vu. His voice shifted when he talked stats, plays, players, and the game. We both understood it. I grew up watching it with my dad. It's one of those topics that kept us close. In 2019, it felt like we were in the red zone. Close to something like freedom with hope in motion. Then I heard about Texas House Bill 1271 and felt like it was the play that could score for us.

The proposed law change would count Vu's good time toward a shot at parole. With the current law and a sixty-year sentence, he needed to do thirty years flat to be parole eligible. If HB 1271 passed, it would require only fifteen. He was already past that. I read every line of the bill like it had his name buried in the footnotes. It wasn't just policy. It was breath.

I got to work. Found legislators. Wrote template letters. Called his family and his friends, the whole motley crew of Fox News devotees who'd never said "prison reform" without rolling their eyes. But this wasn't politics. This was Vu. And once they saw that, they moved. At first, they resisted in the way people do when their worldview is being nudged an inch of center.

"Thao, you know I don't get into all that activist stuff," one cousin said, lowering his voice like I asked him to commit treason.

"This about one of them bills?" asked another relative, suspicious, as if I were recruiting him into a cult.

But the second I said, "It's for Vu," they softened. Not a full conversion, just the tiniest crack where love sneaks through.

His uncle, who once told me he didn't trust government unless it was a government willing to fight against communism, whispered, "Well, if it helps him, I'll sign my name ten times."

His brother's friend, the one who used to brag about how "tough on crime" he was, said, "Vu's like a brother to me, just tell me what to write in the letter."

Jackie's husband, whose family treated Fox News like scripture, cleared his throat and said, "He's my brother, too. Make the letter. I'll sign it."

Jackie said she'd vote blue next time but wouldn't tell anyone.

They called me back with questions, with follow-ups, with genuine hope in their voices.

"What's the update?"

"Did it go through?"

"Do we need more signatures?"

"Is there anything else we can do?"

Their politics stayed the same, but their humanity cracked open just enough to let empathy in. They weren't necessarily fighting for "prison reform," they were fighting *for him.*

I joined a Facebook group for Beto families. It's one of those digital gathering places where hope, despair, chili recipes, gossip, and legal strategy all sat side by side like mismatched furniture. That's where I recognized Sarah from her profile picture and remembered observing her during visitation. She stood in front of the vending machine with a loose circle of wives and girlfriends. She spoke with a mix of fire and fatigue. She was saying something about how "we need to get together if we're gonna make a difference," her hands slicing the air. So I sent her a message.

She replied almost instantly, "I remember seeing you at visitation."

It startled me that she recognized me. Maybe that's what trauma does: it makes archivists of us all. We memorize faces, stories, and the way someone's hope is expressed in their posture. She had written a post about needing letters from victims of crimes that would attest forgiveness for the perpetrator. I sent her a letter I'd written as a victim of gun violence. She wrote back again quickly. Told me it moved her and that she had shared it with her organizing team. They wanted to include it in the campaign. It was about surviving violence. About how forgiveness isn't theory, poetic, or abstract. It's slow, cellular work, the kind that's so profound that it rearranges you from the inside out. I had forgiven Glenn Shelton and understood his actions weren't about me, but the aftermath was about me and my recognition that the event changed my life in many ways for the better.

HB1271 wasn't just about legislation. It was a test of whether we meant what we said when we define prison as a place for "rehabilitation." Of whether we saw people like Vu as capable of redemption and worthy of a second chance. In the journey of vocal politics, I was on a parallel road with a quiet journey. The one I didn't talk about. The one growing louder inside me. I let myself imagine it, really imagine it. Vu walking out, free. Not in chains, not broken. Just him. And me. That hope had weight now. It wasn't soft or abstract. It lived with me.

Slept beside me. I started to believe maybe, just maybe, all this noise we were making might move something. Might be enough.

But every time I brought it up to Vu, he'd meet me with that stillness he'd perfected. That kind of stillness that knows too much. He'd say, "I've seen bills like this before. They never make it." I know he wasn't trying to crush me. He was just living in the truth he knew. He was trying to spare me the breaking. "You shouldn't get your hopes up," he said.

But it was too late. My hopes weren't just *up*, they were soaring. Running. Jumping. Me believing so hard and so fully in him being a free man that it started to shift something in him. A crack in the caution. He began to ask me questions. Talked to the fellas inside. Asked what their people on the outside were doing, if they were writing, calling, pushing. He was letting it in. Letting the hope do a slow, quiet walk around his chest.

I sent him a copy of my letter, the one Sarah's crew had slid into the packet for the legislative committee. He read it. Then he passed it around inside like a special kite. When he wrote me back, he said, *They're grateful, babe. I'm so proud of you.*

But what he didn't get was, there was no need to be proud. This wasn't charity. This wasn't some noble cause I could walk away from. I was fighting because I loved him. Because this was home work. Not homework. Home Work. And I was ready to do whatever it took to get him back where he belonged. And for the first time in too many years, I let myself dream the whole sequence like it was already unfolding. The bill would pass. We'd prep the parole packet. He'd walk out. We'd build life from scratch. Not perfect. But together.

I believed it. *I let myself believe it.*

Fighting for HB1271 felt like we were deep in the red zone. It was the last stretch. We had clawed and hollered our way down the field, yard by yard, heartbreak by heartbreak, and now we were staring down that goal line like it owed us something. And maybe it did. When the public hearing came, it was like a group parole packet. Testimonies poured in, real stories, hard stories, stories soaked in pain and love and long years of waiting. We outnumbered the opposition so heavily, it felt like they couldn't ignore us this time. We had the momentum. The bill actually hit committee before the session clock ran out. That never happens unless something's shifting. And the committee chair? The one holding the pen that could move it forward? He'd been quoted in the news. He'd talked that prison reform talk before. He'd said the right things and said them pretty loudly, too. That felt like a sign. Like maybe all the pleas we mailed in, all the hope we scribbled in margins and attested to in testimonies, had found a listener.

We were so damn close. I could see it. See families reuniting. See a system doing something besides punishing. Victory didn't just feel possible. It felt inevitable. Like it had already happened in some parallel world where justice isn't a coin toss.

But hope in that red zone is a dangerous thing, too. Because the closer you get, the harder the fall hits if they swat the ball out of play. I knew that, but I wanted to win.

It was during this time that we experienced a different victory. I received an email from the Asian American Writers Workshop, which is the publication where I submitted Vu's essay that he had written at my request.

January 20, 2019

Dear Hoang Vu Tran (and Thao Ha):

I write as an editor at the Asian American Writers' Workshop. Thank you for sending us "My Name Is Chino." We were grateful for the chance to read it, and were struck by its self-awareness and humility. We're happy to report that we're interested in working with you to publish a version of this piece.

January 21, 2019

My Dearest Vu,

I want to give you some great news. Remember the essay you wrote and I submitted? It got accepted! Congratulations, Babe!!! Please give me a call or write me as soon as you can to let me know whether or not you'd like to move forward in working with them. You always said you'd like to be a better writer, right? Here's an opportunity for it, and you're getting feedback from professionals! I'm so excited for you, but I want you to be fully comfortable with moving forward. After you decide, I'll let them know your answer. Again, congratulations, my Love! I'm so proud of you!

January 30, 2019

Hi Babe,

It took me a while to start this letter to you since your last letter has been tormenting me the past few days. This is the first time I can smell your fragrance and it was so overpowering that I was overwhelmed with visions of me holding you. I held you close to me with my eyes closed, wondering if anything in my life has ever been this perfect and knowing at the same time that it hadn't. Love, these images make me want to keep my eyes closed but the thought of opening my eyes makes it one day closer to being with you and that thought excites me more than anything.

The journey of 1,000 miles begins with a single step and that first step began for me when you showed me there's hope beyond these walls and a love that's still burning after all these years. This existence of mine came to life since you have awakened a part of me that I thought was gone. When I wrote the essay, I did it because I know you wanted me to. I never, ever thought it would be accepted so I was very surprised. Thank you for believing in me. I will continue with the editing process wholeheartedly since it's still my gift to you even though I'm nervous. So that you know now, don't be mad at me if it gets published one day and a lot of women start writing me knowing I'm a hopeless romantic (haha the last time you got jealous you wouldn't even speak to me for 24 years). I think this writing opportunity is a miracle because of you. Let me share a quote so you know how you made me feel. "There are only two ways to live my life. One is as though nothing is a miracle. The other is as though everything is a miracle."—Albert Einstein. Looking around my surroundings I see no miracles, but I can feel it, so my surroundings disappear until there's just you and me.

I thought a lot about what you said, about how writing can be therapeutic and how it helped you cope with your struggles. I like to try it but sometimes when I try writing about things that haunted me or what I struggle with, my mind goes blank. It's funny because being an introvert, I should be able to write my thoughts out more easily rather than speak it but it's not. Maybe it just takes time for me to release myself mentally from this prison of my own mind.

Ahh, the prison of the mind. This prison doesn't need bars. No guards. No count time. You can be strolling down the street in full sunshine, latte in hand and still be locked up hard. Sometimes the mind's grip is tighter than the cell block. There's no lockdown louder than the snide little voice in your own head tellin' you, *You ain't shit, change ain't possible, the story's already written.*

A physical escape is dogs, helicopters, recapture, headlines. But liberating yourself from your own stitched-together mythology? From every lie you've inherited and every myth you've repeated to yourself over the years? That's the real jailbreak. That's the kind of escape that doesn't end in cuffs and a mugshot. That's the one that ends in clarity and a sense that life might finally be lived instead of merely endured. Mental freedom is the miracle. That's what lets you see the world with your own eyes, not borrowed ones. But the problem is, we don't know how to drop those chains. Half the time we don't even know we're wearing them. We're too used to 'em. We think our pain is our personality. We think the past got the final word.

So when Vu told me he'd started thinking about all this, *really* thinking about it. I felt it. Hope. Not that wishful, cross-your-fingers hope. I'm talkin' about real hope. The kind that makes your spirit light and your eyes soft. The kind that makes you believe, *Damn yo, he's close.* Like he was in the red zone of his own mind, one good play away from something he'd never tasted before. *Freedom.* Not good-behavior credit. Not parole. Not early release. *Freedom.*

I told him once about the Laws of Attraction, about how the energy we put out doesn't just float. It *returns*. How our thoughts, even the small ones, start shaping the ground we walk on. I told him it isn't about magical thinking. It's about accountability. Alignment. About knowing the Universe doesn't respond to what we *say* we want, it responds to what we *believe* we deserve which then delivers the clarity for the decisions we make to *earn* what we deserve.

When he told me he was reading up on it, I wondered how he was reading the same material in a place where information is rationed like food. Where knowledge is contraband. And of course, his answer was so perfectly Vu. He held awe in a low-key way. The kind of answer that reminded me why I kept believing in him, even when he couldn't fully believe in himself yet.

February 24, 2019

Hi Babe.

One night while I was working, I thought about what you said about the laws of the universe and wanted to read more on it because I found it interesting. I was sweeping and mopping, and when I looked down, I saw these two booklets on the floor—The Law of Attraction and Laws of the Universe—and no one was around. Kinda creepy, huh? I've been asking around to see who it belonged to but no one knew what I was talking about. I shit you not.

I knew Vu wasn't gonna bullshit me. That just wasn't him. But still, the way he said he found those books didn't add up. It was baffling. Strange in that *too-perfect-to-make-sense* kind of way. Maybe he mentioned something in passing, and somebody, quietly and carefully, dropped the books in a common area like a secret blessing. Or maybe it was something bigger. Something unnameable. Coincidence? Maybe. Divine timing? Could be. All I knew was, they came. And it felt like a gift. Like the Universe was saying, *You're ready now.* Whatever it was, he had them. And once he did, everything shifted.

Our weekly phone calls had become ritual, sacred even. Like communion. We carved out time and held it close, just for us. Thirty minutes a call is what Securus decided, but that limit was a joke. As soon as it ended, he'd hit redial. And again. And again. We'd go for hours. Three, four, sometimes more. Our voices wove through the static like two people stitching a life back together with sound and sentiment. One moment we'd be talking about the rumble of the train in the distance while I walked the neighborhood at sunrise, the next we'd be deep in Arthur Schopenhauer, Sylvia Plath, or Marcus Aurelius to untangle the world like it was yarn in our hands. Vu's reading habits informed these conversations, and it was the first indication to me that Vu's mind was opening with the same speed and expansion of his heart.

There's something deliciously absurd, yet profoundly human, about discussing German pessimism with a man serving a life sentence. Schopenhauer made more sense in that context than anything elsewhere. Plath sneaked her way in, too. Her honesty was so sharp it felt like she was telling the truth for people who had lost the ability. Marcus Aurelius, one of our favorite life coaches, reminded us that even in confinement, the mind could still practice a kind of Stoicism that felt almost rebellious. Reading and discussing those works together did something for us. They cracked open small windows in the mind like tiny portals that let air in where there seemed to be none. Their writings weren't exactly escape routes, but more like maps. Each one traced a route through pain, beauty, despair, dignity, and the maddening miracle of still choosing to live. They made us ask better questions of ourselves: What do we fear? What do we owe the world? Who are we when no one is watching? And maybe that was the greatest gift of all. That literature, in all its unruly brilliance, made our lives feel larger than the circumstances could shrink them. We weren't just talking about philosophy or poetry. We were talking about survival, love, purpose, and the stubborn insistence that our lives, our stories, were not finished yet.

Life doesn't always let your mind stay wandering in the lofty expanses of the universe or the soul. Philosophy is lovely until real life taps you on the shoulder and asks, *And what are you going to do about the people you love who see the world entirely differently?* Eventually our conversations drifted back down to the terrain of news headlines and human messiness, where ideas stop being abstract and start shaping the power structures that can control actual lives.

His newspaper of choice was *USA Today*. He'd flip to the sports section first. Always. That's how we found ourselves talking about Colin Kaepernick. The kneel that ruptured one of America's favorite pastimes and exposed things we knew were festering under the fabric of the country. The noise, the outrage, the backlash. We were in lockstep in the belief that it wasn't really about football. It was about bodies. Black ones. Brown ones. Caged ones. Beaten ones. Loved ones. It was about choosing to kneel when the world tells you to stand, choosing to stand when silence would've been easier. Philosophy helped us understand the moral architecture of it all, the Stoics reminding us to discern what we control, Schopenhauer whispering about suffering's universality, Plath naming the darkness most of us pretend we don't feel. But the real challenge wasn't intellectual; it was personal. It was the question of how to live beside people we loved when their ideology had the power, quite literally, to shape the fate of the communities we cared about.

Our people—friends, family, neighbors, coworkers—many of them were operating under an entirely different ecosystem. Their opinions were like old brick walls—thick, familiar, and immovable. There's a particular kind of heartache in sitting across from kin and feeling like a foreigner. That dinner-table silence after the explosion when a wrong word gets said or a belief is spewed that stings. It bruises the heart. The writers we immersed ourselves in gave us language of the ache, but real life demanded something harder. Staying in relationships without surrendering your conscience. Loving them without shrinking yourself. Seeing the trap some call tradition and still choosing not to step inside it.

With Vu, I didn't have to translate any of that. We both knew what it meant to love the folks who raised you or were raised with you while knowing their worldview could trap you in places where they can't feel your suffocation. That tension sat with us, but instead of hardening us, we found something with each other that was more comfortable than agreement: we found understanding. Somewhere in that space, my feelings expanded. It wasn't just love anymore. Not for me. My feelings had already rooted deep, but what was growing now? It was respect. It was admiration. The kind that makes you feel more yourself in the presence of another, your wholeness with another, and if they were holding up a mirror, for once, you liked what you saw.

Respect and admiration have a way of deepening when action follows intention, and his next move made that unmistakably clear. I received a copy of the Asian American Writers' Workshop agreement for Vu's essay. They published it and paid him $150. Behind bars, that kind of money isn't just rare, it's radical. I held the agreement in my hands, eyes scanning the lines, smiling at the signature. And there, scribbled at the bottom, under Vu's name, was a note to Daniel, the editor.

"As I stated in my essay, it was a gift, so it doesn't seem right for me to receive any payment. But I would be grateful if you sent the person who inspired me (Thao) some flowers—phalaenopsis orchids. Whether it's $50 or $150 worth. If that's not possible, please donate it to TIFA (Texas Inmate Families Association)."

And just like that, I remembered: this man, this mind, this voice could not be caged.

I read it once. Then again. And again. And then the tears came. Not all at once. Not dramatic. Just slow. The kind of tears that sneak up, soft at first, then hit you all at once. *Damn, I'm so proud of him.* It made me miss him so badly. Because what washed over me wasn't just pride. It was yearning. That deep, aching kind that sits in your throat and then begins to spread. I wanted to hold him. Not just in theory. Not just in thought. I wanted arms around him, skin on skin, heartbeat against heartbeat. I wanted to feel the joy of that moment settle between us like sunlight through a window. I wanted to say, *You did that*, and see his smile stretch in real time, not just through a letter or a call. But it wasn't just about the accomplishment. It was the way he carried it. The way he folded me into it. The way his joy made room for me, like I was part of the work, part of the win. That handwritten note to Daniel? That was more than gratitude. That was love in motion. That was his way of saying, *I love you, and this is ours.*

And yet, yearning doesn't magically negotiate with the Universe, and life can't always bend the world to match the heart. I wanted to believe that if I just wished hard enough, loved deep enough, stayed soft enough, that the Universe would meet me there. That all those Law of Attraction folks were right. That the energy you send out boomerangs back with blessings tucked into the center. But life isn't math. It isn't always a one for one that balances out in a karmic ledger. It isn't always fair or mystical or poetic. Life is messier than that. Part timing, part systems, part sheer human chaos. It's wanting something with every cell in your body and still being told *no*. The truth is, I've wished before. Prayed before. Poured my light into the world like it was currency. And sometimes? I got left empty. Not because I didn't believe hard enough. But because the world doesn't always bend the way it should. Or it's not the path meant for you. Or it's not the right time for that path.

I've come to learn that expectation is like a wound. We tend to it with belief and hope, as if those things alone could heal the hurt of what is. We say things to ourselves. *If I want it enough. If I stay good, stay bright, stay strong.* As if the world will reward us for how gently we asked, or how boldly we demanded. But life is not a scorecard of virtue where good deeds automatically earn rewards. Expectations can come with a fist sometimes. Or a loss you didn't plan for. Or a bill that never passed.

HB 1271 taught me that.

It taught me how reality arrives uninvited, unwanted, and knocks you back with both hands, hard blows, and then it waits for you to understand that control, the control of anything out of your control, is never part of the Universe's deal with you. On the final day of the congressional session, the bill was left to die in committee on April 11, 2019. No movement. No explanation. Just silence. The truth landed with the force of something heavy, and the hope I'd been holding on to like a candle lit in prayer, tumbled out of my palms and shattered. The pieces lay at my feet.

Vu called and tried to console me, even poking fun at my optimism. "I had a feeling it would end up dead before it even made it to the floor. Remember I told you not to get your hopes up? So, can we chalk this up to one time that, between you and me, I was right?"

He made me laugh, and I appreciated the lightheartedness, the way he tossed out humor like someone trying to guide me away from broken glass scattered across the floor. For a moment, it worked. But the relief was brief. With my lack of discipline and control in accepting what I couldn't control, I was angry. I was heart-sore. I was impatient. I wasn't ready to crouch down and sweep up the shards at my feet, glittering in that cruel way shiny things do when they break. I was painfully unaware that I chose to navigate the mess with bare feet. The devastation didn't creep in. It struck like a single blow, sending every expectation I'd constructed tumbling into the same wreckage. Then the math hit: the bill had failed before, it had failed again, and it would almost certainly fail in the future. He wouldn't be eligible for parole for another eight years. Eight years, another set of shards added to the pile. I stared at it all—doubt, fear, questions, wondering whether I could survive walking this path without slicing myself open, wondering why the idea of waiting felt less like devotion and more like stepping deeper into a room full of broken glass. Women have waited decades for their men. So why was this such an unbearable thought for me? Why did the idea of waiting feel like a prison of its own?

April 30, 2019

Hi Babe.

Earlier today, my unit ran outside recreation and that's a rarity, like an every blue moon kind. Supposedly, we're allowed these recreated periods every day but since it's understaffed, they don't run it. I never go out there for the simple fact that it makes me depressed. But for some reason, I went today so this is like the first or second time being outdoors in twenty years. When I stepped outside, I had this unusual feeling of wonderment. It seems as if everything was breathtakingly beautiful regardless of the razor wires, the double fences and the gun tower. You and I know it's not. As I took my first breath I nearly choked since I'm not used to breathing clean fresh air anymore. I spent the whole time staring up at the sky. I wished the sun was still out but it wasn't since it was late and the sky was already darkening. Wishing, hoping, and wondering what life would be like for me beyond these fences was what I was doing. Now you see why I don't come out here. The longer I stood there, the more I wanted to return to my coffin with the knowledge that the next time I step out again, it would be for me to go home. Thinking this, I enjoyed the rest of my time out there. I wonder what you were doing at the time. I wonder if you were looking up at the sky during this time. I also wonder which direction is toward Oceanside. That way when these fences disappear, I'll know which direction to walk toward. For me, home is not a place anymore. It's you. "I always have many roads to travel, but I'll take the one which leads to you."—Amit Kalantri the Mentalist.

These past few days have been a struggle for me since I felt the hurt and disappointment you are feeling over HB 1271. I don't blame you since in a way, it broke my spirits somewhat. Even though I don't show it. We are connected to a point where our feelings or moods will carry on to the other without speaking. It upset me that I have difficulty finding the right words to comfort you during this time. "Occasionally in life there are these moments of unutterable fulfillment which cannot be completely explained by those symbols called words. Their meaning can only be articulated by the invaluable language of the heart."—Martin Luther King, Jr. I thought a lot about what I wanted to say but when written, it comes out sounding thoughtless. I can never be that when it comes to you.

Dealing with these emotional feelings of mine is somewhat new to me. From the first day of incarceration, I learned to suppress everything I'm feeling. It's what works for me. I realized now why every incarcerated individual acted and lived differently. Their mental state, emotional feeling or even their actions are most likely reflected upon the conditional states of their loved ones. Whether their loved one is feeling happy, sad, pain, or suffering, we feel it, too. The only difference is that it is amplified for me since we have more time thinking about it. Maybe with this explanation you'll have more of an understanding of what it is I go through with each and every day for you. Even if I don't show it, but somehow you know it. "One must learn to love, and go through a good deal of suffering to get to it, like any knight of the grail. And the journey is always towards the other soul, not away from it. To love, you have to learn to understand the other more than she understands herself, and to submit to her understanding of you. It is damnably difficult and painful but it is the only thing which endures."—travel writer D.H. Lawrence.

Vu had a knack for using quotes well. What he couldn't quite articulate in his own words, he borrowed them from writers he loved, stitching their sentences into something that felt entirely his. Reading his sentiments related to the failure of the house bill made my heart ache. My eyes blurred with tears as I moved line by line, and even after they dried, a dull pressure settled in my chest remained, stubborn as a bruise.

I could feel myself retreating long before I admitted it. My letters, once easy and steady, slowed to a trickle. I'd open a blank page and stare at it until the guilt grew so loud that I left the sheets on my desk and went to bed without writing a word. On the phone, I sometimes let silence do most of the talking. Pauses that stretched too long, answers that landed flat. I wasn't brave enough to say the things gnawing at me: the doubts, the fear of eight more years, the question of whether I had the stamina to love someone through time that seems as if it refuses to move. Every time the prison number flashed on my phone, a small dread flickered in me, not of him, but of what he might hear in my voice. I knew I couldn't fake joy, not with him. My tone would betray me—thin, melancholy, pulled taut in places where warmth used to live. He'd ask how I was, and I'd offer tender, vague answers, the kind that try to hide but never fully succeed because he knew me all too well.

It was a quiet retreat. The sort that doesn't make any dramatic sound when it happens. Just fewer words. Longer pauses. Silences that suddenly feel awkward. A heaviness he could surely feel. And instead of stepping toward him, toward the tenderness and the terror of telling the truth, I inched backward, hoping he wouldn't notice the distance widening. This retreat rattled me. It made me question everything. Had I ever loved him the way I told myself I did? Or was the love so intense that the ghosts we'd both inherited kept breaking into the present? Dark thoughts crept in, stealthy as thieves, happy thoughts stolen, the mind filled with disarray from the wreckage of the robbery. I was locked from the inside: a mental prison held me hostage. I began thinking that even if he walked free, then what? Freedom wasn't even the finish line. Because we would be staring down another fight: his order of deportation, another kind of cage.

I tried to convince myself, or bargain with myself, that maybe the bill's failure was for the best, a twisted kind of grace. Maybe the bill failing spared us from an even crueler outcome. If he had been released in 2019, while under the first Trump administration, he wouldn't have stepped into the sunlight. He would've stepped into Immigration and Customs Enforcement (ICE) custody. The thought sat in my gut like a stone.

What haunted me most was the way his fate seemed to have been decided not just by the choices he made but also by laws that had already measured and priced his worth in this country. Clinton's 1996 Immigration Reform and Immigrant Responsibility Act (IIRIA) turned immigration into a punishment machine, expelling people as if citizenship were the only armor. If he had been a US citizen, things would have been different. But he wasn't. His case happened in December 1996, just months after the law passed. Even still, the law was retroactive. He was fucked either way.

His parents naturalized as citizens in April 1991. It was six months after Vu's eighteenth birthday. If they had become citizens just a little earlier, he would've derived citizenship automatically. That's how I got mine. But his timing, like so much of his life, had been unforgiving. When his case came through, he stood before the system as a green-card holder, a legal resident. And with the conviction, the government seized his legal papers and replaced them with a deportation order.

That was the reality. That was the burden we carried. I asked myself, could I carry it any longer?

On my worst days, I caught myself wondering if confinement was the only thing protecting him. Maybe it was a messed-up kind of mercy that he wasn't eligible for parole yet. Sitting in that cell, stuck in the same four walls under fluorescent lights day after day, might've been the only barrier keeping ICE from exiling him. I hated thinking like that. Hated trying to twist my rationale, the contortion of confinement into "protection." But some days, that was the only thread of hope I could hold onto. Maybe by the time he got out, Trump would be gone, and maybe, just maybe, the next president would remember what it meant to protect people like us.

For decades, Vietnamese refugees with final removal orders lived in a kind of legal purgatory. They were technically deportable, but pragmatically stationary in the United States. The protections weren't perfect, but they existed. And they didn't arise from compassion. They emerged from geopolitics. After Congress passed the 1996 IIRIA, the United States attempted to deport thousands of Southeast Asian refugees. Vietnam refused. At the time, the two countries were still rebuilding diplomatic ties and Hanoi did not consider postwar refugees to be Vietnamese nationals. Some had fled as children, some were born in refugees camps, and some were born in the former South Vietnam, a nation that no longer existed. From the Vietnamese government's perspective, these individuals were essentially stateless.

Legally speaking, the United States had other options. Under 8 U.S.C. § 1231(b)(1)(C)(iv), the section of the Immigration and Nationality Act governing post-order removals, the government may deport a person to *any country* willing to accept them when removal to their country of nationality is "impracticable, inadvisable, or impossible." In theory, that meant a Vietnamese refugee with a final removal order could have been sent to a third country when Vietnam refused to take them back. The statutory authority was broad enough to allow it. But in practice the US government never exercised that option for the Vietnamese community. Instead, immigration authorities used a kind of uneasy stalemate. Vietnamese with final removal orders were released under Orders of Supervision—administrative agreements requiring individuals to report regularly to ICE, comply with efforts to obtain a travel document to Vietnam, observe movement restrictions, apply for work authorization cards, and live with the knowledge that deportation could be triggered if the diplomatic landscape shifted.

The result was precarious but offered some type of stability. These men and women lived and worked openly in the United States—raising children, cared for aging parents, building businesses, volunteering in the community—while technically remaining under active removal orders. Their lives were proof of a quiet truth: Even when the law allowed for dramatic action, the government often relied on practical restraint and diplomatic realities. The restraint held for decades, crating an informal understanding—never guaranteed, always fragile—that as long as Vietnam refused to accept them, these refugees could remain on American soil.

In 2008, after years of quiet negotiation, the United States and Vietnam signed a Memorandum of Understanding (MOU) that formalized new rules. Vietnam agreed to accept deportees, but only those who had entered the United States after July 12, 1995, the date of diplomatic normalization between the two nations. Anyone who arrived before that date would not be subject to deportation under that agreement. For the next decade, the MOU functioned as a structural protection. "Pre-'95" refugees with criminal records still had deportation orders, but Vietnam consistently refused travel documents when it was requested.

Then, beginning in 2017, things shifted. ICE began detaining pre-'95 Vietnamese with removal orders for deportation. In response, in February 2018, a class action lawsuit titled *Trinh v. Homan* was filed on behalf of pre-'95 Vietnamese challenging the government's detention practices. While the result of the lawsuit provided a temporary injunction against ICE, halting the deportation of pre-'95 Vietnamese with final removal orders, it made clear what the community had already feared—the 2008 MOU's protections were fragile. The effects rippled through communities and fear spread throughout the community impacted by old criminal convictions. For me and Vu, seeing the whole picture and living it was its own kind of exile. It was an isolating experience. It was lonely as hell. Not the kind of lonely you feel when you're by yourself, but the kind that settles in when you're in a crowded room full of people who love you but still can't see you. Vu's parents. My parents. Aunts. Uncles. Siblings. Lifelong friends. Church folks. The whole damn community, it felt like. All of them cheering and riding for Trump. Clapping for him like he was the one who gave them freedom, like he saved them, as if he'd personally carried them across the ocean, like he hadn't already marked people like their own sons, daughters, relatives, neighbors, friends, church members, and coworkers for removal.

I tried talking to Vu's parents. Sat in their living room, hands clasped together tight, soft voice, heavy heart, doing everything I could not to sound angry even though I was furious. I laid out what Trump's policies were doing to Vietnamese refugees. To *their* son. To *our* people. And they just nodded, offered me tea, eyes drifting away from me, and changed the subject. Work, who was having a baby, what China was doing. Like if we didn't say it out loud, maybe it wouldn't be true. But it was. And that silence? That silence was screaming at me. It was the kind of silence that pretends to be peace but really, it's just fear dressed up in tradition. The quiet became heavy, and I could feel it unraveling my patience slowly, the way a draft chills you one degree at a time. My stubborn tendencies made me incapable of leaving well alone, and so I brought it up again. Not because I thought there could be a breakthrough, but because pretending otherwise felt like I would be participating in the denial. I couldn't pretend I didn't see what it was doing to Vu, to me, to us. If I stayed quiet, the noise in my head would get louder.

His mother finally said, "Being deported to Vietnam is not such a bad thing. We can send him money, and he can live a happy life there."

"What about being separated from family?" I asked.

She shrugged it off. "We can go visit him. Taking trips to Vietnam would be fun. And he could live more lavishly there with the money we send him than he would here in America."

Her optimism hung in the air like heavy perfume—sweet, overwhelming, and impossible to breathe through. But I understood. The way someone sees the world is shaped by survival. People don't invent their worldviews out of nowhere. They inherit them from the landscapes surrounding them. Fear, once learned, becomes a kind of homeland. The older generation of Vietnamese Americans had been forged by fire, shaped by the collapse of a country they carried in exile. The long shadow of communism followed them across the oceans. What communism did to them—what they witnessed, what they fled—carved wounds so deep, even the word *democrat* felt like a threatening echo of the past.

Trump's team knew this. They poked at the scar and called it safety. They shouted *socialist* and *communist* like slurs, and something in our elders flinched and ducked on instinct. In their memory, the Republican Party became refuge. A placed where strength meant safety, even if the party today was enforcing policies that could disappear their own children and build walls to exile us again.

Somewhere in these contradictions, I began wrestling with questions I didn't want to ask. Could I love Vu fully when his family adored the man who would destroy him? Could anything we build survive in a household where silence was more valued than truth? Our conversations turned sharp, circular, exhausting. Blame hung in the air. No room for nuance, no space for real questions. Only shame, frustration, and the quiet surrender that comes when you realize loving your elders means accepting they will never see the thing that is breaking you. I stopped bringing it up. Stopped asking. Stopped hoping for a different angle. Because how do you argue with someone who believes exile can be "managed" through a wire transfer?

I asked my father once what he would do if it were his brother, if he weren't a citizen and he was deported for the crime for which he'd already finished his prison sentence.

He said nonchalantly, "That would be a consequence we would just have to accept. We could give him money to help him start over in Vietnam."

As if displacement was a line item. As if exile was just a minor inconvenience, a problem fixed by Western Union. I wanted to scream. But I didn't. I swallowed the sound of disbelief and digested it into my heart where the other quiet sorrows lived. The days stretched. The nights grew heavier. HB 2171 was dead. But Make America Great Again was alive. And in the chaos of my soul that followed, what remained was grief and the terrible thought. *What if he doesn't come home at all?*

Vu and I had the conversation one early Friday morning. His voice steady, mine fraying at the edges. "If I'm deported, I'll accept it," he said. "At least I won't be in prison anymore."

I wanted to meet his resilience with my own, to take his words and cradle them like a source of comfort. But I couldn't. I was selfish. My mind latched on to what it would mean *for me*—another fracture, another distance too vast to close. Once again, we would be apart, separated by more than just walls and gates, by more than just time.

I tried to imagine the ways I could hold on. Flying to Vietnam on my breaks, carving out stolen moments, making space for something that would be a logistic challenge to fit. But was that really possible? To reassemble the connection by stringing together bits and pieces into something resembling a life? That wasn't the life I wanted. Perhaps, again, it's just a life I would have to settle for. A life I'd always accepted, a life of *almost*, of shrinking to fit inside someone else's circumstances. But settling had already taken so much from me. I had spent years, decades, a lifetime settling. Settling for men who could not meet me where I stood. Settling for love that asked me to reshape myself, to make me contort my freedom to their constraints. Settling for relationships that drained more than they ever poured into me. I had done my time in spaces that left me empty. I had done my time convincing myself I was happy when I wasn't. Pleasing everyone else at the cost of me, smiling through dissatisfaction. A championship-level people pleaser. Didn't I deserve more?

But then came the counterattack, the trauma-laced rationales that were the hemmed-on dress of an eldest daughter of refugee parents: What about sacrifice? What about gratitude? What about faith in something bigger than me and my own comfort? What about *me* meeting someone where they stood? What about the laws of attraction, the forces of the Universe, the belief that love could bend even the most rigid realities? Why was I so unbendable? So rigid? So self-centered and so selfish? What the hell is wrong with me?

The noise in my mind was raucous, rattling the bars of the cage I had locked myself in. I wanted to scream, to curse the universe for its timing, to walk away before the crisis of my own contradictions crushed me entirely.

And that is exactly what happened.

I began to shut him out. The old pattern, one I knew too well, crept back in, whispering that the only way to protect myself was to retreat. I wrote less. I spoke less. I *felt* less. Because the intensity of confusion and hurt swelled past anything I could contain.

He sensed it. He asked more frequently if something was wrong. I told him it was just a disappointment about 1271, that I would get over it in time. But it was a polite lie, a lie to keep the dam intact. It wasn't just about the bill. It was about everything the bill represented. How hope could sprout and be ripped out at the root. How dreams, no matter how carefully cultivated, could be denied with a stroke of a pen. How control, my old friend that fought so hard to keep, was slipping through my fingers like water running from cupped hands. I didn't want to talk about it. Not the fear, not the way the future felt like an elevator dropping too fast. Not the suffocation, not the way my nerves rattled like loose change in a dryer. I didn't want to talk to him about *anything*. I wanted to be alone. I wanted to disappear into silence, to create a distance so wide that he would walk away first so I wouldn't have to watch myself do the hurting. If I avoided him long enough, maybe the eventual break would feel less like breaking and more like inevitability. I convinced myself this was logical, responsible even, that time would make it make sense. Maybe we could meet again in the future. *We had already lost two decades*, I thought. *What's another eight years?* If we had found our way back to each other once, couldn't we do it again later, when life felt less like a battlefield?

But logic was a poor mask for fear. He told me he felt me slipping away. He said it gently, the way you'd speak to someone who'd forgotten their own name. I lied again. I told him I was just busy with a film project and that I was overwhelmed. He believed me, or at least accepted it because kindness sometimes requires pretending you do. He had always been patient, always understanding with me, even when we were young, he'd hold space for me. I know it hurt. I know it landed somewhere deep. He wrote to me a quote about distance, a lifeline in words, from something he read by an American author known for her candor:

"Distance is not for the fearful, it's for the bold. It's for those who are willing to spend a lot of time alone in exchange for a little time with the one they love. It's for those who know a good thing when they see it, even if they don't see it nearly enough."—Meghan Daum.

Vu's love of reading while incarcerated sharpened his mind and honed his skill for choosing quotes that fit the moment with surgical precision. His gift wasn't insisting I absorb his quotes; it was selecting ones so well attuned to the circumstance that they lingered on their own. The words pressed me gently, asking for reflection. I let the intention sit with me, but I couldn't quite feel I deserved to be in that space. The quote assumes that distance is noble, even romantic, and that it was the territory of the brave. Brave enough to be okay with being alone and loving someone who was worth the abundant value of brief but extraordinary moments with them. I wanted to believe. To be bold in that way. But fear had me by the throat, stronger than my will. The deeper I loved him, the more it hurt. I used to resent his parents for not visiting: they said it was too painful to leave. I'd scoffed. But now, I got it. The more I loved him, the more afraid I became that our story wouldn't end the way I dreamed. I drifted in and out, like a tide too scared to touch shore. Safer to keep love at arm's length. So I rebuilt the walls he'd chipped away at with every ounce of tenderness, patience, and determination he had.

And this is the part I didn't want to admit, not to him, and not even to myself. Daum was writing about courage. I was practicing avoidance. One is an act of love. The other is an act of survival dressed up as strategy.

And maybe that was the worst part, realizing I wasn't the tragic heroine of some impossible love story. I was pulling the emergency brake before the train even left the station. I was choosing comfort over distance, over the risk of being known. I was afraid. Fear bred avoidance. Avoidance bred distance. Distance became a cycle I could not escape. And it was unfair, so *deeply* unfair. Because all he had done was love me. And all he had ever been was a good and gentle person. With every act of kindness he offered, every moment of tenderness he extended, my fear only deepened and made the ground under me shake harder. The more he reached for me, the more I feared what it would cost to hold on. I wanted the love. I wanted the future. I wanted what I *imagined* for us. But wanting didn't stop the terrible ache of knowing how easily love can vanish, how quickly a life can split open. I could not hold on to love without already grieving what could be its inevitable loss.

13

Voices on the Margins

DISAPPOINTMENT HAD LONG SINCE MADE a home in Vu's life. He told me that he and his family had grown accustomed to it, that every step along this endless road of incarceration had led only to more letdowns, more doors slammed shut, more hope chipped away. They had learned to accept it, not just as an occasional sorrow but as an inevitable truth, too. Setbacks were expected, losses scheduled like routine, a rhythm of disappointment so steady it no longer startled them. They had resigned themselves to the cruel mechanics of a system that kept them bound, existing within its unyielding limits. It made the journey bearable. It is what it is. Keep calm and carry on.

But I hadn't yet learned how to live that way.

I have known disappointment in other corners of my life and have let its bitterness rest on my tongue, sometimes until it numbed the rest of me. Each time it came, I walked through its corridor of shadows, hands grazing the wall, learning again that sorrow isn't a punishment but a passage. On the other side, life waits and asks only that I keep walking. And when I do, when I step back into the light, I see that what once broke me has cleared a space for something truer, born from the wreckage of what I thought I wanted. But with Vu, I did not know how to carry it. The weight of it was unfamiliar, unbearable. I didn't know how to tend to the bruising of my heart, how to sit with the ache, not let it consume me, and let it pass. To keep calm and carry on. Let the next day be an opportunity to love still and to hold on to him because it was worth the momentary agony. *This too shall pass.* Nope. Didn't know how to do that. So I did what I always did when sorrow became too much. I pulled away. Vu—tender, perceptive, and steady—sensed the change in me before I could even name it myself.

May 24, 2019

Babe.

To be honest, it does bother me when you go quiet on me all of a sudden. I wished I could read your mind in those moments and know what you're thinking of. Too bad I can't so can you please tell me what's really bothering you? I can't stand it anymore. You once said that I am your best friend, and as best friends, we should always be able to talk to each other about anything, right? I want my best friend back. We never had this problem before and we are not about to start now. Do you hear me, Thao Le-Thanh Ha? I have this powerful need in me to know, to understand, and to help if I can. It doesn't matter what it is that you're feeling or going through, I want to share the burden with you. I mentioned once that whatever we do or go through, we'll always do or go through it together. I meant every single word of it, through the good and the bad times. "To love means never to be afraid of the windstorm of life, should you shield the canyons from the windstorms you would never see the beauty of the carvings."—Elisabeth Kubler-Ross.

I've been grasping at straws on what's been going on with you, I couldn't help wondering maybe I might have done or said something to hurt or sadden you. Did I? There's a lot of things I can deal with but that I cannot. Never would I want to see you hurt or sad, especially because of me. I would rather walk away. Being emotionally involved is all new to me after all these years so I don't know what to do when you shut down on me. It's frightening and a heartache. To get through it all, we need to communicate, to understand and carry each other when needed. With our current circumstance, it's going to be a difficult struggle as it is, but without communication nothing is possible. If I could take your pain and suffering away, I would do so in a heartbeat.

June 7, 2019

My Dearest Vu.

I sat with your words for a long time. I had never done that before, usually writing back to you the same day I receive your letter. This was not just an interruption of our journey together, it was a disruption. Sensing the urgency and distress in your words, it tormented me. I never wanted you to go through such feelings. You have already suffered enough as an incarcerated man. How could I have done this to you? Why did I even write to you to begin with? We fell into our love again, and from this agonizing experience of knowing you weren't coming home any time soon, I wanted to run away from it again. It was a triggering reminder of the heart throbbing anguish we faced in 1997 when you were first sentenced. Incarceration was designed to break the spirit of the incarcerated, and in this structured process, it tears apart the spirit of those who love them, turning us into stone if we let it, and I let it. I crumbled. But I could not avoid it any longer. With each passing day that I waited to respond, you had to go through a passing day of unknowing.

I am so very sorry. I felt horrible about hurting and confusing you. I confess there were moments when I wondered if I could keep doing this and truly be a good partner to you. In addition, I got upset with your sister sometimes when she talked about perspectives that go against mine when it came to politics. I felt like the odds were stacked against us, and in the times of fatigue and weariness, it was easier to lay there and think until my mind went numb than to write these thoughts to you. As one week turned into two then three and so on, I got more stressed about writing to you because I felt so bad about how much time had passed. It was a snowball that kept rolling down a snow packed mountain and became so enormous that it was overwhelming and unconquerable. It weighed down my spirit. In my nature, when I'm feeling miserable, I want to be left alone. I have never been good with confronting these kinds of feelings. My coping mechanism is to avoid them at all costs.

In this experience, I started to wonder if my love for you was coming from our past and that in the present it was not the same. I'm a different person, in a different place in my life, living a different kind of life, and I am unsure if I could be on the sideline waiting for us to be physically together again. I thought I could, and those rekindled flames between us had sparked so many imaginations of us together, but not of us together like this. It is so fucking hard. While you're incarcerated, it feels like we can only have a partial relationship, and my heart yearns for a full one. Some women have managed to do this and stay with their partner. I am too weak. I have not dealt with my traumas that anchor me below surface and keep me from breathing in our love. I feel suffocated, perhaps life cannot be lived to the fullest when loving someone inside prison walls.

I wonder if my feelings of love for you were warped because of your circumstance. Are my feelings of love wrapped up in compassion, empathy, nostalgia, or anything of these sorts? Did I want to save you from feeling lonely and in despair? As I questioned these ideas, it wrecked me. You always told me you would be fine. Would you be fine if I walked away and in 8 or 9 or 10 or 30 years, that our love would withstand the years, and we could be rekindled again? Would you be fine if I live my life with someone on the outside until the day you were a free man and that I would choose you? I love you, Vu, and I always have, yet I confess that being in a relationship while you are incarcerated is something I am not sure I can handle emotionally.

Please know that this was the hardest thing for me to do. To tell you my truths. To love you while knowing that I was not living my best life while you were incarcerated was a painful recognition. To believe that someone else might be what I need to make my life feel whole hurt because I knew it would hurt you, too. Love and devastation seem to be what defines you and me, then and now and perhaps, forever. This was my whole truth to you. That was all I could give you—my truth and the tragedy that lies in the truth. I am so sorry, my love.

June 18, 2019

Love,

Now you see why I struggled with my decision when you first asked to write and then to visit me? I am vulnerable when it comes to you and I knew it. With you I knew the possibility of the devastation that comes with our kind of love due to my circumstance. I accepted it. For any amount of time with you I was willing to pay whatever the price a thousand times over. I felt the devastation once before and knowing how painful it would be but still if given the chance I'd do it over and over again in a heartbeat. I am sorry for the pain and suffering that you are feeling. I am feeling the same. Know that if I could shoulder them for you I would. I love you. Never would I ever want to see you hurt. I am dazed, confused, and hurt deeply. Words never came as easy for me as it does you and at times like these, they don't come at all. I only write to honor your wishes that speaking on the phone would be difficult for you. This has got to be the hardest thing that you ever asked of me. I will try to do so using my own words and not the quotes I once loved. Know that everything I ever wrote to you were true and as it is. I wrote with my heart. Loving you has been the most beautiful and the most devastating thing that has ever happened to me. I do agree with you that love and devastation does define you and I. What you love the most will always hurt you the most. From the start, I knew it would be this way due to the circumstances. But still I couldn't stop loving you and loving you wholeheartedly. Our kind of love has its way of always wanting more and more of it. It's never enough which creates a problem. But until my circumstances change, it will always be a painful feeling for us. I have thought of setting you free. Easier said than done since there was no way my heart would let me do it. I gave up on us once, and it's the worst decision I ever made. No matter what you do, you are not getting rid of me that easy. I'm not pushing for a night, not for a week, not for a month, not for a year, but for a lifetime with you.

When you wrote that you wondered if this love of ours was out of nostalgia or my circumstance and that maybe your feelings for me were from compassion or sympathy, it hurt me deeply. Is this why you love me? Is this the love that it is? I am not going to accept that nor am I going to believe that. This love is real. I felt it deeply every time we're together. It felt it deeply when our fingers are intertwined. I felt it deeply when I kissed you. And I felt it deeply when you trembled in my arms when I held you. I have never wondered about this love of ours so I need you to dig deep in your heart for this answer. I do need to know this. This can be an easy answer for you if you use your heart and not that PhD mind of yours. But if your love for me is out of nostalgia, compassion, and empathy, so be it. Please be honest and real with me. It is the least you could do for me. I love you regardless. Maybe it's better this way so that it doesn't hurt you as much. Maybe it's better this way so that you'll be able to love someone else. And maybe it's better this way so that you can find happiness elsewhere.

However, the more I thought of what I want for you, it made it better. I've always said that my love for you is unconditional, and it is. When you love someone this much, you think of them first. You think of their well being. You put their happiness first before yours. Love, I will always do these things for you whether I'm in here or out there. Please don't think I'm mad at you. I am not. If anything, I'm mad about the circumstances and the goddamn 1271. As long as you still love me, I'm never going to give up on us. But I do want more for you. I want what you think is best for you. I want you to be happy. Writing this has been a struggle for me. Just know that I'll hold your hand through all this.

He asked me to lead with my heart, not my head. As if it were that easy. As if I hadn't trained myself out of that a long time ago. Love, for me, has never been soft. It has always come sharp-edged and attached to warning signs and contingency plans. I've lived by logic. Measured my steps like landmines might explode beneath me. Built entire parts of my life inside invisible spreadsheets and formulas—risk, consequence, loss mitigation. Reason wasn't just a shield. It kept me from slipping into the kind of chaos that love so often had promised. But then there was Vu, and my heart wanted to reject the script. But I didn't know how. How do I not listen to the careful arithmetic in my mind that was on auto-compute? If I hadn't understood him, if I hadn't believed that what he felt for me was honest, I would've left. I've done it before. Many times before. Made the clean break. Pulled the ripcord. No apology. No explanation. Just gone. Easy. Efficient. Formulaic.

I wanted to stay. But it also pissed me off. To feel this tethered. This exposed. This vulnerable. Like love had snuck in and rearranged the furniture in my bedroom without asking. The chaos wasn't just his incarceration; it was the war I waged daily with the parts of myself that wanted to run. His family? Too much. My own disillusionment? Louder than I wanted to admit. The fact that I couldn't have him the way I needed? Unbearable. I wanted to let go. I swore I *could*. But something in me, call it stubborn or stupid or faithful or loyal. Whatever it was, it made me refuse. Pain is supposed to be a price worth paying for a love that never asked permission to take root inside me.

And as if distance and disappointment were the only tests left. But another test came with a name: Francis. We had been friends through our exes, bound by years of inside jokes and NBA playoff rivalries. He loved the Warriors. I swore allegiance the Rockets like it was still the '90s. Every April, we bet, small stakes that somehow became a ritual, a way to mark the time. He always won. But 2019 felt different. The Rockets had the edge , and I said yes to another wager. First, it was bragging rights. Then a meal. Then tickets if my team won. But if his team won? I had to go with him to a Coast Guard event. He was a reservist. I was sure I had it in the bag. But like clockwork, the Rockets choked, and the Warriors surged.

I lost. And I had to honor the bet.

In the weeks leading up to the event, Francis and I talked more than we had in years. What began as playful texts about basketball slipped into the soft terrain of real life. We caught up on the wreckage of our lives. His divorce. His broken engagement. My mishaps and misadventures, the tangled mess of my dating life, Mr. Hot Mess, and, of course, the ache of Vu—the life sentence, the reunion, bureaucratic cruelty of deportation, and the loneliness of loving someone behind bars. He listened without judgment and was the kind of person who didn't interrupt, who stayed present even in silence. When I cried about Vu, about the slow unraveling of everything, he didn't rush to fix it. He just listened. That kind of stillness was its own kind of grace. When my emotions steadied, he asked tenderly, "What can I do? *Tell me how to help.*" I promised that if there was anything—anything at all—I would ask.

Francis was safety made in the flesh. He had the calm of a man who had already survived himself and had the steadiness of routine—morning coffee, workdays that ended at five, homework with the kids, one weekend a month with the Coast Guard. He treated me with the kind of care that asked for nothing in return. When I forgot to eat, he showed up at my door with groceries and whipped up culinary masterpieces from the *New York Times* recipes. He set the table and plated the dishes like an offering. When I was sick and contagious, he dropped off medicine and soup at the doorstep with a text and photo to check the door like a personal courier. When deadlines swallowed me whole, he sent playlists labeled *for breathing*, each song carefully selected like a 1980s mixtape, a reminder that someone was thinking of me. He'd check the locks before we left, refill my gas tank without telling me, and text me when storms rolled through: *Drive safe. Roads are slick.* And he extended that gentleness to Pork Chop, too. Dog sitting when I was out of town for work, picking up treats without being asked, wiping muddy paws before letting him back inside, and sitting on the floor with him like he was a child who needed steady company. Pork Chop adored him, in that uncomplicated way dogs love the people who show up for them. It mattered more than I let on.

He never asked to be let deeper in. He simply stayed near, circling at a distance that felt like protection, not control. Doors opened, a hand on my back when the world felt too much, dining reservations to celebrate the joys of deep conversations between us. He made ordinary moments feel like shelter. I was drawn to it—the ease, the predictability, the quiet promise that someone would always pick up when I called. After years of chaos and of crisis love, that kind of gentleness felt almost radical.

And yet, even in the comfort of Francis's steadiness, Vu's name still lived inside me like a pulse. I could not end things with him, could not unlove the person who had taught me how to open my heart in the first place. So I tried to live in the space between, between loyalty and longing, between what I wanted and what I owed to the people I loved. It began softly, the change of course you only recognize after it's already happened. A text in the morning turned into texts throughout the day turned into calls at night. One afternoon, while strolling Seaport village and giggling over the follies of Filipino uncles, he placed his arm around my shoulder and squeezed. It felt nice. One evening, I felt him leaning into my shoulder while watching a movie, and I didn't move away. It wasn't passion that pulled me in first, but peace.

On the night it shifted, we had a post-dinner session listening to 1990s R&B while hitting the hookah pipe he gifted me. Somewhere in that late-night conversation about nothing and everything—our parents, civility in politics, the weight of expectations, the people we once were and no longer could be—he reached for my hand. Just that. No words. Just a warmth that moved through me like a confession I hadn't meant to make.

When he finally spoke, it was the soft conviction of someone who had already made peace with whatever would come next. "Thao, we don't know what the future holds. We can go at any time. Live your life to the fullest. Love as much as you can in this life before it's over. And no one can predict the future. Who is to say that if we gave us a try, we would know how long it would last? And if it lasts until the day Vu is free, I would never make you choose. You would have to go with your heart. And if you chose him, I would be blessed with the years we had together. It would probably hurt deeply, but your happiness is what I'm all about."

He said it without judgment. Just truth. And in that moment, I saw him not as a replacement, not as a consolation, but as a man who wanted to be with me without possession. The kind of love that doesn't cage you but opens the door and waits. The kind that stays even when it knows it may never be chosen. That kind of offering felt too generous, too impossible. Like something torn out of mythology or a scandalous romance novel. But the offer also made me feel seen and heard.

I couldn't keep it from Vu. I'd promised him that I would share whatever struggle I was going through. Swore on everything that mattered that I'd give him the truth of whatever I was feeling even if it wasn't pretty—raw, messy, no filter, no shine. Even when it hurt. *Especially* when it hurt. Even when every part of me wanted to wrap it up in silence and call it protection. Vu once hit me with a quote widely attributed to Lao Tzu but apparently not actually from the *Tao Te Ching*: "Being deeply loved by someone gives you strength. Loving someone deeply gives you courage." I didn't really get it then. Thought it was pretty. Thought it sounded wise. But it didn't live in me until that moment, and I needed to be brave, holding the truth in my hands like something burning and still choosing to hand it to him. Not because I wanted to. Because I *had* to. Because love, the kind that makes you stay when it'd be easier to run, that kind of love doesn't let you lie.

The phone connection crackled faintly, that thin hum of distance between us. I was crying before the words even landed. Saying *I'm sorry* on a loop. Like repetition could ease the betrayal. Like guilt could undo what already *was*. But he stopped me. Not with anger. Not with silence. But with something that I considered worse because I didn't know what to do with it. He stopped me with love. A quiet love. The kind that doesn't scream. The kind that listens even when it wants to shatter.

"Don't say sorry," he said. "Everything will be okay. I love you regardless. I just want you to be happy. And when I'm free, I will never make you choose. I'm going to write to you and explain more. I got to go now. Love you always, don't ever forget that."

June 21, 2019

My Dearest Thao:

I don't want to see you saddened or crying over this anymore. It is what it is. We understood that it was a difficult circumstance we were facing when we started this journey. But never have I ever wanted nor have I ever expected you to stop living your life for me. From the start I felt that this relationship was unfair to you. I even told you that it will be a lot harder on you than it is on me but you wouldn't listen and neither did my sisters. That's not to say I am ever giving up on us. I Am Never Going To Do That. It's just that when you love someone deeply you do what's best for them and see to their happiness. One thing about me is that I have always thought of you first since we reconnected. I know what it is I wanted. You once said that we should define our relationship

> differently on our own terms and not on the norms of society. I believe we should also but it's easier said than done. Hopefully some way, somehow, we will find our own way. No matter how difficult it is. I will leave you with this to think about. Yes, there are times that I wanted to tell you to move on so that you can find happiness. It's like an ongoing thing inside of me on that decision. You say I'm part of your happiness. Well, you're my everything to me so there's no way it makes me happier for you to move on. When you love me at my lowest point in my life, I know I am loved. There is no way I don't ever want you in my life and when these walls come down, I'm going to want you even more. Until then, live your life as you please. Just know that when I'm free, I want you wholeheartedly. You should not have to choose. Your heart will know what to do.

I came to understand the difference between loving someone and wanting to *possess* them. Both men, in their own ways, taught me that. Neither tried to cage me. Neither demanded that I choose. They simply *loved* me, freely and without claim. You'd think that kind of love would make things easier, but it didn't. If anything, it made it harder. Because when no one holds you captive, you have to face the truth of your own freedom and what to do with it.

With Vu, love was forged through distance and impossibility. With Francis, it grew out of presence and steadiness. One taught me how to endure, the other how to rest. Together, they dismantled every notion I had about love being a bargain, a trade, a set of conditions. They offered it to me with open hands and asking for nothing back except honesty. And that made the weight of it even greater.

Some of my friends understood. Others didn't. They thought freedom was easy, that it meant release to do as you please with whomever you please. But I learned that freedom in love comes with its own ache. Both loves were invitations to live fully. To walk my own path knowing I was held regardless. And when no one asks you to choose, the decision becomes your own, and that can feel like standing on a cliff with no map and no guardrail.

While I was living it, guilt was what I felt most. But when I think back to that time, what stays with me isn't the "triangle" people imagined, but the grace that existed within it. It was a rare symmetry of two men who understood that love is faith. Faith that when you give someone the freedom to move as they wish, their decisions and actions are the truest reflection of who they are and what they feel. When you remove control, demands, expectations—there's no obligation left to hide behind. No guilt, no fear, no performance. It's because their heart led them there. And that, I've learned, is the only kind of love worth keeping. The kind that is uncoerced, unclaimed, and therefore, real.

A couple of weeks after the phone call with Vu, while on my family's summer vacation, I received a message from Daniel Gross, the editor of Vu's essay from the Asian American Writers' Workshop (AAWW). His words spilled onto the screen.

Dear Thao,

I hope you're doing really well. I'm writing with some very exciting news! AAWW will be publishing Vu's essay in the near future, and we recently came across an opportunity to share it more widely. We were invited to participate in the Asian American Literature Festival, hosted by the Smithsonian Institution. This year, the theme is caregiving. Will you be speaking to Vu this week? If so, would it be possible to relay a message to him?

> We would love to:
>
> —display his essay at the festival
> —record a phone call with him reading the essay out loud so that we can play it at the festival
> —ask readers to send Vu feedback via postcard
>
> We chose Vu's piece in part because he writes about the emotional support he received from his network, including you. If you're okay with it, we'd display his essay with a dedication to you. The goal of all these efforts would be to help Asian American readers engage with his writing.

Vu's voice was rising, breaking past walls meant to silence him. I was moved and honored to witness his journey. But around the same time, I faced a dilemma—loving him while feeling something for someone else in the free world.

My sister was taking her family to Seattle. My niece begged me to join. Francis had invited me before, and the trip felt like the perfect chance to share a city we both loved. But Vu's essay was being featured at a festival that same weekend—the one where his words would be on display, where I could stand in his place, take it all in, and bring it back to him like a gift.

I was torn. Seattle with family and Francis, or the festival, for Vu?

Francis would understand. Hell, he might've even offered to come. But my niece's excitement tugged at me. She'd been promised I would go on this trip, and I couldn't let her down. I told Vu, and he understood. "It's the right decision," he said. "I'll keep writing. That won't be my last publication. Maybe we'll go together next time, babe!"

I asked Daniel Gross to take photos. He did, gladly. When I sent them to Vu, I heard the glee in his voice. The pride. He told me about postcards from readers, strangers moved by his words. There was humility in him but also awe that his story had broken through the bars. And it was reaching people. For real.

Vu spoke with pride when he shared, "My favorite was from a young Vietnamese American woman. She wrote that his essay had reminded her of the importance of family, of bonds she had let slip away. She told him that because of his story, she would reach out, try to mend what had been broken."

His words, written from a place of captivity, had moved someone into action, had reshaped the trajectory of a life. That was the power of his voice. That was the impact of his writing. I loved that he shared this writing experience with the men inside. It didn't surprise me that they were inspired, that they asked him to help them write their own essays. When he told me they wanted to get published like him, I acknowledged his achievement while encouraging him to consider his own power to lead: "Not an easy thing at all, my love. But if you mentor them, you never know what can happen."

I wanted more for him. More than just his own voice on the page. I wanted him to share his power. When I asked him to guide them in writing their stories, he didn't hesitate. Of course he didn't. He had never denied me anything. I was grateful to him and to the men who entrusted me with their words, who allowed their essays to be shared in my class, to be read by students who might otherwise never be asked to confront the humanity of someone incarcerated. When I told him we should mimic the festival, have my students read the essays and write postcards to the authors, he agreed, offering more than just permission. It offered wisdom.

August 1, 2019

Thao,

I'm okay with anything you want to do. As I said before, it was for you to do as you want since I gifted it to you. I actually think it's a great idea. Literature is meant to be shared. I do hope the stories of my writing journey, as you say, can inspire someone else. I owe it to pass on what was passed to me. This single year of writing has been very therapeutic for me.

In under two months, he rallied a dozen men, collected essays, and sent them to me fast. I laughed when he said more didn't make the cut. He wasn't playing. He gave it his all. The essays aligned perfectly with my class on mass incarceration. But they did more than support the lesson. They broke the wall between theory and reality. Raw, vulnerable, and unfiltered, the writing pulled my students in like no textbook could. These weren't just systems or statistics. These were men with sentiments of regret, resilience, and survival etched in every line.

It was a victory for us, but not without pain. Especially for Vu. He knew I was spending time with someone else. Some calls turned quiet, his voice clipped. I'd done that before too. I recognized the distance. After those calls, I sat in the silence he left behind. I could feel his unspoken ache. No matter how much love he gave, the ache of our circumstances still found a way in.

Vu wasn't wrong to feel what he felt. The truth is, the more time I spent with Francis, the more I started feeling something warm. Not just attraction, but comfort. Care. I liked being around him. He was kind in that quiet way, the kind that doesn't announce itself. He showed up. He laughed with his whole body. He was unbound, fully available.

And I was grateful—for his company, for his ease, for his honesty, for his support. Vu knew it. Felt it before I said a word and confirmed it when I shared with him about Francis. And he wanted that kind of tenderness for me, too. Just . . . not from Francis. Not *instead* of him. He wanted it *from* him. But he was incarcerated. So he'd take what he could get. Said as long as he stayed boyfriend number one, he could deal.

He'd ask me on the phone sometimes, "So how's boyfriend number two doing?" And every damn time he asked, something cracked in me. Guilt curled up in my throat like it had been waiting there. Because love like his deserved better than settling. And a love like Francis deserved better than settling. But *who* was I settling for?

No matter how much I enjoyed the freedom of being with Francis, my heart always reached back and pulled toward Vu. The one behind the walls, the one who had no freedom at all. The abundant days, the steady rhythm of a life with Francis—dinners, road trips, long walks in the open air. They didn't feel as deep as the rare, fleeting moments I shared with Vu. Those brief calls, the letters arriving like lifelines, the stolen seconds of connection. Sometimes the scarcity of it made it burn brighter. At times I was blind to it and got lost in the pain of what we could not have. But I was slowly learning what incarcerated love meant and felt like. That the hardship, the distance, the waiting could make me forget the glory of what we had. But then I reminded myself that I could be so consumed by our struggle if I let it eclipse our joy.

But then I'd enjoy my freedom with Francis.

And so, I moved through my days in quiet war. My heart and mind at odds, again. Dueling it out inside me, their swords slashing at my sanity and insanity. One was Vu, the deepest longing in my soul, a love that could not yet be fully realized. The other was Francis, a joy that was here, open and waiting, but my heart could not, would not, take it fully.

I remember the time Vu pulled away on the phone. One minute we were talking, or trying to, and the next, just silence. It had me tasting my own poison that I'd fed to him, and to people before him, dispensed in my own moments of distance, defensiveness, fear. The call ended abruptly with no resolution. The sadness that didn't shout at me, but the way it subtly settled and stayed stung. Then, a few days later, a card showed up with an apology inked into paper. We talked the next week, and there was no dancing around it. He laid bare what he was feeling and why he pulled back. He said the things he hadn't been able to say in the prior call. Then he said something graceful and poignant. "Saying sorry is more than words, sweetie. It's a promise to recognize the fault in yourself and try like hell to do better." And the way he said it? I don't think it was just for me. It was for him, too. For the boy he once was and the man he was trying to become. And maybe most of all, it was for the kind of love that asks you not to be perfect, but to be honest when you fall short.

Francis was like that, too. He's the kind of man who didn't just say sorry. He *meant* it. The kind who apologized with his heart, not just for the mistake but for the harm, too. Always trying to grow. Always reaching toward better, not just for himself, but for the people he loved. He understood the mess I was and was in. He understood in a way that I didn't expect and didn't even fully understand myself. I told him about the writing project for my class. He embraced it, encouraged it, asked questions about Vu and about how he was doing. I shared that when Vu struggled, he coped by eating honey buns, and when he was spiraling, he'd down a dozen of them in one sitting. Francis laughed, this short, surprised sound. Then his energy shifted with a pause, a moment of contemplation. "We all got our ways of coping, Thao," he said. "He has it rougher than we do. Exponentially." And he didn't say it like some throwaway line. He said it like he saw Vu and decided not to judge it, but to hold it. And I felt that. Then he looked at me and asked, "How are you doing? With juggling all this. You okay?"

"No, not really. Not sure what I'm doin' sometimes. Sorry." He nodded, touched my shoulder and said, "That's okay."

I guess it was. Not fixed. Not figured out. Just okay. And sometimes, that's the most loving thing someone can give you. The space to not know.

As the months stumbled along, it wasn't just Vu's writing that was blossoming, it was *him*, too. He was blooming backward, like breath returning to lungs you didn't know had collapsed. His messy journey and his magnificent mentorship became the brightest, most blistering light of 2019. We didn't just talk, we wrestled with poetry, with sentence structure, with how feelings too complicated to fully comprehend could be transfigured into language. He had regularly sent quotes to me, but then the fragments borrowed from others morphed into ones he penned. Then came poems. First, it was other people's. Then his own. Like he finally believed he had something worth expressing and knowing how to express it.

On my birthday, he gave me a poem. Yes, he wrote the poem, but what I really mean is that he *gave* me a poem, he *gave* me something that held parts of him he said he'd never given to anyone. He said he loved how he lost himself in the making of it. It made the days go by quickly. And that it also cost him something. It was the price of vulnerability. It made him uncomfortable. Discomfort in a sense of losing some sort of masculinity that he once held as a high-value commodity in the streets and in prison. How it healed something, too.

Timeless beauty is all I see
How Heaven made you just for me
Angels cried when we two parted
Of your absence had me broken hearted

Lingering lost love kept life incomplete
Every thought and dream, someday we'd meet

To finally realize we are destined
Half a lifetime our love never lessened
Acceptance of this love we share
Nothing in life that you and I couldn't bear
Hands of time have already foretold

How this everlasting love of ours unfolds
Age after age, life after life, we search for one another's soul.

I love all his poems. They carry me someplace just outside language, where you don't just read the words, you *feel* them, like really fucking feel them. Where longing gets a pulse. The way he laid those lines down, the way he built a bridge between what we say and what we ache to say. Each line he wrote was a kind of spell. And I kept falling further into him. I didn't think love could do that, didn't think it could *grow* like that, so quiet yet echoing long after into the dusty corners of my heart and making them sing from the way he expressed himself. The way he wrote about longing and despair and hope like they were old friends he'd drank beer with all night. I hadn't known that love could be read out loud like that. Hadn't known it could sound like poetry and still feel like home.

His writing journey became my beacon, illuminating the untapped power of words, the promise of sharing a voice that had once been silenced. His essay, along with those of the men he mentored, did more than fill pages. They moved through the world, landing in the hands of my students, stirring something in them that I could not have predicted. When I collected their postcards, I hadn't expected the depth of care woven into each message. Encouragement, forgiveness, and hope were scrawled in ink. Some students sent pictures of mountains and forests, trails winding through the wild, offering glimpses of a world these men had not seen in years or maybe had never seen. Others illustrated their thoughts, like the one Vu told me was his favorite. It was a pair of hands cradling a heart, *HOPE* marked in its center, a quiet prayer in neon pink and black.

One student wrote a poem just for him. How perfect, how fitting, that he would inspire poetry. That his words would awaken words in others. That something born in captivity could bloom into freedom for someone else. I loved how much he loved the poem. I loved how much he inspired others to write. I loved how deeply grateful those men were, not just for the students who had written to them, but for *him*, for mentoring them, for showing them that their voices mattered.

All the incarcerated men sent notes of thanks, but there was one letter that stood out among the rest, one that exemplified the vivid description of transformation. He wrote that the experience had changed him, that through this exchange with my students, something inside him had *opened*, as if he had been set free from the demons that chained him to his past and given him permission to start again. He found the courage to quit drugs.

That is the power of writing. That is the power of connection. That is the power of being heard. These voices, voices on the margins, held a power in them that the world so often refuses to acknowledge. These were men the world had long stopped listening to, men whose existence had been reduced to headlines and numbers. Society is more comfortable seeing their strength as a force of violence and harm and never tenderness. But their confessions were not asking for pity or forgiveness or to convince someone of their innocence, but rather a plea to see their humanity. Reading their words, I felt a quiet kind of astonishment. It reminded me that transformation rarely arrives with fanfare. Sometimes it slips in gently, through letters passed between people who might never meet, and changes everything.

"For the first time in my life, I feel seen. I feel heard."

How many of them had spent their entire existence being ignored, discarded, erased? And I thought, *What if we could heal more of this pain?*

Imagine the collective wounds we could mend if we met them with compassion instead of condemnation. Imagine the burdens lifted, the broken souls pieced back together, through something as simple and profound as understanding and empathy. Words of forgiveness. Of hope. Of encouragement. Of love. Imagine the moment a man in the depths of his own regret reads something from a stranger, and for the first time, sees himself as something other than a lost cause. Imagine how that single act could set his spirit free.

14

Home

BY THE END OF 2019, I truly understood the power of words. The way they carry love, longing, regret, hope, and everything in between. Vu had been teaching me that long before I realized it.

In prison, reading had become his way of slipping past the razor wire. He once told me that a good story felt like an open field, something he could run through when the reality around him was narrowed to concrete, metal, and shady characters. He devoured Westerns for their grit and romance novels for the parts of tenderness that was absent in a place like prison. His favorite was *The Notebook,* though he tore the cover off so the other guys wouldn't know he was reading a sappy love story. Books softened him. Writing sharpened him. Both shaped the way he reached for me.

His reading deepened over time. He started reading more nonfiction, poetry, and self-help books. As he widened his genre selections, his letters grew more textured. He wrote with candor he never claimed as talent, only as a version of how he lived his life—wearing his heart on his sleeve. When we were young, we talked for hours, curled up in the dark like the world might end if we stopped speaking. When life pulled us apart, our love adapted. Ink on pages, sketches full of care, poems bridging the silence.

Calls came once a week, but we stretched them, redialing again and again. One of my favorite memories lives in those marathon calls before my holiday trip to Houston. Eight hours one day, eight the next. Thirty minutes at a time. Just our voices, rising and fading, steady and sure. Those words, that rhythm, it felt like home. And I always wanted more.

December 18, 2019

Thao,

I'm missing you so much it hurts. I'm thinking about our amazingly long conversation we had on the phone. To be exact, two wonderful days totaling 16 awesome hours. Em yêu ơi [my darling love], it is very obvious some things seem to never change between the two of us. When we interact with one another, we seem to lose focus of the world around us and the track of time. It doesn't matter whether we are writing letters, talking on the phone or face to face. You have a way of captivating me and making me feel as if I'm still 19 years old. My love for you will always be this way. I'm very lucky to be loved by you. Throughout my whole life, you were always there for me when I needed you. One call and you would always come running no matter what. I know you truly love me. When this circumstance of mine is behind me, I will always be there for you. This time around, it will be me running to you. To the day I take my last breath, I will always come running when you need me.

I wanted to run to him for Christmas, to press my palm against the cold glass and see his face, to make the distance between us feel smaller, if only for a fleeting moment. But he worried. Worried that too many obligations would pull me in too many directions, that I had already stretched myself thin with all the traveling that year. He told me I needed to be present for my family, for my friends, that I should let myself rest. I fought him on it. *You are of utmost importance to me.* I told him I *wanted* to see him.

Francis knew, too. He wanted to come to Houston with me. He offered to drive me to the prison, willing to sit in the parking lot and wait, content with a book in his hands, waiting. But Vu wouldn't allow it. He feared it would create tension between me and Francis. He spoke with quiet conviction, his words threaded with care, with concern, with the quiet sacrifice that had become second nature to him. And so, I relented. He got his way. But in the silence that followed, in the echo of unspoken words, something lingered. A letter arrived, his handwriting familiar, steady, but carrying the trace of second thoughts.

December 28, 2019

Since I made the decision about our visitation, I've been in my feelings. Not that I regret the decision because I don't. It's just a sadness I feel for the missed opportunity of spending time with you. But you know how I am. I will always do or say what I think is best for you. At the moment, I'm thinking if I keep opening this big mouth of mine, I will never be able to see you again. Next time you mention coming here, I won't say anything. I don't care who wants to take you. I don't even care if your dad wants to take you. That's saying a lot since you know how scared I am of your dad.

May this new year bring you a lot of fortune along with good health and an abundance of joy. I do hope this letter of mine finds you safely at home and in good spirits. It is also my hope that it has you missing me like never before. I write that because it's only fair since that's all I seem to be doing. Thinking of you and missing you. It's all your fault for spoiling me. Now I keep wanting more and more of you. My last two Christmases have been miraculous and memorable. Simply because you spent them with me. I can't remember ever being so happy. Thank you for loving me and sharing your precious time with me. I loved every second of it. For those moments, I was in your world with you. It was ethereal. Love for me is to hear your voice. Love for me is to be closer to you. Love for me is everything about you. Loving you is all I've ever needed. Loving you is everything to me.

I am looking forward to the new year. I bet you didn't know that the incarcerated population celebrate New Year's day more than any other holiday. Do you know why? It's one more year of time served. For myself, every new year that arrives, I get these feelings of excitement and anticipation, but also anxious and frightful all rolled into one. Does that make sense to you that I feel this way?

Yes, it does. Living through his words, seeing through his eyes, I learned to understand his world and the slow passage of time, the way it expanded and compressed, a cruel and predictable tide. But one more year ending meant one more year served, and that was one more step forward, another mile behind him on this journey of a thousand treacherous miles to a dream fulfilled.

The excitement, that rush of knowing he was inching closer, the glimmer of something beyond the walls that held him.

The anticipation, looking ahead, willing freedom into existence, hoping so fiercely that it became the very air our souls ached to breathe.

The anxiety, the gnawing worry that time was an avalanche, that the years, relentless and unyielding, might smother our will to keep going.

The fear of doubt that creeps out from the darkest corners of the mind, the fear of tragedy. *What if that day never comes?* What if fate is unkind, and this story is left unfinished? What if freedom is nothing but a mirage?

I processed these thoughts and emotions, and I could not let another opportunity slip away. Without question, without permission, without hesitation—without even the fear that he would worry, knowing I had just been in Texas—I booked my travel to see Vu in January, the week before spring semester began. A decision made not with logic, but with longing, with the quiet desperation that only love and distance can create. The need to see him in the flesh, to trace the contours of his face with my eyes, to hear his voice unfiltered, unrecorded, untethered by time delays or the static of prison calls. The hunger to be near him, to break the cruel barrier of absence, to exist in the same space again. It was the same ache, the same gravity that had compelled me to reach out after nearly two decades of silence. The chance to sing with him. To joke with him. To ponder with him. To eat potato chips and sip RC Cola together, the cheap mixture of salty and sweetness tasted like luxury when I was with him. These were the only things I wanted to usher in the new year. No resolutions, no grand plans—just *him*.

I thought of Francis, and my mind drifted through the journey we had traveled together over the past seven months. The kindness in his heart, the sharp angles of his good looks, the quiet generosity of his spirit. His devotion was steady, his tenderness pure, his presence unwavering. But there was always something about Vu.

I reflected on the chaos, this storm of my own making, the war between longing and surrender, pulled between the comfort of what was possible and the torment of what was just out of reach. *Chaotic love.* It wasn't just circumstance; it was my own soul in turmoil, trying to bend the impossible into existence and loving someone in captivity while attempting to live freely with someone else.

It was the inability to choose me and Vu as we were that drove me mad. The inability to embrace the love we had without grievances over the love we *could* have.

What is fate but a thread woven through the fabric of time, tugged and twisted by the choices we make, by the roads we take, or avoid? What is destiny but the quiet pull of something greater, something inevitable, a force that neither distance nor doubt can sever? Jean de La Fontaine once wrote, "A person often meets his destiny on the road he took to avoid it." I have spent much of my life avoiding. It was how I survived. Through the trials and tribulations, through the wounds of my past, avoidance had become my shield, my method of coping. When pain loomed too close, I ran. When heartache felt inevitable, I retreated. But there was no avoiding Vu. Not this time.

The force of his love was unrelenting, undeniable, and demanding to be faced. Through the slow passage of time, his actions spoke louder than any promise, louder than any plea. He loved me with a quiet devotion, unwavering, unconditional. His love did not press, did not demand. It simply *was*. It wrapped around me, soothed the chaos within me, brought harmony to the discord of my mind and the madness of my heart.

It was clarity. And for the first time, I stopped running. I stood still, and in that stillness, I *chose*. When I returned from the visit, I knew what had to be done. I had to tell Francis. I had to end it with him. And then I would tell Vu that I chose him. Only him. Not on the phone, but in person. I'd visit him again in March during spring break and tell him with my eyes locked into his.

I thought about writing a letter to Francis, pouring my words onto paper, hoping the ink would soften the blow. But he deserved better than that. He deserved my voice and my honesty, even if it meant he would hear the tremble in it, even if it meant he would hear the tears fall between her words. Someone like him, so kind, so pure, should never have been misled, should never have been given a false sense of hope. Yes, there was attraction. There was comfort. There was stability. There was fun, understanding, kindness, generosity. There were a hundred things that would make most people feel secure, make most people sink into love. But the heart is reckless in its desires. The heart is unruly in its truths. And when a soul meets its mate, there is no explanation, no reasoning, no logic to undo the bond that exists. It is not in the touch of skin, not in the press of bodies. It is something deeper, something unseen. An electric tether, an inferno that neither time nor distance could extinguish. How could I explain this to Francis? I didn't know how. But I would have to try.

February 2020 came, and with it, the obligations of life. I flew to Houston to celebrate my nephew's fifth birthday, a milestone and a moment that mattered. From there, I traveled to Washington, DC, for work. I sent Vu two postcards, tiny fragments of myself, whispering across the miles how much I missed and loved him. When I returned, there was another speaking engagement. When I finally came home, exhaustion was real. I needed time. Time to recover. Time to gather my thoughts, to find the words that wouldn't shatter Francis. I had avoided having the conversation. But before I could, *he* beat me to it.

At times, Francis struggled with feeling like he was not enough for me. He was uncomfortable with the distance I sometimes placed between us, the quiet ways I pulled away. After the holidays, I had thrust myself into work and barely spoken to him. I had done it on purpose. It was avoidance again, my oldest survival skill, keeping me from facing the inevitable. But Francis was human. And love, especially the perception of unreciprocated love, makes humans ache for certainty. For reassurance. For proof. And when the silence extended too long, when the distance between us must have become unbearable, he did something he had been working so hard to improve upon. He confronted me. "Thao, why do I feel like you're avoiding me?"

I think we had closure. I'm not really sure. I wasn't good at healthy closure. I wasn't good at tidy endings. I'm sure I was bad at communicating in a way that would have honored the dignity he deserved. When I finally sat with Francis and tried to explain why I was ending our relationship, the words felt clumsy, like I was rehearsing a script meant for someone else's life. I told him his world didn't match mine, that his need for more time, more attention, more companionship was something I couldn't offer. I said it gently and firmly, or at least I think I did, framing it like it was care, that I was thinking of him, like I wanted him to have the kind of partner who could meet him where he stood. I told him he was a good father. That his children were amazing kids. That they deserve a good stepmother, someone steady and present and willing to shape her life around theirs. That he deserved better than me. That I was holding him back from what was best for him and his kids.

I told Francis what he needed. But I never once said what I wanted.

Instead, I packaged it as kindness and sacrifice. The truth was delivered sideways and edited. It was the closest I could get to an ending, even if it wasn't the whole truth. And in the aftermath, he understood and even encouraged me to allow my heart to love who it loves.

After years of reflection, I'm writing what I wish I could have said then.

Dearest Francis,

I want to be honest, although, I'm afraid of stinging your heart. For much of my life, I abandoned truth to avoid the discomfort that comes with difficult conversations and broken relationships. I could give you explanations that buffer the hurt, but to barely scrape the surface would discount and dishonor the kind of honesty you deserve. I am grateful you gave of your whole self to me. I am grateful you handled the many difficult times with grace, compassion, and understanding. I am grateful you gave us a shot knowing that the future could never be predicted. I thank you for assuring me that you would never make me choose. But I did. And this is the part that feels hardest to express. I choose the person who fits me in the shape of who I want to be. It's easier for me to tell you that our ending is some kind of sacrifice on my part so that you can find someone who fits your life more seamlessly. But that would be another half-truth wrapped in good intentions. It's not my place to decide what is best for you. The truth is that in balancing two relationships—one tethered to Vu, a man behind bars, and one with you, a man in the free world—I learned something unruly about the nature of my own heart. And I know it sounds perplexing, maybe even unfair, but the love confined to concrete and steel is the one that feels like mine. Vu's love feels like home—steady in its own fractured way and rooted in a history I can't shake. Your love, no matter how great or earnest, feels like stepping into a house already built, with obligations waiting in the rooms. The idea of being absorbed into your family terrifies me. I don't want to be folded into domestic routines that aren't mine. I don't want to contort my calendar to meet your desire for more time together or to pick up the kids at soccer and swimming and basketball. I know you never expect that of me explicitly, but I understand it in the way it shows up as gentle disappointment in your eyes when I decline. And it shows up as tiny fragments of resentment in me when I oblige. I can't share my life that completely. I've spent so long caring for everyone else that I don't want a life that requires me to feel burdened. But there is something deeper than all of this, something harder to explain without sounding mystical or naïve. You deserve to know that, too. I was attracted to you, and I care for you. I was drawn to your steadiness, your warmth, the way you offered joy and structure in equal measure. You showed up with generosity, patience, and a kind of goodness that anyone would be lucky to receive. Many others would have stepped toward that kind of love without hesitation. But the heart isn't persuaded by what makes sense. Desire doesn't answer to logic, and longing doesn't negotiate. What pulls me toward Vu is something older, something that lived beneath the surface of everything I tried to reason through. It's a melody I can't quiet, a knowing I can't unlearn, a connection that kept beating even when the rest of my life told me to move on. It's not about touch or promises. It's the way our histories fold into each other, the way memory still sparks in places I thought had gone dark. It's a force I can't untangle. Unfortunately, I don't feel these things with you. I owe you that truth, even if it's landing on you imperfectly. I'm so sorry. Although I'm saying farewell, I have many hopes and dreams for you. I wish for you to fall in love and for that person to fall so fucking madly in love with you, too. I wish for all the beauty that you are to be the beauty of who she is. I wish for you to be loved in the way that you love. With sacrifice, with kindness, with abundance, with tenderness, with honesty, with humility, with devotion. Unconditionally.

15

Incarcerated Love in the Time of COVID-19

THE WORLD STOPPED. A TERRIFYING stillness settled in as the pandemic crept in like a shadow, unseen at first, then everywhere. For me, it began on March 13, 2020. My college shut down. Classes moved online. The world began to close. Flights grounded. Prisons locked down. My spring-break visit to Vu evaporated in an announcement on the Texas Department of Criminal Justice website that all visitations were suspended until further notice. The country came to a standstill. We experienced fear, uncertainty, and the realization that individual control was just an illusion. We were allowed to move only for essentials such as groceries, hospitals, and police stations. Life turned into waiting, ruled by shifting dates and shrinking hope. Life became a waiting game, measured in increments of restriction, in ever-extending deadlines.

Two weeks, they said. Just two weeks.

Two weeks stretched into months, then kept going. I was saddened by the disruption because the visit I planned wouldn't happen, and I didn't know when it would be available to us again. And it wasn't just about the small, human miracle of showing up for him. I also wanted to sit in front of him, look into his eyes, and to let my presence accompany the words I wanted to say. That this love was real. That I was his and only his. That what was between us wasn't nostalgia or fantasy. I was his without negotiation. He once said important things deserved presence. So I waited, thinking that a future date on the calendar could be decided on when visitation opens again.

I was disappointed about what was put on pause for him, too. He'd written with excitement about an author scheduled to come give a talk at his unit, a writer we once stayed up late discussing. He was eager to hear the words live, to hear the man's voice and see the man beyond the pages. His letter carried that hope.

February 10, 2020

My Dearest Thao:

Remember when you shared with me the allegory of the carrot, the egg, and the coffee bean? The reason I brought it up was because I recently read an article on it. It made me understand the full concept of it. Not that your explanation of it wasn't good. For me, I just have to read it to understand it better. So if I imagine prison as a pot of boiling hot water, and I must decide how to react, I can choose to be the carrot and turn soft, allowing life and circumstances to beat me down. Most carrots are weak, vulnerable, and depressed. Believe me, no one really chooses to be a carrot. They just are. Then there is the egg which turns hard on the inside. The eggs are mad, and their hearts become hardened like the yolk of a hard boiled egg. This could have easily been me. As a matter of fact, I was the egg at one point in

> my life. But seeing too many circumstances of the carrots and eggs made me choose to be like a coffee bean, which changes the pot of boiling water into a pot of coffee. The one that is always smiling no matter what, being positive through the storm, and always helping others when needed (unless they piss me off that is haha). The guy who wrote the two books, The Change Agent is one and The Coffee Bean is the other, is doing a tour of all 104 Texas prison units. I'm wondering if he's the same one you read about the coffee bean. I haven't read any of his books, only read a bio about him. Incredibly inspiring since he is a formerly incarcerated person. It will be a while before he gets here, but still, I can't wait to hear his presentation. Remembering that reminded me of your "Life After Life" presentation. I'm almost there and the realization of it is for me to wrap my mind around it. I know my circumstances are different from others but it doesn't change my outlook. The thing that I have to think about is where do I begin.

I had agendized this conversation topic for the visit so that we could explore together how he could start adjusting his outlook to believe that he will come home someday soon. The topic of choosing to be a coffee bean in hot water would come after my confession, of course. Or, I figured we could have the coffee-bean talk on the phone. But even phone calls were rare. One-hour time limits shrunk to five minutes. When I did hear from him, he told me the line of men waiting to make calls was unusually long. Too few phones for the urgent circumstances that affected everyone. It would be days or even weeks before it was his turn in the line. When he could make calls, he told me he dialed me first. He knew I'd be worried, and he knew I'd be responsible enough to let everyone in his family know that he was alive and that he wasn't sick. Just hearing his voice felt like air after drowning.

Still, the fear stayed. His unit was among the worst hit. The virus tore through overcrowded cells with the efficiency of a brushfire. I worried for Vu. For our elderly parents. For my sisters who worked in hospitals. One of them, a PA, was reassigned to COVID duty. She told me she was ready to quit rather than walk into that storm.

Then another call from Vu came. *I missed it.* My phone was on silent. I was in a Zoom meeting, saying things that suddenly felt pointless. My chest sank when I saw the missed call. Then his sister rang. *Had I heard from him? Was he okay?* I told her to call the unit since someone in the family was surely on his medical release form. Her pause cut cold and sharp through me.

"What form?" she asked.

Disbelief hit hard like a physical blow. How could she not know? Without that form and his signature granting permission, if something happened to him, we'd get nothing. No updates. No calls. We would be shut out from the truth of his condition, his existence. The horror of it gutted me. He was caged, and I was caught in the chaos of not knowing. I couldn't eat. Sleep came in fragments, haunted by looping dreadful thoughts. Then, a month into lockdown, a letter came. His handwriting. Proof of life.

April 20, 2020

My Love.

It seems forever since the last time I've written you. I do apologize for that. Please understand that there are always reasons why I choose to do the things I do, the way I do them. But even though I haven't written, doesn't mean you weren't always on my mind. So much more than you will ever know. Babe, I miss you. I miss talking to you. I miss the sound of your voice. But it is what it is, the circumstance of life's restrictions for us and also for now. We do what's best for us to get by. When missing you hurts too much, I deal with it the only way I know how. I tend to try to ignore or more like try to keep you off my mind, but that's like a constant battle I can never win. See how impossible it is since I am writing to you now.

During this Coronavirus crisis, my unit is greatly affected. They are under order to practice incarcerated social distancing. Yes, you read it correctly. It's so stupid but at the same time comical on how they are doing it. Damn near impossible to do if you ask me. Let me tell you. First, they put 50 of us TOGETHER and wait to go where we are supposed to go. For example, to eat, we'll wait TOGETHER. Then when we get to the chow hall, they separate us 6 feet apart and seat us two to a table. Once we're back, they put us back TOGETHER again. I don't think this is what the CDC had in mind when they ordered the incarceration style social distancing. Then there was an exposure so we have been on a full lockdown. So much has changed around here during this desperate plight of incarcerated social distancing. Through all of the chaotic, hectic, problematic and confusing state, some good came with it. We are living in a lot cleaner conditions. That's saying a lot. The warden came to our dorm and started slipping and sliding because the floor was wet due to it being so humid. That day was also gloomy so it made the dorm look like a dark, nasty smelling dungeon. He took one look around and said with sympathy and compassion, "You guys deserve to live a lot better than this." Hearing this, I just knew we (meaning the porters like me) are all screwed. For as long as I can remember, it's always the inmates' fault, never the unit. While waiting to be fired, I was surprisingly amazed when a clean up crew showed up that same day. They cleaned up the form from top to bottom. That's not all. The very next day, the paint crew came around and painted everything. You wouldn't believe what color my dorm is now. Aqua blue!!! I am not joking. The very same color you love so much. This has to be some kind of coincidence or is your universe just wanting to mentally torture me? Now everywhere I look, I'm being reminded of you. It's all good though since I love the color myself and the new look around here.

April 24, 2020

My Dearest Vu.

I cried reading your letter knowing the environment you were living in, how dangerous it had become due to this virus and how impossible it was to maintain social distancing in a prison. I fully understood what you meant about hurting too much and ignoring and trying not to think of me . . . avoidance. We have always been so very alike. But I had promised to be honest with you. I have been so stressed about the pandemic. Everyone is scared. People are sick and dying. I am so worried about my family. I have been tracking the cases at your unit, and I am so worried about you. I have fallen into another bout of what I feel is depression. Mail is disrupted. And I understand that they're not allowing you phone calls. When you did call me that one time, I am so fucking pissed that I missed it. How could my luck be so bad? I literally feel sick. I haven't told anyone. But I promise that I am working on getting better. I am doing my best to take care of myself. I hope you are ok, my Love. I don't know what I would do if anything were to happen to you. I pray to the Universe that you are okay.

May 1, 2020

Babe.

Do you promise that you are okay? I do hope that you are well and getting better. I need you to be healthy. I started this letter not knowing whether I wanted to kick your butt or thank your universe that you are feeling better and improving everyday. I can't believe you would hide the fact that you were sick from everyone. What if something would have happened to you? I, for one, would not know what to do. You brought everything that is bright and joyous to my life. I love you more than you will ever know. I see it's okay for you to worry and have anxieties over others but others can't worry over you? You have to understand that it's part of loving someone. You worry about them no matter what.

Everything is okay with me, and I am well so please don't worry about me. I promise that you will know if I am not. Remember the strength and resilience you always say I have, that will always be there. If anyone should be worried, it should be me. Two weeks ago I wrote you a letter but never finished it or sent it out because I sensed something was wrong with you. Many thoughts ran through my mind. Now I wished I would have sent it so you wouldn't worry so much. Since the coronavirus hit my unit, it has spread like wildfire. It is the most frightening and most terrifying time for us, to say the least. Every dorm is on medical restriction or quarantine except D-wing where I am. For the moment, we are the only dorms with no symptoms or confirmed cases. Which also means we are the only ones able to work. There is way too

> much work and not enough workers. Most of us are working 12 to 14 hours, 7 days a week. We are all tired. It's to a point where some are hiding under their bunks to avoid going to work. Last time I checked, the kitchens are a day late on our Johnny sacks. They are trying to get the surrounding units to help make them for us. I don't know what will happen when my dorm goes down. Today, they tried to move everyone on D-wing to the gym, but we refused. They say it's for our safety, but the reality is, they need room for the sick. In the end, they ended up shipping about 100 of the sick to another unit.
>
> Babe, I wrote you right back as soon as I got your letter. I did not want you to worry so please don't worry about me. I am okay. Can you please take care of yourself for me? I love you with all of me so please remember that. Be well, my love.

I told him not to worry. He said the same. But anxiety led me to think his words were used for comfort, not truth. Words used in the way people use gauze—thin and temporary, meant to soothe rather than heal. I needed more than his reassurances. I needed facts. I searched the Texas Department of Criminal Justice website, scrolled the rows of case data. Positive tests. Medical isolations. A tally of bodies turned into numbers. Then I found the Beto Unit. It housed just 3 percent of the prison population but 37 percent of all COVID cases. The math was a flare in the night. My stomach dropped. I'd read how prisons kept the sick among the healthy, where the air was thickened with contagion, where men breathed the same recycled air. Dread wrapped itself around me. I couldn't sleep.

On the next call, I reminded him to sign the medical release form. If he got sick, we'd know nothing. He could vanish into state custody, and we'd be left chasing silence. I told his sister to write, to call, to push for a wellness check. She was worried, too. I tracked numbers daily.

Beto's count rose. So did my panic. I ate in morsels. Work was done in snippets. I tried to escape into things I never used to care for such as mindless television. *Tiger King* of all things. But even absurdity on screen couldn't distract me. Everything circled back to Vu. Loving him had steadied me. Now, it was like walking through a field of smoke and landmines with a lantern.

One morning, I made myself sit still and meditated. Breathing in, breathing out, letting the rot in my body settle into something that resembled order. My thoughts slowed down, and the panic that had been crashing like waves on my nervous system subsided. For clarity, I counted the calendar. April was ending. July was close. It had been nearly two years since we'd found each other again. Seven more until parole. Then five. Then three. Then one. Then done. I held on to that math the way some people hold rosary beads in a prayer.

And I needed to write. To tell a story about me and him and our struggles. Very few people in my orbit knew he existed. I wanted them to know about incarcerated love in the time of COVID. But it wasn't just that. I hoped to give something more. I wanted to name what so many of us might be feeling in those days. A sharing of the complexities we faced and the collective trauma we were experiencing in a dim world where so many of us were blindly living, stumbling through the dark, pretending we could see.

There's a strange salvation in turning chaos into language, how sorrow shaped into sentences becomes something you can hold instead of something that holds you. Words let me open the door of my mind, let the thoughts walk out instead of pacing the cage in my head. Words became release. And so, I wrote a blog entry and shared it on my social media accounts. It was my offering to the Universe, a confession made in the privacy of my desk, a way to say that loving Vu from a distance was both the thing that buoyed me and the thing that hollowed me out. That I was proud of him. For the man he had become. For the things he taught me. For the published essay with the Asian American Writers' Workshop. I included a link to his essay "My Name Is Chino."

Positive words filled the comments section and the direct messages of my inbox. I copied my blog and sent it to Vu in a letter. I included the comments from strangers who had delivered tenderness from across the void—lines of admiration, of empathy, of grief shared. My favorite read: "Wow. The tragedy of this situation is crippling. I am stunned and have no idea what to say—if anything. This hurts me on so many levels, but I know not nearly the level it does for Vu and you. Where there is peace, may you both find it."

Peace. What does peace feel like in a world unraveling? What does peace look like when he was there and I was here, and no amount of longing, no force of will, could close the distance? What does peace feel like when you are powerless? In isolation and solitude, I reached for peace in the only place I knew at the time. *Us.* Our love, even in its chaos, had always been a kind of refuge.

The evening after I posted the blog, I found myself reaching again for something familiar, something stable. I settled on the couch with a cotton throw draped over my legs, and Pork Chop curled against my feet, his warm weight grounding me in a way nothing else could. He lifted his head once, as if checking on me, then tucked himself back into sleep, his quiet presence reminding me I wasn't entirely alone in the room or in the world.

I pulled out the old letters. One by one, I peeled back the years and traced our history in ink. From 1992 to 2020—every page a tether, every word a pulse of something still alive between us. And in that moment, with Pork Chop breathing softly at my feet and the past unfolding in my hands, I felt it. A small whisper: *You are still here, and so is he.* Something close to peace.

Until my phone buzzed. It was a Facebook message from his mother.

"Thảo cháu khỏe không? Bác chỉ nói nhỏ cháu nghe nha đừng buồn bác nha, khi cháu có any information or mail from Vũ do not put in Facebook you can send to our children because I do not want other people know about him because public all people can see it that make me sad. chúc cháu nhiều sức khỏe trẻ đẹp thanks Thảo."

[Thảo, are you doing well? I ask you quietly, don't be sad with me okay, when I have any information or mail from Vũ do not put in Facebook, you can send to our children, because I do not want other people know about him because public all people can see it that make me sad. I wish you good health, young and beautiful, thanks Thảo.]

I never told Vu about this. I would never risk altering the way he saw his mother. I loved her, respected her, and understood the world she came from. She asked me to take down the blog and delete it on my social media. But I could not do as she asked. If only she had read the words of strangers in their admiration, their grief, their recognition of his humanity, perhaps she would have understood why it mattered. Why people needed to know his story, why his words deserved to be read, why his existence could not, *should not*, remain unseen, like the shoebox of his photos she tossed in the garbage. Maybe it was her way of coping with the idea that he'd never come home. Maybe it was her own ceremonial way of saying goodbye to her son. I get it, I really do. Vietnamese parents often love in silence. They were raised in a place where speaking pain could cost you more than bearing it, where secrecy was not a flaw but a shield from losing face, a way to protect the family from humiliation. The idea that suffering could be spoken, shared, laid bare for the world to witness was foreign, uncomfortable, and even shameful. Suffering was something you hid, not something you brought to light. To name it, to share it, to let others witness it felt like breaking a sacred rule.

To me, though, it was the opposite. It was a step in returning him to a world that had forgotten he existed and to my world of people who never knew he existed.

A month later, I received his letter.

May 29, 2020

Babe.

I miss you. I miss you. I miss you. I think about you all the time and can't help myself. I know it doesn't seem like it since I've taken so long to write back to you. I'm sorry. Though it's not my intention since I started this letter of mine a week ago and this was as far as I had gotten. Not that I don't have nothing to say but the complete opposite, just at the time I have difficulties formulating my thoughts into words. It's weird when I write to others, it doesn't take me much time or effort at all. I just write. But when it comes to writing to you, on the other hand, my thoughts, my feelings, my mood, my handwriting, the pen, the papers, and everything in between has to be just right. My first sentence done took more than 10 sheets of paper due to the fact that I felt my handwriting didn't seem right for some reason. So over and over again, I rewrite it. I am not embarrassed to admit that I am a dumb ass as long as you understand me and know where I'm coming from. That's all that matters to me.

One difficulty I have most is not wanting to darken my letters with the sad circumstances of my surroundings. I feel it defeats the purpose of writing you. For the simple fact that my purpose is to bring you joy, amusement, laughter, love and desire for me if I can. But even though I tried, somehow you already know. Like when reading your social media post (not sure what that is),

I was shocked and surprised at the range of your knowledge on what's been happening here at Beto. Some of the things I didn't even know. Some with so much detail I kept wondering, how the hell did she know this or that, or are you writing someone else besides me at Beto? I'm playing. But seriously, you wrote about I wing, dubbed the "death wing" by the inmates and the guy that jumped off the third floor. Very accurate. And here I am trying to shield you from these ugliness so that you wouldn't worry and be apprehensive for me. Not knowing that you already know.

Your writing has always amazed and enthralled me. I love how you put things into perspective. It touched me deeply that you have the strength and courage to share me with the world outside. I am overwhelmed with love for you. Most would rather deny my existence than face the backlash of being associated with me. Not you. You come running toward me during my darkest moments with these bright lights of love, hope, encouragement, and inspiration. Time and time again, this cycle keeps repeating itself. You somehow freed my inner demons and set me at peace with myself when you wrote "Then he was sentenced to 60 years, taking the fall for his buddy who pulled the trigger. He refused to testify against him, even if it meant it would free himself." I have always wanted to scream and shout to the world that I didn't do this. Don't know why that's important to me after all these years, or maybe it's reading your words and knowing that you believe me.

You say it's a crazy life out there, but it's a crazy life no matter where we are on this Earth during this damn time—free world or incarceration, we're all struggling to make it through the day. I've seen some strange things lately that's been fucking with my mind and emotions. Never have I ever known or seen anyone go home out the front gate of Beto. Now, 5 have left off this wing alone. My neighbor was one of them and didn't even know it. When the officer woke him up by telling him—his family been outside waiting since 6 this morning. He kept saying—man, this has got to be a dream. I've waited 40 years for this. After hearing that, I yelled out to him—man, get your shit and get the fuck out of here!!! Everyone laughed while inside I felt agonizingly. Then the next day I walked up on someone I've known since I got here. He was crying. Come to find out, he received an FI one (a notice of favorable parole action) after 32 years of incarceration. For him, it was bittersweet. Bitter because he needed an address within 10 days. But as sweet as his FI one is, he's not sure what's going to happen. I didn't realize so many people on my wing are waiting to be released. Not used to that. Back then, there were two ways of leaving, either do day for day on your time or get life flight out.

As for myself, it's the same old, same old. Not much going on here beside working. At times it can be exhausting, but it's a lot better than being stuck in the cell so when my cell door opens, I run out. Guys are getting frustrated with this and are fighting. Myself included. It's understandable, just like animals when you have them caged up too long. What keeps me grounded are my books, and I have plenty, so that helps. Other than that, I am well and am doing okay in these circumstances so please don't worry, okay? Without you (my ultimate bliss) in my life, there's only pain and suffering for me. I love you.

Please don't worry? How could I not?! A foreboding sense of doom came to me, a quiet, relentless terror I couldn't shake. I fought against it the only way I knew how. With meditative prayers whispered into the stillness. *Everything will be okay. Vu will be okay.* I repeated it like a chant, willing the words to become truth, as if speaking them enough times could bend fate in our favor. Then, finally, he called. We got five precious minutes. Five minutes to unravel weeks of waiting, five minutes to hold on to his voice. It was never enough, but it was everything. His voice was steady, but I could hear the soft anxiety behind it.

"They finally got me to sign the medical release form," he said. Relief flooded me. At least now, if something happened, we would know. We wouldn't be left in the dark, waiting, helpless, powerless. But then he sighed, and his words struck something deep inside me. "All these twenty years, my family never cared about this form until you pushed it." A pause. A subtle exhale. "I guess it's better late than never."

The melancholy in his voice cut through me. Better late than never. But *why* had it taken this long? I wanted to tell him that he deserved more than *better late than never*, that he deserved more than being an afterthought. But five minutes disappears faster than you think, and there was never enough time for all the things I wanted to say. So instead, I just held on to the sound of his voice, trying to memorize every syllable before the line went dead.

We could have never predicted how fucking important that piece of paper would be. And yet, it was everything. A single signature, a line of ink on a document, became the thin, fragile thread connecting us to the truth of him. Without it, his family and I would have been left in the dark. And still, even with it, the waiting for updates was always filled with anxiety. A month passed before I heard from him again. A month of gnawing dread, of restless nights, of checking the mail with a sinking heart when no letter showed up. When his letter finally arrived, my hands trembled as I tore it open. My eyes scanned every word, but one passage held me hostage, an echo that has never faded.

July 6, 2020.

As for myself, I am very worried about my health. I tried to hide it from you since I didn't want you to worry, but I should have known. You have too many tattletellers on your team. Here's

> what's been going on. For the past three weeks, I have been experiencing extreme nonstop abdominal pain. Been in and out of the infirmary many times but only to leave with non-aspirin. I promise to fight through this, but if something unexpected happens, know that you are the love of my life. I love you dearly.

I read it once. Then again. And again. Each time, parts of my heart splintered, like hairline cracks spreading through the architecture of my chest. The words lodged themselves in me, sharp as shards of glass. He was *worried about his health*. He was *in pain*. He was *fighting through it*. He was pushing through it *alone*. And I was *helpless*. This was a new kind of torture, one I had never endured before. Loving someone behind bars demands a kind of endurance some people never have to imagine. But loving him in the era of COVID, when death drifted through ventilation systems, lurking in the very air he breathed, when sickness spread like smoke seeping through the dorms, when medical neglect was not just an accident but a condition of the institution, this was its own brand of terror. I clung to hope the way the drowning cling to the surface, desperate, shaking, convinced that if I just kept flailing, I wouldn't go under. I pictured the crisis would pass and of the moment visitation would open again. I thought of Whoopi's gregarious greeting and Officer Tran's warm smile. If flights weren't running, I would drive. I would cross states, deserts, highways and byways, whatever waited between us. Like always, I would come running. Because I had made a promise. I had agreed with him that when it came to the most important matters, the truths that defined life, I would speak them in person. I *still* had not told him the one truth that had been burning inside me all this time. That I was *his*. That he was the only one I wanted to love. That he was, in every *real way*, the only one I had ever truly loved.

16

I Will Try

EVERY MORNING, VU AWOKE TO a world that tried to break him, and every morning, he fought back. A hundred pushups, five hundred sit-ups, a thousand burpees. His body was a machine relentless in its endurance. His friend Long once told me that Vu could grab a pole and hold himself suspended, parallel to the ground, as if gravity had no claim on him. He moved like a force of nature, up and down three flights of stairs as a porter, scrubbing away the filth of a world that would never be clean. He ran circles around the young dudes, outpacing them, outlasting them.

But no amount of strength could hold back what was coming. A silent, unseen illness crept into his body, something that stripped away his power, that left him weak, breathless, and broken in a way I had never imagined him to be. Like everything else in prison, pain was just another sentence. It was one served in waiting. Illness did not grant mercy, and neither did the system that held him captive. Medical care moved at the speed of indifference, shackled by bureaucracy, buried under layers of neglect. For weeks, he tried to see the medical team, putting in request after request, and each time, a note would come back letting him know he would be scheduled at the next available appointment, as if pain was an inconvenience and suffering was routine. He didn't have COVID symptoms, so he wasn't a priority. He had severe back pain and a severe stomach pain that killed his appetite and stole his sleep. When he was finally seen, they handed him ibuprofen.

They *refused* to send him for outside treatment because his condition "wasn't severe enough." They *denied* him phone use, silencing his voice when he needed it most. They *forced* him into desperation, so much so that he had to risk everything just to be heard. Jackie told me he used a burner phone to call her. Whispering through the static, he told her what he couldn't tell me himself. "Sis, I need you to call in, fight for me, help me get through this." Then she told me Vu and his friend Jordan, the owner of the burner phone, were debating. *Should they tell me? Should they risk my disapproval?* They knew how I felt about contraband, about the consequences, about what a single misstep could cost him. Yet, in the end, pain overruled principle.

"Don't tell her, bro, she gonna be mad," Jordan advised.

"Okay. Okay. Jackie, don't tell her."

"Vu, she gonna know anyway. She aint' dumb!" Jackie said vehemently.

"Okay. You can tell her. Tell her I need her to know I'm okay. Tell her I love her."

I felt nauseous. Vu had always shielded me from the darkness of his world. If he had stopped pretending, if he had let the facade fall away, then I knew it was *bad*. *He asked for help.* Worse still was knowing that, even in his agony, he was thinking of *me*. And he wasn't okay.

A week later, through fevered breath and a broken system, through the crackle of an illicit phone, his voice reached me. Not strong and steady like before, but weak, unraveling. He didn't ask to be saved. He didn't have to. His words carried desperation. His friend held him up just to get him to the phone. Just to say my name.

It was worse than I'd let myself believe.

July 6, 2020. Babe, my feet are so swollen I can barely walk. Jordan had to help me get to the phones. I've had back pain for months but in the last couple weeks, it's gotten so bad that I can't sleep at all. I can't eat anything. I feel dizzy all the time. My voice is so hoarse the phone system didn't recognize my voice to let me call out. I'm glad it finally worked this time. I need your help calling medical. When you talk to them, get their name, and record the call if you can.

To advocate for him, I had to enter the labyrinth of prison healthcare—a system built not to heal but to delay, to dismiss, to deny. The deeper I dug, the more fury burned inside me.

Call after call. Pleading for and demanding a transfer. *Just get him to Galveston.* I wanted him sent to the University of Texas Medical Branch (UTMB) there, the one place in the entire Texas prison system equipped to treat severe medical issues by someone resembling real care. Let an actual doctor see him, someone with a specialization and a conscience. But every time I reached out, the Beto Unit met me with the same rehearsed dismissal. *We have your request. We'll get back to you.* That was their answer to everything. A bureaucratic lullaby in an attempt to pacify, not to help. Days passed. Then a few more. No follow-up. No urgency. No acknowledgment that a man's health was unraveling while they hid behind scripted lines and sometimes dead phone lines. Then I called the warden's office and left a message. They didn't call back, but the day after, I heard from Vu.

July 17, 2020. Babe, I love you. Please don't worry. They're finally gonna send me to Galveston. I'm in severe pain. But I'll see a specialist, so I'll be alright.

Relief should've followed, but rage hit instead.

"They didn't help until I collapsed," he said. "Nurse Reed just walked away. I told her, 'Fuck you. When I die, I'm haunting your bitch ass.' She hates Black Lives Matter. She's a racist piece of shit."

She left him crumpled on a filthy floor as if a man's body was abandoned paperwork. As if his pain was an interruption to her shift instead of the very reason she wore the uniform. In that moment, something hot and ancient rose in me—vengeance, or the closest thing a heart can summon when helplessness has nowhere left to go. She wasn't just a nurse; she was a symptom of a system trained to step over men like Vu, treating his suffering like routine debris.

After the call, I did what I usually do when fear threatens, I went looking for answers. Doughboy told me that getting sent to Galveston meant it was serious, an emergency. He'd been shipped there once for a broken jaw. The only consolation was that family could visit. But it was 2020. Hospitals, like many other spaces, were locked down. I called anyway, hoping. A woman on the line confirmed: yes, policy allowed visitors. But no, not now. Not during COVID.

The words landed like stones in my throat. I swallowed what I couldn't change and convinced myself it was something minor—kidney stones, gastritis, anything treatable. I had to fight the urge to consider a type of catastrophic condition that his brother Van had hinted to me. Van told me Vu had asked him about the symptoms of stomach cancer. That he'd read an article in *USA Today* about a lady's diagnosis and wanted to compare. I wrote it off. I needed to. I told myself it was his fear talking, his pain and delirium blurring the edges of reason. But part of me, quiet and trembling, recognized some truth beneath his inquiry: Sometimes the body knows before the world is willing to listen.

The next day, there were no calls, no updates, just the thick, nauseating quiet of not knowing. The weekend came and went. Silence.

Monday arrived, then slipped away, carrying nothing but unanswered questions. By Tuesday, my nerves were stripped down to wires, strung so tightly that every vibration of my phone sent a tremor through my body. I kept imagining worst-case scenarios until they blended together, a carousel of horrors. Then, at last, a call from a number with a Galveston area code flashed across the screen. My pulse spiked. My fingers fumbled so badly I nearly dropped the phone.

A calm, measured, professional voice greeted me. Too calm and too composed for what I sensed coming. "May I speak to Miss Thao Ha?"

"This is she."

"Hi, my name is Dr. Wilson from UTMB hospital in Galveston. Your boyfriend, Mr. Hoang Vu Tran, has been in my care."

I inhaled and held the breath inside me, waiting for him to continue.

"As you know, he was referred to us for severe stomach and back pain. We did several imaging scans and unfortunately discovered a mass in the pancreas. Based on the size of it, it's likely pancreatic cancer."

The words sliced like a blade—sharp, deep, unforgiving. *Pancreatic cancer.* My body trembled. The air thickened, pressing against my chest. My voice barely surfaced through the panic.

"Do you . . . do you know what stage it is?" I muttered.

"That's a good question. Given that we see masses in the nearby organs, the cancer has likely metastasized. Unfortunately, this means it's stage four."

Stage 4. The world tilted. My throat tightened, my breath shallow, unsteady. I pressed my fingers against my temple, gripping on to something, anything, to keep from falling into the abyss that had just opened beneath me.

"Okay . . . what are the next steps?" The words scraped out of me, fragile and weak.

"We'll do a biopsy to understand more about the cancer and what treatment options will be available. It will take a few days, so I'll call you again if that's okay with you. Mr. Tran said he would like you to be the primary contact."

"Yes, that's good with me." I swallowed hard, forcing down the terror clawing up my throat. I had to ask. I had to know. "What is the likelihood of survival?" A breath. Then, the truth I wasn't ready for.

"Honestly, it's terminal. Maybe up to a year. Depends on how far it's spread and if he responds to treatment."

Terminal. The word detonated inside me. It didn't feel real. It felt like the air had been sucked out of my world. "Okay," I whispered, barely audible. "I should . . . I should tell the family. And you'll call me back as soon as you know anything, please?" I begged.

"Yes. I'm sorry to give you such bad news. But we will do our best to take care of Mr. Tran."

"I do have another question. Because this is a prison hospital, is the treatment different from a free-world one? I'm wondering if there are options if we are willing to pay for it."

He didn't hesitate. "The hospital is affiliated with MD Anderson's cancer center. He'll get the same treatment as any free-world patient. I'm a doctor with UTMB, and I do work outside the prison. Please know he is in the best of care when it comes to cancer treatment. I want you to know, just because they're inmates, we don't see them as such. We don't know what they did or why they're in. We see them as patients. I promise you that."

"Thank you for the reassurance. I'll wait to hear from you again."

The call ended, and with it, a small, fragile world I believed I could keep together. Everything after was noise and not-noise, breath and not-breath. Everything blurred into a kind of trembling. Grief didn't show up quietly. It came like a thunderclap splitting the sky of my chest. There was no shushing it, no bargaining. It was a fuse already lit, a countdown without numbers, only the knowledge that it was winding down toward an end I could not stop. No mercy, no off-switch.

Just this horrific knowing. This brutal, awful knowing. He was dying. And the place he was dying in wasn't meant for life.

My hand released the phone before the rest of me understood what surrender meant. It hit the floor with a crack, like a door slamming shut on a future that evaporated. My knees gave out next, folding beneath me as if the earth itself had loosened. I wrapped my arms around my stomach like I could hold my insides in, as if pressing hard enough could keep the loss from breaking through and keep him inside me a little longer. But grief came anyway. Loud, tidal, full, and holy in its devastation. Screams rose of out me like a creature that had slept in the hollows of my body for decades, waiting for this precise moment to be awakened.

"My God, my God, my God. Oh my fucking God, why, why, why?!"

I'm sure it didn't even sound like language after a while. Only raw sound, stripped of meaning. Just syllables soaked in pain. Just a loop of sounds my lungs kept pushing out. My face was wet—heat, salt, desperation spilling faster than I could breathe. My shoulders rumbled like the grief was trying to beat its way out of me. I rocked. Forward and back. Forward and back. The way a child rocks in the dark when no one comes. As if motion alone might trick the pain into moving on. But it didn't. It stayed. Dug in deeper and rooted, burrowing until it anchored itself in the hollow where hope had been. Its dark tendrils coiled itself around my ribs and squeezed until my muscles seized and my limbs gave out. I slumped into the floor, palms down, knees cracked, face pressed to ground, like bowing deep, like protest, like surrender.

"God, why? Why is this happening?!"

And then, there was a softness. A small, steady weight against my side. I turned my head, and there was Pork Chop. Big black eyes, dark as night, staring at me like he knew. Like he knew what I'd lost and what was still being taken. He didn't make a sound. He just leaned in. Nudged his little furry face into the curve of my neck like he was trying to keep me from falling apart completely. I gathered him into my arms. Buried my face into his fur, letting myself vanish there, like he could hold the burden for however long grief might allow. My sobs shook both of us. I looked up at the ceiling and howled, raw and cracked and open, a howl torn open by love and terror and the unbearable truth taking shape inside me.

"He's gonna die, baby," I whispered into his fluffy ear, the words catching in my throat. "He's gonna die in prison."

I've got no memory of how long I lay curled like that, lost in the abyss of sorrow. Time had stopped, collapsed in on itself, like a star giving up its last light. But through the fog of devastation, a new thought cut through me. It pierced me clearly. *His family.* I had to tell them. I sat up suddenly, too fast, and the world swayed. I yanked the hem of my shirt and dragged it across my face to wipe the tears, the spit, and the snot—every grief that spilled out of me had drenched my face, my neck, my hair. My hands were shaking as I reached for the phone, dialing with trembling fingers. Jackie answered on the first ring.

The moment I spoke the words, the grief transferred like an electric current jumping from my chest into hers, sending Jackie into the same spiraling horror. A wail filled the receiver, raw, high, and unrestrained, disbelief and devastation colliding. We sobbed together, two women tumbling together through the same dark tunnel in a loop of insanity, neither of us able to find the bottom of this grief, no solid ground beneath us, just the freefall. "I have to go," Jackie choked out finally. "I have to tell the rest of the family."

She hung up, and silence settled in again, thick and suffocating. But even through the haze of my own sorrow, another sharp, clear, and heartbreaking thought. *His parents.* How could they bear this? Their beloved son, the one they had cried over for decades, the one they had prayed for and begged the world to return to them. The son they carried in their blood even when the world locked him away. He would not be coming home. His father had been right all along. The prison system had buried his son alive. And now, it would bury him dead.

I pressed my back against the wall, curling into myself, knees pulled tight against my chest. The trembling had quieted, replaced by stillness. My body had given up its fight against grief, surrendering instead to a paralysis so deep it felt like possibly death, too. A spiritual death, perhaps. A dimming of interior stardust. Tears continued their silent descent, tracing cold, damp paths along my skin. I thought of my family, but the thought of speaking to them, of forcing words through the torn place in my throat, felt impossible. Instead, my mind drifted to him alone in a prison hospital bed, suffering in a sterile, indifferent room. Surrounded by machines instead of love, fluorescent lights instead of faces, wires hooked into his wrist instead of warm hands. The thought plunged me into an abyss so dark, so fathomless, I feared I would never climb out of it. My heart crumbled into dust, splintering into the marrow of my bones, filling every hollow space inside me with agony.

I moved to the couch, pulling my knees into my body again, searching for some form of solace in the contortion. The room had grown cold, evening shadows settling in. I reached for the throw blanket draped over the armrest and wrapped myself in its softness, but warmth eluded me. Pork Chop hopped up beside me, his tiny warm body pressing against mine. His rhythmic breath and soft little snorts were the only sounds left in the house. I stroked his fur absentmindedly as daytime gave way to dusk, then dusk surrendered to darkness. The sky outside dissolved from a slate to black, swallowing the last remnants of light. I blinked heavily, my swollen eyes burning from the explosion of grief. My head fell against my knees, and I wept quiet, exhausted sobs that held the same refrain: *My precious Vu.*

He was suffering, trapped in the torment of both body and mind. And I could do nothing. No way to reach him. No way to hold him.

No way to console him. No way to whisper that somehow, everything would be all right. And in that helplessness, I realized I was trapped, too, alone in my own quarantine. Sealed off by COVID, by distance, by the invisibility of isolated suffering. No one could reach me either. No one could hold me or steady me or promise me I would survive this. Vu likely had the same crushing thoughts, probably wishing he could reach me, too. He and I were two people drowning in separate rooms, unreachable in different kinds of cages, without a way to call out for each other, without a way to comfort each other, without a way for either of us to break through. I drifted into a deadened state, somewhere between wakefulness and oblivion, unsure if sleep overtook me or if I was simply a zombie, awake but living dead. When I found consciousness, the world outside was still cloaked in midnight. It was dark and silent. I closed my eyes again, but the quiet kept speaking a sickening truth.

He has cancer. He is dying. He won't survive this.

I stayed awake inside a silence that wasn't silent at all. It was a space swollen with everything I couldn't say and everything I feared I'd have to say soon out loud. Pork Chop was still nestled beside me, his small frame tucked against my shin. His warmth was soothing, like the small flames of a campfire, subtle but steady. A fragile comfort in the wreckage of a living nightmare. I titled my head and placed it gently on his back. Tears streamed into my ears. I let them fall freely, let grief wash over me like tidewater reclaiming the shore. Eventually, it pulled me under again, and I cried myself back into the void.

There were no meetings on my calendar, no obligations taking up the morning. At 5:30 a.m., my phone alarm chimed as it always did. I reached for it, silencing its gentle insistence with a slow press of my finger. I did not rise. I let my body sink deeper into the quiet disaster of the morning after. For a moment, I lay there, absorbing the rare stillness of Wednesday mornings. Finally. I slept. And though it was only for an hour, it was merciful. In those roughly sixty minutes, slumber exorcised the demons of shock and disarray. I awakened with an alertness. There is only so much sorrow the human heart can hold before it revolts, before it rallies, demanding movement, demanding action. There was no more space for despondency. I had to do something. The hands of time would not wrangle me back into paralysis. Not when his life was slipping away with each passing second.

I called Jackie. Her voice was strained with grief thick in her breath. She told me their mother collapsed when she heard the news, choking on her tears, her body crumbling under the shock of the inevitable. The family was stunned into a silence that felt unnatural for their loud, loving, bustling home. Hearing of their suffering ignited me. It was a fire that burned through the haze of my own despair, torching the helplessness and clearing the way for conviction. I would not sit and wait for death to steal away what was left of our time with him.

Doing what I typically do when my world feels like it's caving in on itself, I went hunting for answers. Slipped into research mode like it might save him. Like it might save me. A friend who taught at UCLA, bless her, tapped into the UC library system like it was a hotline to medical school. She sent me everything I asked for, every medical journal, every peer-reviewed study, every microscopic footnote. I stored files until the download folder looked like a database for a dissertation. I copied every passage that felt like clues to a life-saving solution and pasted them into a document where I tried to craft a life-extending narrative. I wasn't just reading or studying; I was trying to rewrite a future. Trying to out-study grief. Trying to be the expert love needed me to be. Because when the system won't give you mercy, you dig into the cracks with your brain and hope something breaks loose. I had to find a way. Even if there wasn't one.

I dove headfirst into the cold, sterile language of pancreatic cancer. Neuroendocrine, Ki-67 proliferation index, somatostatin analogs, poorly differentiated, rare neoplasms. I rolled these clinical terms around in my head like maybe if I understood them deep enough, I could translate them into something human. Something hopeful. It wasn't just cancer. It was a pancreatic neuroendocrine tumor, extremely rare, slow-growing if you're lucky, silent until it isn't. Nonfunctioning, like the systems we were up against. Studies covered things like targeted therapies—everolimus, sunitinib—that seemed like magic pills he probably wouldn't even have access to. They said prognosis depends on staging, on whether it's resectable, on how fast it's multiplying, how far it's gone. I kept reading anyway. Had to. I kept digging for peer-reviewed hope, for some footnote that said: "He might live."

As I assembled the puzzle pieces and linked them to his medical records, the emerging picture was dismal. Stage 4: the cancer had spread to other parts of the body, not resectable. Ki-67 index: 95 out of 100, an ultra-fast rate at which cancer cells are dividing and multiplying. Poorly differentiated, nonfunctioning: does not produce hormones that cause recognizable syndromes, thus often diagnosed late.

How long does he have? Not much. What can we push for? Not much. What can we do to become the kind of person who can break down a door that won't open for people like us? Not much.

But . . . I refused to let them let him die alone in a cage like he didn't matter. Like he was just a number, a body, a line in some dusty-ass file nobody ever reads again. I wouldn't let the same system that almost broke his spirit be the one to bury his body. No. Not like that. I wanted him home. I needed him home. I needed him to die with his name in someone's mouth, not in a medical log. I wanted his last breath to be wrapped in love, not in fluorescent lights and cold concrete. I wanted his mama's voice nearby. I wanted *my* voice nearby. I wanted him held.

And if I couldn't save his life, I could damn sure try to *dignify* his dying.

So I turned to the law. Not because I believed in it. But because it is the only language the system is willing to hear. I dug through statutes and case law like maybe somewhere in all that cruel bureaucracy, there might be room for mercy. I found stories of men let out with bad lungs and weak hearts because COVID might get to them before the state could. If they could show compassion for that, surely they could show it for this. Because this was cancer. *Cancer is COVID's older, meaner cousin.* It eats everything. It doesn't wait for permission.

"Compassionate release." That's what they called it. What a fucking joke. The criminal justice system is not designed to hold pain gently or to make room for repair. It was built to punish, to disappear, to warehouse bodies marked as disposable. Compassion doesn't live in places where grown men die on cold floors while nurses look away. It doesn't live in solitary cells where people scream into walls that never answer back. It sure as hell doesn't live in paperwork that takes months to approve a Tylenol or denies a dying man the right to say goodbye.

They call it "corrections," but what are they correcting? Grief? Poverty? Survival? Trauma passed down and weaponized? The only thing getting corrected is a person's access to dignity. To autonomy. To being seen as human. Compassion would mean recognizing that harm doesn't get healed through cages and that no one gets better by being broken. But the system isn't interested in better. It's interested in control. In silence. In punishment as profit. In punishment as policy. In punishment as spectacle.

Let's not be fooled with the buzzword *compassionate release*. It's soft language made to pad the edges of violence. Because at the core of it, this system is not about humanity. It's about managing death. It's about making people disappear and calling it justice. And if compassion exists in that place, it isn't because of the system. It's despite it. It's the people on the inside who still choose to love. Still choose to protect each other. Still choose to hope. That's where humanity is.

Compassionate release is a phrase made to sound tender so that the public don't choke on the truth. There's nothing compassionate about the way they let bodies rot in cells while the world keeps spinning. Nothing humane about a Nurse Reed standing over him while he writhed on the floor and choosing not to care. Choosing not to see him. I can still feel the heat in my chest when I heard how she sneered at his pain like he deserved it.

My hands curled into fists before I even knew it. This wasn't just about him anymore. This was about all of them. Every person in the system who tried to make him invisible. Every breath that was stolen in silence. Every dying moment that should've been met with a hand, a prayer, and a name.

This fight was about justice. About dignity. About making sure the forgotten are remembered before they become ghosts.

The legal path ahead was clear, yet uncertain. We chose the Medical Release with Intensive Supervision (MRIS), which is essentially medical parole. A week after that first devastating call, Dr. Wilson phoned again. His voice was steady and clinical, delivering a truth that felt like a dagger. The pancreatic neuroendocrine tumor had spread to the stomach, the kidney, the liver, and the lymph nodes. It was a stage-4 death sentence. Eight months, he said. Maybe more. Maybe less.

And then, a gift. A rare permission. Dr. Wilson authorized a phone call. More than that. It was a video call. When the screen flickered to life, my chest momentarily lifted up and out at the sight of his face. The contours I had memorized, the eyes that always held something unspoken. A prison guard's phone was our bridge across time and distance, across sickness and sorrow. I wanted to press my fingers against the screen, to trace his face, to pull him through the pixels and into my arms. But even in this moment, even with the cruel countdown hanging between us, he had his own ideas.

"Baby, they said I got eight months left. I wanna go back to Beto so I can talk to you and my family on the phone. They don't have phones here at the hospital, so these calls they givin' us are rare. If all I got is eight months, let me do that time with access to the phones."

"No, babe." My voice was sharp, urgent. "COVID is still spreading. And it's hot as hell right now. At least you have AC in the hospital. And eight months is only an estimate. You could live longer. Dr. Wilson told me they were going to give you treatment like any patient in the free world. Please, do not ask to go back to Beto."

I knew that inmates had the right to refuse treatment and sign themselves back to their home unit, to die in the shadows of concrete and steel. He could have ignored me. He could have made his own choice. But he listened.

"Okay, baby. I will do this for you. I will try this chemo thing," he said, his voice soft, uncertain. "But I heard chemo can kill you."

"The cancer is already killing you," I said, my voice gentler now, cradling the truth as softly as I could. "Chemo will be hard, but you are strong, and you have to fight through this. I'm gonna get you a lawyer and request a medical parole."

"No, baby." A pause. A sigh. "I can't put that burden on you and my family. Lawyers are bloodsucking thieves. My family spent so much money on me, and look at me. I wasted it."

"Please." My plea was quiet, desperate. "Let me and your family figure this out, okay, love? I need you to understand and just let us take care of you."

A silence stretched between us, heavy but full of understanding. When he finally spoke, his voice was barely above a whisper. "Okay, baby. I trust you."

Later, Jackie asked if I had cried when I saw his face on the screen.

I didn't cry in that moment. Not when we were connected. Instead, we smiled, we laughed, we clung to the sheer joy of hearing each other's voices, of looking into each other's eyes through that narrow frame. I took screenshots of the call, capturing the way his eyes crinkled above the mask, the way they still smiled.

"You're beautiful," he told me.

"I miss seeing your handsome face," I told him.

"I love you," we said, unison.

Within days of that conversation, his family had arranged a call for me with a parole attorney in Austin, one who had handled MRIS cases before. His voice was steady, practiced, full of the kind of measured confidence that lawyers always seem to have. He assured me there was a strong case for release given the conditions we had laid out. I knew better than to trust a lawyer's optimism, but I had to believe him. Even if he was wrong, we had to try.

The cost was staggering—a minimum $40,000 to file the writ, with additional fees for medical expert witnesses. But the attorney had connections, he said. One of the nation's top specialists in Vu's type of cancer. The kind of doctor who could testify in a way that the parole board would have to take seriously. Hope sparked in me, fragile but bright. Days later, chemotherapy was scheduled. A small step toward the impossible dream of survival. But nature, indifferent and cruel, had other plans. A hurricane barreled toward Galveston's shore, thrashing against the city with wind and water, a force that felt personal in its timing, in its intrusion. I called Jackie to update her. The defeat in her voice was immediate, thick with exasperation.

"Sis, it's like nothing ever goes Vu's way. He's fucking dying of cancer. You said it's an aggressive one. And the day he's supposed to start treatment, they cancel because of a fuckin' hurricane. Like what the actual fuck?"

I felt the same fury. The same helplessness. But something in me, some stubborn, desperate belief, kept whispering that it would be all right. I called the hospital and asked to speak with Dr. Wilson. A day later, he returned my call. His voice was calm, reassuring. Once the storm passed, treatment would resume immediately.

"What if the power goes out?" I pressed.

He promised the hospital had generators, that the machines and medicines would not stop, and that Vu would not be left in the dark. And for once, a promise held true. A nurse practitioner called soon after the storm settled to confirm that chemotherapy had begun. He had tolerated it, and they would monitor his body's response. I clung to that update like a lifeline, a small victory in a war I knew we were losing. Then, another gift. A rare FaceTime call. His family saw his face and heard his voice. When Jackie called to tell me about it, her words were careful, hesitant.

"He told us not to put up the money for the lawyer," she said.

My stomach clenched. I knew him too well. He had agreed to it with me, but he had probably spent days thinking about it, letting the guilt settle in. He couldn't bear the thought of his family carrying that financial burden again. Not after all they had already lost his court cases. Jackie sighed, frustration laced with love.

"We're not listening to him," she said. "We're gonna find a way to get it, even if we have to sell the damn house."

His parents had already made their decision. They had been saving for years, waiting for the day they could do something for him. They would use that money to bring him home. If love alone could have freed him, he would have been walking through the gates that very moment.

I couldn't stop thinking about the money after my conversation with Jackie. It wasn't about whether his family could pull together the resources. I knew they could and they would. The struggle that weighed heavy on my heart was knowing how much it pained him to be a burden. He carried guilt like an anchor, dragging it through the years, convinced that every sacrifice his family made for him was undeserved. I thought about offering to pay, but I knew there was no way in hell he would accept that. His pride was sewn into every part of his being. His family, undeterred, pressed forward, pooling the money and securing the attorney. But even as things moved forward, I felt stuck. What would this do to him? The mind of a cancer patient had to be fortified and resilient enough to withstand the ruthless war being waged inside his body. Chemotherapy was not just an assault on the cancer, but an unraveling of the self, stripping strength, diminishing will. His spirit needed to be whole if his body had any chance at surviving.

Then the attorney called. Said he'd met with Vu. Said it was worse than he thought. Said Vu told him reading was a struggle now. Letters blurring, pages dancing out of reach. Said he was in a wheelchair, couldn't stand long, couldn't make it to the bathroom without help. That split something in me. Not snapped. *Split.* Like grief finding a new corner to crawl into. There wasn't time for guilt anymore. Not his. Not mine. Whatever pride had kept him from asking, whatever hesitation I still held, I had to let it go. He couldn't carry this alone. Couldn't *fight* this alone.

Then came the doctors, holding words like weapons wrapped in white coats. Said the chemo slowed things down, *maybe just a bit*, but it didn't shrink the tumor. Didn't reverse a damn thing. The cancer was still there, slithering its way through him, his stomach, his kidney, liver, lymph nodes. And now, maybe his brain. They said a lumbar puncture could confirm it.

I should have known. The way he struggled to read. The way his words stumbled. The way his letters, once meticulous and written in the calculated perfection of a man who had spent decades with nothing but time, had become scattered, uncertain. A letter arrived from him while he was still in the hospital. I hesitated before opening it, fearing what I might find. His handwriting, always so careful, so deliberate, was now deathlike on the page, letters malformed, as if his hands no longer obeyed him. His words, once fluid and precise, were tangled in confusion, sentences breaking where they never had before. It was as if I was witnessing the slow unraveling of the man I loved.

Hi, Love.

At the moment, I don't understand a thing. All I understand is the pain and suffering. What's most that's important to me is the decision you make for yourself and my family. Babe, I hope you think clearly and know what you are up against. The first months I thought this is the worst that's to going to happen to me. I am wrong. Babe, it's very important that I can talk to you. Please make it happen because that's the only you can understand me. Can tell by my writing. Or at least get my lawyer to talk to me. I need for things get back normal so at least get back to my unit if nothing else at least used the phone and hear your voice. After the first month, I didn't know what to do. I wasn't even able to read your letters or understand. When I did start to understand, all I did was cried. What true cannot be denied. Babe, everytime I started picking up the paper, I start crying all over once again. Whatever you decide is always ok with me. Remember I'll love you with my life. Please know I truly love you. One thing you should always know, I'll always cried over us.

After reading his letter, I wept. Not just for him, but with him. His pain, his fear, his reluctant hope that bled through every word. It stained the page with the blots of his suffering. I shared the letter with his family, and there was no hesitation in their response. Desperation fueled them.

They wanted to proceed, to push forward, to leave no stone unturned. There was no room for doubt.

Late into the night, I pored over every piece of legal information I could find, my mind tangled in the red tape of a system designed to keep him ensnared. A medical release was not freedom just yet. It was only a crack in the door, and even that came with shackles. He had the deportation order. And that order sat like a shadow over every word I read. Because even if he was granted compassionate release, even if the state finally acknowledged the truth of his dying body, he would not be going home. In the federal system, a deportation order meant ICE would be waiting at the gates to detain him, to take him to another cage. That realization sent a chill through me. Even in his dying days, they would not let him leave their legal grasp. There would be no recognition of the human being unraveling in front of them. His body, frail and failing, still had a heartbeat, and he would simply be handed off from state prison to ICE detention, like passing along a package instead of a dying man.

If we had any chance of truly bringing him home, we would need more than a medical parole attorney. We would also need an immigration lawyer, someone who knew the intricacies of deportation defense, someone who could fight to keep him from being detained at the gates of freedom. The next morning, I called a friend in Dallas, an immigration attorney. He explained the complexities and the legal maneuvers we could attempt. He offered to do it pro bono. I wanted to argue, to insist on paying him, but he refused.

"There's a way," he said, his voice measured, careful. "An attorney can physically show up at the release site and, if ICE is there, make a case on the spot. Sometimes, for reasons we don't understand, ICE doesn't even show. It's random."

Random. I didn't trust random. Not when every step of this journey had been shadowed by systemic cruelty. I couldn't afford to rely on chance.

My friend hesitated before adding, "There's just one issue. If I go, they might not listen. I'm Vietnamese. Sometimes, law enforcement . . . well, they don't respect us the way they do white men. If an older white attorney shows up, they're more likely to defer."

It didn't surprise me. But it cut anyway. Even in death, whiteness held the key to mercy like it was something always earned. I couldn't risk it. I called the attorney handling the medical parole and asked for a name. He gave it without hesitation. I searched the name. An older white man. Pale eyes. A mouth used to being listened to. When we spoke, his voice was calm, practiced, and certain. His fee was $10,000. So now, the cost of his freedom, *just to die outside a cage*, was over $50,000.

And yes, it was worth it. Of course it was.

But still, the thought of Vu knowing, *truly knowing*, the price, the hours we'd work, the things we'd give up, the weight his impending death would place on the backs of those who loved him most, it made something twist in me. Like a knot in a rope pulled too tight, holding but barely.

I called Jackie. She heard me, the quiet fear behind my words. Vu would see himself as a burden. Again. When he was young and fighting for freedom, he thought it was worth it. But this burden wouldn't be worth it to him. He was dying anyway. Why fight it? Why spend so much after already spending so much on a chance that was slim to none anyway? *Let me die. Let me die without bearing the guilt of my family's sacrifices. Let me die knowing it would bring me peace not to be an encumbrance.*

She agreed. And it was her idea to start the GoFundMe. A kind of reaching. A way to say, *We're not alone, Vu. It's not our money. It's someone else's.* "Write it, sis. Please." she pleaded.

I recoiled at the thought. I hated even thinking about it. The asking. The *needing*. I wasn't built for that kind of vulnerability, especially not when it came dressed as public desperation. It wasn't like his family didn't have the money. They did. And they were ready to pay every last dime. GoFundMe was for folks who had nothing left. Folks drowning. This didn't feel like *that*.

Or maybe it did. Maybe I just didn't want to admit it.

I sat there in the density of my own discomfort, choking on pride, trying to dress it up as principle. Sat with the shame of asking, the weight of wanting to believe we could carry this alone. And then I read his letter again. Heard his voice again—tired, soft, full of that kind of reluctant grief that doesn't show up in tears but in the way a sentence dies halfway through. He didn't want to be an albatross. And I realized—if asking, if *begging*, could lift even a sliver of that weight off him . . . if it could make him feel even a little less guilty, a little more free, even now, then fuck it. I'd do it.

I'd do anything to make him feel lighter. Happier. Less alone in all this. Less of an albatross.

So I swallowed the pride that had been embedded in my psyche for most of my life and wrote it all down. That first draft? It was fire and fury. I wrote like the words could burn a hole through the system. I wanted folks to *feel* it. To see what it meant for him to take the fall for Trí. To sit in a cage for a crime that wasn't his, because silence was loyalty, and loyalty was survival, and survival always came at the cost of someone like him. I tried to make the whole thing about justice. Tried to write it like a case file mixed with a sermon. Tried to beg people to hate the system and hate Trí as much as I did. To rage like I raged.

Jackie read it. She didn't like it. "Sis, this isn't you. You're not an angry person. And Vu already forgave Tri, remember? I don't think people are going to be interested."

I didn't know how to respond. I stayed quiet. Then she continued, "You want to know what I want to know? I want to know why you love my brother so much. Look at you. You're educated, beautiful, accomplished, make movies, give to charity, and inspire people to be better. You can get anyone you want. So why the hell do you love my brother so much? Why do you spend all your waking time trying to be a cancer doctor and then a lawyer when you're already a professor with a PhD? Why do you love him, sis? Why are you doing all this for him? If you write about that, I think people will want to give. Because if they understood why you love him, maybe they'll love him, too."

Clarity.

In the final version, I confessed every messy, beautiful, tragic thing about us. I laid it bare. Our love, our ache, our last-ditch hope for time. I wrote for the hope that people might love him for the reasons I did. To understand the boy he once was, the man he was becoming, the light he carried while in the darkness of incarceration, and the life disappearing inside him. To know our beginning, our separation, and our reunion. To ask for a gift, a final act of love—the gift of letting him die with dignity. I wrote it in a blog post and linked it in the GoFundMe page. I asked the world to help bring him home. And they answered. Not just with donations—though more than $70,000 poured in, a tidal wave of generosity I could never have anticipated—but with care, with attention, and with a reach that stretched far beyond anything I imagined. The blog went viral, passed from device to device, country to country, heart to heart. People from all walks of life and all over the world sent messages to share that they cried, that they prayed, and that they had never seen love held up against a system like that.

I wanted Vu to know what had happened. I wanted him to know we got the kind of money that would not just meet the receipts but also ease him from the distress of being a burden on us. Most of all, I wanted him to know that he was loved, that people cheered for him and rooted for us, that one of the donors called it an epic love story. I printed the blog and the comments with a note to ask a nurse to read it to him. I sealed the envelope and mailed it to him—a thick stack of love letters to the Dirty South.

17

Smile for Me When It's Over

CANCER IS A MOTHERFUCKER. IT wrecks the body the way termites take a house, quietly at first, tunneling through the beams you thought were solid, until one day you touch a wall and realize it's soft, hollow, and already gone. It wrecks the spirit in a more violent way, like a robber who kicks the door off its frame and storms straight in, grabbing what it wants with both hands—your calm, your courage, and the sense that the world is still yours to shape. It overturns the furniture of your mind, rips open drawers you'd kept sealed for years, and shouts its violence into every quiet corner. Your spirit is utterly violated as the part of you that once believed in tomorrow realizes it's been expertly robbed.

I kept asking him to hang on. Just hold tight a little longer. As if endurance could be summoned the way a commander calls in his troops. I don't know if I believed it myself or if I just needed to say something that didn't feel like goodbye. Hope is a strange reflex. You repeat it the way you check a locked door, knowing full well the house has nothing of value in it. Then one night, my phone lit up a little past

10 p.m. I froze when I saw the area code. It was after midnight where he was. I answered.

The screen opened to darkness, except for his face, washed in the soft white of a hospital lamp. I heard a nurse hovered behind him say, gently, "Go ahead, Mr. Tran, she's on the line." She shifted the angle of the light, trying to help him see me better. I watched patiently as he tried to lift his head. His voice came out cracked, like it had been scraped against gravel to get to me. His face, my God. It was sunken, collapsed on itself, hollow in a way I wasn't ready for. His cheeks scooped out, his eyes floating in the hollows. Like his bones had started to whisper through his skin. It hurt me in places I didn't even know could ache. It's a particular ache that comes when you watch someone you love dying on a phone screen in real time, pixel by pixel, breath by breath. You think you're prepared, maybe you've rehearsed moments like this in your mind. But nothing prepares you for the sight of someone slipping away while you're helpless holding a phone like it's a lifeline instead of as an instrument of witness. It changes you. Not in the poetic way we sometimes think we could claim. But in the blunt, clinical way, permanently and without permission.

The nurse didn't have to let the call happen. But she did. Maybe it was professional humanitarianism, or maybe she recognized the look in his eyes, the kind of fear that doesn't respond to anything in a hospital cart. They weren't treating him anymore. No more procedures. No more optimistic schedules taped to the wall. No more promises. Just "transitioning." That's what he said, "They're transitioning me." He told me they put him in a van to move to hospice. Somewhere between the van and the rolling bed, he fell.

He said he was scared. He couldn't walk. Couldn't sit. Couldn't eat. The cancer had touched everything. Pancreas, stomach, liver, adrenal glands, his neck, his lymph nodes, his brain, his bones, his skin. He kept scratching his face from the itch. His body was giving up piece by piece. He'd lost forty pounds, almost 20 percent of himself gone. They call it cachexia. What a cold, clinical word. One-third of cancer patients die from it. When your body just wastes away. It gives up the grand project of being alive. Nobody tells you that when they say, "We're doing all we can."

"Baby, I'm trying to eat, but it hurts so bad," he said. "I need help using the restroom. I can't do anything myself. I just lay here."

That was the moment I broke. The first time I cried in front of him. I'd been holding it down for weeks, showing up with a smile, performing competence and calm, and acting like my strength could pull us both through. The steady tone, the brave little scripts—I wore it all like armor. But his voice undid me. It had the unmistakable quality of someone trying to wrap love around surrender. And the way his face held a kind of stillness that wasn't peace. Just the exhaustion of a man who had reached the limit of what a human body can endure. I clenched my jaw, pushed the hurt back where it came from, and reversed the tears by force of will. I smiled, but it wasn't real. It was the smile you had to put on, like armor that had already been dented one too many times.

"I'm so sorry you're suffering so much, babe," I said. "You still look so handsome to me." He smiled. Weak, but real. The kind of smile that says *I needed that more than I knew*. "I'll start making calls first thing in the morning. I'll do what I can, I promise. I love you, honey."

Then he said it. Soft, shaky, but clear, "Babe, I can't take it much longer. I feel like the end is near. I need you to call them tomorrow and please ask them to do something for me."

I already knew. Didn't need him to say it. Sometimes the most loving thing you can do is not deny the truth. Not smother it in hope just because you're scared of what it means. Folks say you should never speak death into the room. But I believed in honoring pain. In telling the truth back.

"I'm so sorry you're suffering like this," I told him. "If you feel the end is near, I understand. You do what you need, please. If you have to let go, then let go." That's when the tears came, hot and fast. I didn't try to stop them this time.

"Babe, don't cry, please," he whispered. "It's okay. I'll be fine. Just need you to push for me so I can come home to you, okay? I just wanted you to know how I'm feeling because I'll always be truthful to you. I do feel a lot of pain. But I promise I'll keep fighting for you."

That was him. Even at the edge, still thinking about me. Still holding on for love.

I tried. I swear to God, I tried. I called every number I could find in their directory—UTMB Oncology, Chief Medical Officer, Chief Nursing Officer, Vice President of Clinical Support Services, Inpatient Operations, Hospice Coordinator, and more. I begged. I pleaded. I asked for anything that sounded remotely like help. *Can he be reevaluated? Can you transfer him sooner? Can you give him stronger pain medication? Can you give him a feeding tube? Does someone check on him more than once a day?*

I begged. I pleaded. I didn't care how desperate I sounded. But the responses were flat and routine, coming from the voices of people whose daily protocols and regimens outweighed their emotions. Their humanity was held hostage in the iron cage of bureaucracy. *We did what we could. He's already been evaluated. Pain management has been ordered. He's on an IV drip. You'll have to wait for the next medical review. You'll have to wait for the next scheduled hospice transfer. I'm sorry, ma'am, there's nothing more we can do to save him.* All we had left was the attorney's word that a hearing was coming soon. *Soon.* Whatever that meant. *Soon* is a useless word when someone you love is running out of hours.

I'll never forget that third call. It was a week after the last one. The corrections officer said we had five minutes. That was it. Time portioned out like rations. Vu asked her for more. She said no and said she had work to do.

I watched him scratch his face, then scratch his temples, small frantic movements. His hand and fingers looked fragile, thinned by the miles of cancer crawling underneath. Then he pinched his temples, like he was trying to hold his head together, as if something inside was trying to pry it open. And still, he kept his eyes wide open, focused on me. Like he wanted to memorize me just in case he'd never get another chance. Then, he wiped a tear from his eye.

His voice cracked through the static. "Babe, they're sending me to hospice. I'm in so much pain. I got like eight cancers. Even brain cancer. I can't think right. Can't even read your letters. I don't think I can do this no more. I tried for you, but I can't live like this much longer. If I go, they ain't gonna save me. I don't want them to break my ribs. I signed the DNR. I'm sorry, babe."

I replied with words I'll always remember because you never forget what you say when you're terrified it might be the last time someone you love hears you. "Listen to me, babe. Do not say sorry. I need you to hear this. Can you hear me clearly?"

He nodded.

"I love you so much. I have loved since the moment we laid eyes on each other twenty-eight years ago in that karaoke room. I will always love you as my future continues, and never without you, because you run through my veins and into my heart and throughout every fiber of my being. I can feel you, babe. You are always with me. And because I love you more than I could ever say in words, I want you to understand what my actions are saying when it comes to you. My love, I will be okay with whatever you feel is best for you. Please do what you must, even if that means you have to let go so you can have peace. I will stay strong and accept whatever happens, whenever it happens. Fight or go in peace, it's okay with me. You have fought so hard already. You've hung on this long. Thank you for fighting. Thank you for being so brave. You are so handsome and such a beautiful person to me. When it's your time to let go and you come to the place that will bring you peace, remember these words as my last words to you here on earth. Sweetheart, you best damn visit me in my dreams and let me feel your presence. I'll take you in any form. Know that I'll be there someday, too. Do you remember the lyrics of that country song you wrote to me back then about two people always waiting for each other? You wrote that because you always wanted to be romantic. It was your way of asking me to wait for you. Well, it's going to be your turn to wait for me now. I promise, when it's my time, I'll come search for you. I'll see you on the other side. I love you so much."

There are goodbyes that announce themselves. With ceremony. With closure. With time.

Sometimes, there's no goodbye. Unexpected death. Unannounced.

And then there's something in between. There are the goodbyes that arrive already in motion before you know how to name them. I'll never forget how it hurt to say goodbye without *saying goodbye*. I started sobbing so hard, the kind of crying that folds the sounds of desperation into shaking. I don't know if he made sense of what I just said or what made it through in the blur between us. I wanted to stop crying. I punched down on my pain. I never wanted him to see me like that. Not because I was ashamed of the tears, but because I knew they would make him sad. Like last time. When my pain became his, and neither of us could carry it without making the other stumble. So I breathed in. Deep and sharp. Pulled the ache back into my spine, stopped crying, and found the words I needed.

"I need you to know," I said, slowly, each syllable balanced on the edge of my breath, "until it's truly over, I'll keep fighting for you out here. I still got the lawyers. We're still trying to bring you home."

And then, like he always did, like love still gave him just enough air to be mischievous, he tilted his head, the corner of his mouth curling into a smirk. A spark in the fading. “Bring me home,” he said. “Is home heaven?”

I smiled. Had to. His smile made mine bloom like reflex. Then he laughed, and his laugh opened something in me that had been closed for days.

“Home is to Mom and Dad,” I said. “But if you don’t make it there . . . Heaven is a beautiful home, too. It’s a place of love. Of peace. No pain.”

His eyes changed. He got that look they always did, the one that made time slow, made everything outside the moment fall away. He paused, holding the space before the truth. “Babe . . . I just wish I was with you. You are my home. I’m sorry I’m probably not gonna make it home to you. This shit sucks, doesn’t it?”

“No, don’t apologize, my sweet love,” I whispered. “They say home is where the heart is. And since our hearts are still with each other . . . we’re already home.”

“You right,” he said. “You always right. Baby, smile for me when this is over. I love you so much.”

The officer had been off camera as a silent witness. But when she turned the screen to her masked face, I saw tears carving soft trails down her cheeks. I thanked her for the extra time. With a trembling voice, she said, “No problem, sweetie. Y’all take care of yourselves.”

She had heard every word. She understood it wasn’t just a video call. It was a letting go, wrapped in tenderness. A prayer disguised as conversation. A kind of bedside vigil, if you can call a rectangle of glass a bedside. I looked at the call log after it ended. Thirteen minutes. Enough time for a lifetime, folded into a goodbye.

Five days later. I was having lunch when my phone rang. It was Vu’s mom’s number. I was hoping they were on the line with him, perhaps he had gotten safely to the Michael Unit prison hospice. When I picked up, I heard his nephew’s pain filled voice, “Bác Thảo, I’m sorry. I’m so sorry, but Bác Vũ is gone.”

The phone slipped from my hand. Not dropped, *slipped*, like my body had already begun to unfasten from the world before I knew what to name it. I slumped into the chair, or maybe the chair rose to catch me. It's hard to say. Grief plays tricks like that. I wish I could sit here and describe it pretty. Give y'all some elegant and poetic metaphor for heartbreak. I want to tell you what it felt like, the color and texture of the moment, the shape of the grief with its weight and edges. But all I can give you is the truth. And the truth is, I couldn't feel a damn thing at first. Perhaps because I'd spent most of my life building myself out of numbness, layer by layer, year by year, heartache after heartache, disappointment after disappointment. Grief didn't arrive as pain. I don't remember feeling it. Not fully. I know it was there, waiting, but I did not greet it.

I had spent a lifetime running drills. Rehearsing detachment like a dance. After learning at a young age to express pain through violence and savagery, I relearned to withhold it instead. My adaptation was to mute pain before it breached the surface, to press it down, smooth it out, and bury it under tasks. Under survival, I had trained my mind to shut the doors my heart kept trying to pry open. So, when it came, the horrifying news, my mind did what I had taught it to do. To shut down the human part and power up the machine. Task mode. Robot mode. Because the alternative? Letting the unfiltered and unedited version of grief strike me all at once? It would've killed me right there. I swear, it would've.

He was dead.

And as chilling as that sentence sounds, what scared me more was remembering how fast my brain jumped into motion. Not into mourning. Not into screaming. Just . . . the next duty. The next assignment. I became efficient. Almost cold. Like walking through a wildfire with my eyes locked on a compass, searching for direction, not noticing the smoke and ash filling my lungs.

The grief was too large, too loud, so I quieted myself into tasks. Pork Chop hovered nearby, sensing the shift before I could name it. He followed me from room to room, watching with worried eyes, nudging my leg every so often as if reminding to stay tethered to something living. When I sat down to make the calls, he settled against my feet like an anchor.

I called Melinda at Brookside Funeral Services. I signed and emailed the forms—the ones I had prepared when I knew the end was near. I handled the preparations, paid the fees, arranged the funeral logistics. Death certificates, timelines, bureaucracies stacked like hundreds of manila folders on the desk of a tidy clerk.

A week before he passed, the medical expert hired for a hearing that would never come sent his report. He said Vu maybe had a month. More likely only weeks. The sentences were written like a countdown. In the stillness after reading it, I called Jackie. I told her we needed to begin his funeral arrangements. Not because we had given up, but because the body doesn't wait. Because the state doesn't pause. And because death is a business. If you preplan and prepay before the death, you save 15 percent.

His parents, still holding on to hope like it was a life raft, didn't want to hear it out. I told them that preplanning helps us stay present. Helps us take care of him, now. Just in case. When they hesitated, I did the unthinkable. I said I'd do it without them. They folded, their hearts reluctantly moved toward pragmatism the way trees bend in a hurricane, by force. We moved together in the strange choreography of death preparation. The purchase of the plot. The casket. The flowers. A white carriage. A white horse. To carry him where his body would rest. To remind the world that he was worthy of beauty even in goodbye. When his date of death came, September 12, 2020, the preparation was done.

Preplanning was a critical timesaver because even after his death, he wasn't fully free from the state. This was a death in prison, and in prison, even your passing comes with paperwork. Even your peace comes with policy. You're on the clock. You're racing against the system just to give someone you love a decent goodbye. There were still rules. Still countdowns. Still deadlines dressed as policy. They said, *Claim him within thirty days, or we'll bury him on state ground.* If you don't get shit taken care of in thirty days, the Texas prison system will bury your loved one in a state-owned plot next to the other dead prisoners whose families didn't have the means to pay or the efficiency to arrange for dignity. His stone would be stamped with his name and a prison ID: 801576. Stern. Bureaucratic. Final. How does anyone prepare for that kind of urgency? How does a family, already broken, meet those terms?

We had been prepared. The funeral home arranged to pick him up from the state medical examiner's office two hours away. I persuaded his family to drive to the site and witness him officially leaving state custody. He departed the system's gates in a hearse.

We chose the church, the priest, and the prayers. The agendas for the viewing, the wake, and the burial. The guests, the travel, and the lodging. The music, the speeches, and the outfits, including his—a dark blue suit. The program design, the obituary, and the eulogy—all of which were assigned to me. I was given a directive by his parents. Do not mention his incarceration. To shrink a life into a page that expresses the truth of his circumstances while honoring his parents' demands . . . how do you do that without rage, without inner violence? I remember the anger. It came back like muscle memory. Rage, that old, familiar shape that I didn't ask for, but it returned anyway. It was curled inside the hollow where grief couldn't reach. Rage at the journey he had walked so bravely and also, at times, so woefully buried in guilt and shame. The miles of confinement, of illness, and of stolen time in the name of rehabilitation. What killed him? Was it cancer? Or was it prison? Cancer took the future, yes. And prison took what came before it. Fuck you, cancer. And fuck you, prison system.

Yet, among all the to-dos and the fury, I remember, in that moment, being strangely grateful for Texas. From a young age, I was drawn to California for its beautiful landscape and impeccable climate. As an adult, I've grounded myself in its pockets of progressive politics and its perceived mercy. But during the pandemic, California closed its graves. No in-person funerals. And no rituals of passage. A friend in San Diego never got to bury his father. But in Texas, we could. We could gather. We could watch the earth receive him. We could say goodbye with our bodies present. And that mattered. Because death is not just an ending. It's a witness. And we showed up to witness. To speak his name above ground. To say, in this brutal country, he lived. And we loved him.

And others did, too.

Even in the dread and in the fine-tuned machine of my avoidant task-taking, there were moments that were luminous and melted the steel in my soul so that I could feel again and cherish the understanding that he was loved. Small mercies. Quiet openings. Too many to name. Too many to carry. But one stayed with me.

The nurse who cared for him in his last weeks, she reached out to me. A text message, plain and unexpected. But her words opened something. A kind of light. She told me stories. Tiny stitches in the vast wound. She said he smiled a lot, even through the pain that made breathing feel like punishment. Even when the morphine didn't work. He laughed. He joked. He thanked them. The doctors, the nurses, the aides, every hand that touched his failing body, he met with grace.

He talked about us. She said his voice changed when he spoke of his family. Of me. Like memory was a soft room he could still enter.

She said he cried when someone read my letters aloud. That when the words broke, he did, too. That he cried when he knew the treatments were failing. When the sentence shifted from "fight" to "hospice." And even then, he found a way to hold divinity close. He said he was ready. That he would watch over them from heaven.

She told me that caring for him was a gift. That people like him made her proud to be a nurse in prison, a place most people try to forget. That she would keep fighting for patients like him, the ones waiting for mercy in places where mercy is rationed.

And in her words, I saw him again.

The way he could connect, even from a bed of agony. The way he left a mark without ever lifting his voice. That was him. That's how he loved—gentle, wide, deep, persistent.

When I wrote a blog to announce his passing, people who had donated to the GoFundMe and people I'd never from before wrote to me. Strangers from across oceans, across languages, across borders that never knew his name, still felt the shape of his absence. They said they cried. Said they saw themselves in him. In me. In us. Said the world lost someone who made it gentler.

And I think that's the truest thing I can say about his passing.

It wasn't just his voice. It was him. The way he was made of ache and kindness, of scar and song. He left, and still, he stayed. Because some souls don't vanish. They just scatter. Into letters, into air, into songs, into every person who remembers how it felt to be loved by him, to be touched by his story and his life, even for a moment.

One of my final tasks was writing the eulogy—ten minutes to speak about him as if language could hold everything we had lost. Each word was a needle passing through skin, trying to sew memory to paper without making it bleed too much. But this, man, this was something else. A eulogy is not a story. It is a spell. A last offering. A bridge between what was and what still aches. For days, I couldn't do it. I sat in silence so loud it hurt. I turned sentences over in my palms like stones. Too smooth. Too sharp. Nothing fit.

And then, on the flight to Houston for the funeral, something opened. Maybe it was the sky, the way the clouds gathered like hands reaching up instead of down. Maybe it was the way the air thinned at altitude, leaving only what mattered. I don't know. But I felt him. Felt him not in words, but in breath. And when the plane landed, someone came to me with a message. Not a voice, not quite. But something softer. From the woman who would become his messenger. She was a colleague at MiraCosta College. Her message came as a text on my phone: *Thao, I heard from him. He said, "Deep breaths, baby."* At the church, I stood before hundreds who came from near and far, some had flown across state lines, and some watched from virtual corners of the world where time zones meant nothing when grief was involved. I tried my best to express, not to impress. The vastness of the love, the unbearable agony of the loss, and the strange joy that he was ours. Still.

But even as I shaped the words, I felt the tension pulling beneath them. I remembered his parents were firm that I do not mention the part of him that lived behind walls. The years taken. The numbers attached to his name. They wanted to keep the truth sealed, as if silence could preserve sanctity. But how could I separate the man from the cage when he carried his dignity through it like light in a locked room? How could I not honor the part of him that survived the world's forgetting?

So I wrote carefully. Bent the language gently, like a blade of grass in wind. Told the truth without naming every brick in the wall.

> My name is Thao. Who am I to Vu that I would get this privilege to speak at his celebration of life? Vu would tell you that I'm his first love, and mostly, he would say I was his best friend. He is my best friend, too.

I would like to honor Vu's life in the best way I believe I know how. Through a letter to Vu. You see, over the twenty-eight years that we had known each other, I think he would agree with me that writing letters and poems to each other was one of our most favorite things to do. We have been writing to each other since 1992.

Before I start the letter, please allow me to start with a few words about Vu with you. Vu was an incredible thinker and a beautiful writer. It was always a delight for me to receive letters, cards, and poems from him. He loved reading letters, too.

To honor his life with words in a letter is what I feel he would enjoy. It will not be a heartbreaking farewell but, rather, a celebration of a man who lived life filled with purpose and intention, and although there were dark moments of despair, as we all have had in our lives, Vu lived with a vibrant smile and held in his heart a true hope for a bright future.

Vu had many admirers. Girls gushed over his good looks, good hair, and adorable smile. I was one of those girls. Guys everywhere respected his loyalty, strength, and relentless way of protecting them at all costs. He was also a protector of his family. His brothers and sisters each have their own episodes and adventures of when and where Vu came to their rescue. His heart was huge, and he wore it on his sleeve. Everyone could feel the love emanated from his presence. But people with big hearts also find themselves in situations where they save others at the cost of themselves. Vu did this for many of us, and it brought a series of heartbreaking events in his life. And yet, he stayed true to the nature of his heart. No matter where he went, he always carried himself with composure, confidence, class, humor, and good cheer. Through the years, many people who knew Vu told me he was their best friend. He was that guy. The one who so many felt was their best friend. I find myself extremely fortunate that he considered me his best friend. And so, this is my eulogy letter to my best friend.

My Most Precious Vu,

I know this letter is reaching you with a smile on your handsome face and that you are in the most sublime and majestic of places. I would ask you how you are feeling, but I already know the answer—you are feeling the sheer happiness that you fully deserve. You are in the glorious splendor of God and the angels that surround you, and you are now one of those angels, too. I have much to say in praise and celebration of you, but I'd like to share my time with some very good friends of yours who could not be here today. They are often voices missing in this world.

Jordan says, "Words could never truly express how I feel. This whole thing has me brokenhearted. I have always looked up to you and have always been able to talk to you about anything. I will always appreciate what you did for me, inspiring me to write and made me believe in myself. It changed my life. I must honor our friendship and keep you in my heart forever, I will keep writing and always tell people who inspired me to tell my story—you. I love you, brother."

Cruz says, "Thank you so much for everything you did for me. I will always remember you as a strong person with the spirit of a twenty-year-old, the poet that would always make jokes and the pillar that would be there to support if anyone needed help. At the end, Vu, I am so happy you finally reunited with your true love and had many rays of light that made you smile even in your worst moments. I hope you are at peace. I will keep you alive in my heart and mind. See you in heaven."

Charles says, "I miss you, Vu. The way you lived your life, I admire it so much. You are one of a kind, and I miss my *potna*, and I cry for you. When I first heard, it was like the air went out of this place. Everybody is thinking about you. Torres said what's up.

Football season won't be the same without you. Never thought I'd miss you this much! Miss Mitchell cried when I told her. We all admire your character and your walk. You got a lot of love, bro. We all love you."

You had numerous friends who loved you, who considered you like their brother. They were fortunate to have been graced by your presence in their lives. You were like a brother to everyone. And hence, your real siblings were most fortunate to have you as their eldest brother, their Anh Hai. Your brothers Dũng and Van wanted to be like you—strong, cool, loyal, and popular with the girls. Your sisters Judi and Jackie Lan could count on you to watch over them, sometimes with the eyes of an Eagle, constantly scanning and swooping in to lift them and protect them from the troubles of the world. I love when we spent hours talking and the stories of your siblings were always a topic of joy and laughter.

Your siblings, your nieces, and your nephews—they all come through the lineage of your mom and dad. You always reminded me to visit them whenever I could. You wanted them to know how much you loved them, how much you appreciated their sacrifices, and that you thought of them every single day. You wanted to be better at communicating with Mom and Dad. It's okay, babe. It is like that for many of us. Language barriers. Generational gaps. Cultural differences. As children of Vietnamese refugees, we all struggled with that. You are not alone. But now, you can communicate with them through your shining spirit as a guardian angel, watching over them and protecting them. You will always be their beloved eldest son.

So many people love you. People who have never met you admire you, respect you, and are inspired by you. That is because to know you is to love you. To feel you is to feel loved. To receive your gifts is to witness your meticulous attention to detail and the love and care you put into doing everything with your best efforts. You taught me so many things. You taught me to love myself, saying to me, "Sweetie, you have to love yourself and take care of yourself. How are you going to help and serve others when you aren't good yourself?"

You truly are like no other. Your soul is so gentle yet also filled with a fiery passion to love and protect. You lived your best life despite the cruel circumstances you were subjected to. You shined like a radiant star despite being cast into a dark and gloomy place. You soothed and counseled and consoled me through so many of my moments of hardship even though you were living in a constant hardship. And now, you are still shining, still radiant, still filled with love, still protecting, still consoling all of us. We know you are here with us, I can feel you, and your soul is holding hands with mine.

Meeting you and loving you twenty-eight years ago changed my life because I met my soulmate. Since then, through everything that we have experienced, you have impacted me deeply and shaped me into the person I am, and you will continue to be part of our lives as we continue to learn and grow. You loving me and wanting happiness for me gives me great strength and confidence to go into the world and conquer whatever goals need to be achieved.

It is my hope that through your passing, we will all remember your spirit and celebrate you by living our best life like you did. Maybe we'll hold our loved ones a little longer, maybe we'll be grateful for what we have regardless of our circumstances, maybe we'll look at our partner sitting next to us and know what a precious gift it is to have them right there with us, maybe we'll serenade love songs directly to the one we want and not sing the songs in our head to the one who got away, maybe we'll love like there's no tomorrow.

You said your favorite poems are ones written by me. And so, I'm going to end with two that I wrote. The first one is for all of us to honor you. The second one is from my heart to you.

And then, I read two poems. One for the world, where words are shared in the open. And one for me and him, where words are kept close, like a kiss between breaths.

Vu Is Free

From the Earth, Vu has departed
Leaving us all, broken hearted
But we must remember he's with God in Heaven above
Shining down on us with his unconditional Love

He would want us to live our lives like today is our last
Do not grieve too much for his painful past
For he is now feeling ultimate joy and peace
His struggles and sorrows have all ceased
He is healed from any disease
And his shackles have been released
He is smiling, trust it, we must believe
Find the strength to smile for him if you can
Seek the sweet memories of this incredible man
Who always gave us his best while he was here
And keep him in your happy heart
Because his beautiful soul is always near.

We Don't Say Goodbye

We don't say Goodbye
It's not meant for us, my dear
Our connection will continue as it has
We have nothing to fear

I will miss who you were on Earth
But I will look to the kaleidoscope skies
And hear your sweet voice singing to me
Those romantic crystal lullabies

I will whisper back
Sweetie, I hear you, it's so clear
I'll close my eyes to see your face
And feel your presence near

I will gaze at the bright moon
And the twinkling stars at night
Thinking of your embrace
Holding me oh so tight

When I'm feeling blue
I'll think of your good cheer
I'll remember our precious love
And it will banish my tears

I'll think of you everyday
Until my time here is through
I'll miss you more than anything
Until I can join you

I know you are my guardian angel
Watching over and protecting me
I know your soul is tethered to mine
Always, forever, in eternity

I know that you are Glowing in a Radiant Peace
My Love, you are truly now free
You can laugh and dance and sing
As the angel you were meant to be

Be Free, My Love
Soar High
But remember
We don't say Goodbye.

At the burial, I saw the person I felt was at the root cause of Vu's incarceration. Tri Vu. He stood near the back, just close enough to be seen, far enough to stay untouched. Grief has a shape, but guilt—it wears a face like his. Still and heavy, as if waiting to be told to leave. Something sharp rose in me. Not grief. Something older. Louder. A wrath shaped like a clenched fist. I turned to an old ex, Sergeant Big Lips, who was standing beside me. He looked good in his suit. Clean lines. A stillness in his shoulders that made the chaos in mine feel a little subdued.

"Why is he here?" I said, not as a question. "How *dare* he show up? What a slap in the face. I swear, I'm gonna go over there and give him a piece of my mind." I meant it. Every word. I saw myself spit in his face, punch his head, and tackle his body. A blur of fists and kicks and history. Like the way I used to fight the bullies who didn't know how to back off. The body remembers rage long after the heart tries to forget. Sergeant Big Lips didn't flinch. He looked straight ahead, voice steady.

"He's not worth it, *em*. I'm sure he feels a lot of guilt. That's why he's here."

Then Vu's brother, Dũng, walked over. I told him, too, half hoping he'd say go for it, half thinking he wouldn't. He looked at me, soft in the eyes. "Sis, it's okay. Vũ forgave him. If Vũ can forgive him, we can, too."

And that was it. The sentence softened me. Because I remembered. I remembered Vu's voice, not loud, but certain. How he spoke of Tri without venom. The way he called him brother still. The way he mourned Tri's losses even after what he'd taken from him. Vu said Tri's life had spiraled. Said he lost people he loved. Said that was punishment enough. Forgiveness, to Vu, wasn't forgetting. It was release. Not for Tri, but for yourself. For us. So I stood still. Let the heat rise and fall. In the end, it wasn't Sergeant Big Lips' calm, or even Dung's words that steadied me. It was Vu. The memory of his grace, how he held his own hurt like water in open hands. How he never let it harden into stone. And in that moment, I let love lead. I stood at his grave, heart beating against my ribs like a reminder. And I was thankful for him. For his lessons. For the way he taught me that even in the shadow of betrayal, we can still choose light.

Months later, the envelope came. Plain. Thin. Ordinary. Inside was his death certificate. I unfolded it slowly, as if the weight might shift suddenly and pull everything down with it.

He died in the ambulance. He was in transit from the prison hospital to the prison hospice, but he never arrived.

Location of death: roadside.

It stopped my breath. Then I returned to it, slow and deliberate, the way he had taught me to breathe when the world grew too large. I tried to imagine it, what it might have looked like and felt like for him. To see through his eyes one last time.

I remembered the story he told when he stood up for someone in his dorm and was jumped for breaking the code. His nose bled for days, unattended. It wasn't until the blood stained everything and marked him like a warning that the prison medical staff acted. They brought him to a free-world hospital. He told me how ashamed he felt that day walking through the free-world hospital hallways, shackled wrist to ankle, his white prison uniform soaked through with blood dried brown in places, still crimson and wet in others. His face streaked, his nose dripping, the fresh wound refusing to stop oozing. He said people stared. And then looked away. And no one asked if he was in pain.

He told me there was a bright side to the incident. Even in the shame. Even through the blood and handcuffs and sorrow of it all. He said the ambulance ride was . . . almost enjoyable. A strange word, I remember thinking. But he meant it. He said he caught a glimpse of the free world through the window. The wide open sky. Some trees. A few billboards. Fast-food signs glowing like distant promises. McDonald's. Burger King. Whataburger.

And I hold this story close in a quiet space where I go when I think of his final moments. I picture him. Eyes open, just barely. The hum of the road beneath. The faint rattle of metal. And through the glass is the sky, I like to think it was bright and blue. Maybe some trees, their leaves dancing in the breeze. Maybe a billboard for something sweet and cheap and forgettable. Maybe a fast-food sign blinking red and yellow like a childhood memory trying to come back. Whatever he saw, it wasn't the inside of a cell. It wasn't the gray ceiling he'd memorized over years. It wasn't the sound of keys or the click of a closing door.

It was the free world.

And maybe he knew it. He didn't want to die in prison, but outside it and through it into something wide, something open, something not yet ruined.

What did the sky look like through that window? Did the blur of light across the glass feel like freedom? Did the wheels turning beneath him whisper of something greater than the walls that had held him? I like to believe his passing was deliberate, a kind of refusal. That even sedated, with his body unraveling, he left on his own terms. A final act of clarity. A parting toward air, toward something that didn't lock behind him.

And most beautiful, most human, most necessary of all, I hoped he knew he was loved. I tell myself he knew. He died in motion. Between two destinations. Between two institutions. On a road that will never bear his name. But on that road, those moments deserve to be remembered. With these thoughts, I smiled delicately for him when it was over.

Epilogue

Feeling the Sun from Both Sides

WHEN I LOOK BACK ACROSS the years traced in these pages, I see now that the story I thought belonged to two people was also the story of a girl born in Vietnam during the war, flown across the ocean as a refugee in 1975, and raised in a modest home among Houston's Vietnamese community. Before prison letters and visits, there were early lessons shaped by displacement and the quiet demands placed on Asian daughters: how to move between cultures without stumbling, how to carry duty without complaint, how to make myself small enough to fit the mold of the "good" refugee child, and how to be grateful, high-achieving, obedient, and silent about suffering. Those expectations shaped me long before I could name them. They taught me how to appreciate, work hard, achieve, stay humble and charitable, and endure.

But they did not teach me how to be whole.

Wholeness came later, slowly, through heartbreak, through disappointment, and through the connection that returned to me decades later. My journey through failures, missteps, missed chances, and loss forced me to confront the messiest parts of myself, parts I had smoothed over with perfectionism and productivity. Each hardship was a step in the long path toward understanding what I had resisted for years: that healing requires not only resilience but also softness; not only survival but also truth; and not only devotion to others but also devotion to the self.

What happened with Vu is tragic, but I choose to see it as a luminous tragedy, one that carved me open just enough to let the truth in. It is sorrow shaped into something that still glimmers when held in the heart. Vu's final words about possibly being deported, written in his published essay, still echo: *To be honest, anywhere is better than to live without hope and the feel of sunshine on my face.* After he was gone, I found myself returning to a line by psychiatrist and author David Viscott: "To love and be loved is to feel the sun from both sides." That sentiment holds the essence of our story and the lessons it carried: that even in the darkest situations and systems, light can find a way through; that love is both devastating and a blessing; that its warmth can remain even after everything else has fallen away.

From the opening pages to the final moments of this memoir, my life has widened in ways I once could not imagine. From my childhood and the cultural expectations placed on Asian women to the systemic violence around us and the impossible love that transformed me, each experience has shaped every part of how I am as a professor, a speaker, a community advocate, and a writer.

I continue to work with people whose lives resemble Vu's. They are men and women navigating incarceration and post-incarceration under the threat of deportation. They live in an ecosystem filled with fear and uncertainty. For those deported, it's a second exile returning to a land they once fled, rebuilding life in a place both familiar and foreign. As an educator, I have learned how fragile educational pathways can be and how easily lives can collapse. To serve these communities with dignity, I hold the unwavering belief that people are more than the worst thing they did. This is a truth that extends beyond the system, reminding me that compassion requires seeing others in the full complexity of their humanity.

Writing has taught me to respect the power of storytelling and to summon the courage it takes to be raw and vulnerable. It taught me that students learn best when their stories are valued, that teaching is as much about listening as it is about instruction, and that an attuned educator is an effective one. It has shown me that narrative can move systems as powerfully as data, and that language can open doors to people whom institutions have long shut out. Writing revealed that in life, reflection is its own form of survival, that truth grows sharper when it is named, and that healing often begins the moment we allow ourselves to put something into words.

Public speaking reminds me that communication is more than content. It is breath, delivery, tone, and connection. In teaching and writing, the same truths hold: students rarely remember lectures word for word, but they remember how they were invited into the conversation. Readers may forget dates and names, but they remember how it felt to be placed inside a moment, familiar or foreign. Life reflects these lessons, too. What we know matters, but how we show up, how we engage, how we listen, how we care, is what shapes our relationships and our impact.

I carry these lessons along with Vu's light with me into every classroom, every meeting, every event, every call from a detention center, and every letter I write for someone seeking another chance. It is not a burden. It is a compass and a reminder of why the work matters. In the work of dignity, it means meeting people where they're at, listening and supporting them as they work through the shit they're facing. It's deep care and compassion. At times, it's tough love with boundaries and reality checks because people deserve truth that hurts over false hope. Dignity is not a fantasy; it is a practice. It is love made into action.

These identities, as professor, advocate, writer, and public speaker, do not compete. They expand one another. They expand me. They allow me to exist with the humility of someone who has lived inside contradictions, who has known love in violent spaces, and who understands the stakes for people whose stories are still unfolding, stories that have never been told, and stories that have rarely been believed.

Standing where I am now, between memory and possibility, I understand something I could not see as a girl or even as a woman writing her way through grief: that our lives are not shaped only by what we endure, but by what we choose to do with the endurance. My story, and Vu's, has become a reminder that even broken beginnings can lead us somewhere honest, brave, and whole.

And as I write this epilogue, I find myself in another season of loss. My dog, Pork Chop, who wandered in and out of these pages the way he wandered in and out of my days, died. His absence has a gravity I was not prepared for. Anyone who has loved a pet knows that the grief is often no less profound than the loss of a human; in some ways, it cuts deeper. Pets witness us without judgment. They fold themselves into the routines of our lives so rhythmically in sync that their presence becomes a kind of heartbeat we forget to notice. Until it's gone.

And then, five weeks after Pork Chop died, my father died. The man who survived war and exile and the long labor of rebuilding, and whose voice was calm, cool, and occasionally mischievous, was suddenly beyond my reach. Both the creature who kept watch at my feet and the man who first taught me to stand were gone. If Pork Chop knew the cadence of my daily life, my father knew its origin story. Losing them both in the span of a month and a breath, there was no emotional intermission, no pause long enough to steady myself. Grief doesn't line up politely. Sometimes it arrives in clusters, daring you to find your footing without the people or animals who anchored you.

I keep trying to understand what this double loss is meant to teach me, what light might follow such an ache. Maybe the lesson is simply that love, in all its forms, leaves echoes, and grief is just the sound of those echoes finding their way back to us.

If the opening of this memoir asked what it means to return, to a person, a past, a version of oneself, then the closing offers this: Sometimes the return is not to where we began, but to who we were always meant to become.

And because of the love that existed in our lives, through various channels and people, and through each other, I know, despite everything, how to step fully into the light, feeling the sun from both sides.

Love letters to the dirty south

Acknowledgments

THIS BOOK WAS CARRIED INTO the world by a community of people whose faith in the story often held me up when my own faltered. I owe deep gratitude to Lạc Sư, whose memoir *I Love Yous Are for White People* cracked open the possibility that my story, too, belonged on the page. To Kirk Wallace Johnson, who first heard my voice while interviewing me for *The Fishermen and the Dragon: Fear, Greed, and a Fight for Justice on the Gulf Coast*, and who became both mentor and compass—teaching me how to build a proposal, reminding me to stay the course, and urging me forward through rejection after rejection. To Carolyn Hùynh, whose fierce belief in this story helped me find my way to a literary agent. To Amy Bishop-Wycisk, the first to believe in my writing, and to Kendall Berdinsky, who carried me across the finish line and stood by me each time a publisher wrote that they "couldn't relate" to my voice. My heartfelt thanks to my editor, Stephen Hull, whose enthusiasm, clarity, patience, and brilliance shaped this memoir in more ways than I can name. To my copyeditor, Zubin Meer, whose keen eye sharpened the details. And to the writers who lent their eyes, ears, and generosity: Laura Kalpakian and Eric Nguyễn, whose reviews contained critique along with care and encouragement with enthusiasm; Thi Bùi and Nguyễn Phan Que Mai, whose check-ins and nudges were gifts of passion and belief; Tony Bùi, Bảo Nguyễn, Andrew

Lee, and Ôanh Nhi Nguyễn, filmmakers who saw the contour of the story long before it fully formed on the page; and Daniel Gross, who honored Vu's voice and, by extension, mine.

My family has been my grounding force. To my *ba* and *mẹ*, Phát and Ơn Hà, who shed their traditional beliefs to become parents who urged me toward a life that felt true. To my siblings—Hiền, Hiếu, and Johnny—who embraced every part of me and every person I hold close; they brought unconditional love, bouts of humor, and soft light even in the darkest seasons. To my niece, Vi Điệp, who kept me honest and brave simply by wanting to grow into the kind of woman she saw in me. And to Vu's family, who folded me into their memories, past and present. A special love to Jackie, whose devotion bridged years and distance and who always said, "Through you, big sis, Vu is always with me."

To the friends who become kin, who invest in your dreams with the same tenderness and tenacity they invest in their own: Fro Arenas, Tín Nguyễn, Quyên Ngô, and Raphael Mimoun, who hold a significant place in my life and whose presence makes the path in life illuminated rather than impossible. They graciously read the messy drafts with sincerity because they wanted this book to live. To the women whose steadfast presence held me together and reminded me that women supporting women is not a slogan but a way of life through everyday acts of showing up, lifting up, and standing guard over one another's dreams; sometimes quiet, sometimes fierce, and always life-giving: Happy Phàm, Krista Warren, Bea Palmer, Ashley Gerdo, Leila Safaralian, Alketa Wocjik, Nora Kenney-Whitley, and Hải Dương. And to the men who showed up as brothers, reminding me that men, too, can be soft, generous, and essential in a woman's inner circle: Sean Davis, Kenneth Nguyễn, Roy Vũ, Tino Đinh, and Kevin Shin.

To my students, who listen to small fragments of my life and ask for more, and who remind me that stories, especially the hard ones, can change how we see ourselves and one another. To my colleagues, who amplified my voice and held space for my work long before it became a book.

To my community—the Vietnamese refugees who saw themselves in my story, and the strangers who once found my blog and rooted for a love they only knew through words. To the women who, like me, pour their lives into community arts and advocacy: Ysa Lê, Thúy Võ-Đặng, Julie Võ, Tú Uyên Nguyễn, Giana Nguyễn, Yvonne Trần, Christine Trần, Theresa Suarez, Lan Dương, Thảo Hùynh French, Jes Vũ, Taylur Ngô, QuyenZi Phàm, Brittany Trần, Chen Gu, Cynthy Wu, and Lý Hoàng-Schmidt—your labor, spirit, and solidarity are woven into every chapter.

To the one who will remain unnamed: the friend, confidant, and quiet anchor who walked with me through the most grueling phase of this process. Thank you for the morning coffee, the meals I forgot to eat, the clean clothes folded like retailed wares, the daily routines you upheld without complaint, and the tender care you showed Pork Chop. Thank you for never questioning my pace, my voice, or my reasons. You made it possible for me to finish this book exactly as myself.

And, finally, to Pork Chop. My loyal shadow, my companion, the small heartbeat who kept vigil beside me through every draft. While I wrote into the quiet hours, he slept beside me, lifting his head each time I shifted, as if checking that I was still there, still writing, still finding my way. His presence was constant—gentle, playful, and faithful in a way that words can only graze. This book was shaped by not only the people who believed in me but also one small dog who loved me through every page.